CROSS-CURRENTS
in Contemporary Australian Art

CROSS-CURRENTS
in Contemporary Australian Art

TRAUDI ALLEN

CRAFTSMAN HOUSE

Fine Art Publishing Pty Ltd,
42 Chandos Street,
St Leonards, Sydney, NSW 2065
Enquiries: info@gbpub.com.au

ISBN 1 877004 03 0

Design: Kirsten Smith
Reprographics: Chroma Graphics, Singapore
Printing: Tien Wah Press, Singapore

709.94
A, M—(20 —A

PAGE 5
ABOVE
Dale Hickey, *Cottlesbridge Landscape,* 1980 (detail),
oil on canvas, 244 x 198.6 cm. Collection: National Gallery of Victoria, Melbourne
CENTRE
Pat Hoffie, *Hotel Paradise,* 1989–90 (detail),
laser copy on board, 145 x 336 cm. Photograph: Elvira Gonzalez Lopez
BELOW
James Bennett, *Bones and Angels,* 1994 (detail),
batik cap/tulis on silk, 115.3 x 235.2 cm. Collection: Museum and Art Gallery of the Northern Territory, Darwin

contents

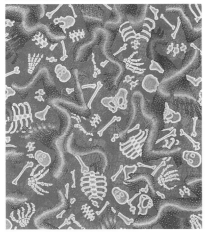

acknowledgments

My thanks go to the many people who have assisted with research. Among them are John Spencer, Dr Jenny Read, Dr Ross Sinclair, Mel Drummond, Dr Conrad Hamann, Angela Italiano, Barry Clarke, Clare Morfett, Neville Walsh, Ted Snell, Ann Stephen, Kel Taylor, Bob Jankowski, Barbara Hall, Peter Kennedy, Jan Martin and Mrs Morrison.

I am indebted to Leigh Astbury for generously giving time to read the manuscript, Sandy Kirby for her valuable comments, and photographer John Brash, who devoted untiring effort in the provision of high-quality reproductions.

Many galleries assisted in numerous ways. My particular thanks go to Sarrah Preuhs of Roslyn Oxley9 Gallery, Dianne Tanzer of Dianne Tanzer Gallery, Stuart Purves of Australian Galleries, Zara Stanhope of the Monash University Gallery and Jan Minchin of Tolarno Galleries, as well as ICI Australia and JGL Investments.

I appreciate the enthusiastic support of Jill Edwards, president of the Art Craft Teachers' Association, at the initial stages of this project.

I gratefully acknowledge a grant from the Australian Academy of the Humanities, which contributed to reproduction costs.

The support and encouragement of the artists involved has been gratifying. Every effort has been made to contact individual copyright holders for permission to reproduce artworks.

introduction

Art Comes Out: Tracing the Development of Contemporary Art

The American art critic Clement Greenberg provided an outsider's perspective on Australia's position in the international art debate during an interview with Paul Taylor, who was to become known as the founding editor of the radical art journal, *Art + Text*, begun in 1981. In answer to the question 'Can major art be produced by an artist in, say, Melbourne, at present?', Greenberg replied: 'One big disadvantage you have in this country might be remoteness — though I'm not so sure of that — but you don't have enough people … You don't have enough millionaires either — neither absolutely nor proportionally.'[1] Speaking in 1980, Greenberg was only the latest commentator to note that Australia's legendary isolation has had a defining effect on its culture. Interestingly, his response to the question contained no comment on the style, subject matter or quality of the art produced. But as the witty definition of Australia by Paul Foss, who took up the editorship of *Art + Text* in 1984, has implied, isolation and population in *terra lostralis* are only part of the story.[2] ➤

Australia's much-discussed limitations of distance — minimising access to information about art in the major centres of Paris, London and New York — are put forward as part of the explanation for the conservative tendencies of Australian artists and their viewing public. Also operating has been a sense of inferiority derived from being outside the main debate, leading to what has been described as 'the cultural cringe', in which anything made, written, performed or achieved in Europe was, in an attitude apposite for a colonial people, automatically considered superior.[3] The well-aired notion that Australian immaturity is directly related to the brevity of time in which it has formed a modern, western cultural identity is also a factor often mentioned in descriptions of the Australian cultural profile.

Through its modern history, Australian art has existed simultaneously in several spheres, stretching itself across the currents from British conservative to French and American avant-garde, while nurturing its own strains of tentative thought. Artists have experienced the contradictory confining pressure of finding voices relevant to an international debate while experiencing the challenge and stimulation of making them original and applicable to Australia.

How then does Australia arrive at the beginning of the twenty-first century as a partner in an international art discourse with collectors of its art around the globe? How has it equipped itself to coin the phrases rather than adopt an already well-honed language? How has it become a centre of debate itself?

Usually considered pivotal in the introduction of modernism to Australia is the first exhibition of international modern art in 1939.[4] For many, this was the first time work by the internationally historic artists included had been seen other than in reproduction. As has been well documented, the arrival of the 'French and British Contemporary Art' exhibition marked an important moment in Australia's progress through to modernism and international postmodernism, even though the ideas and styles that were adopted as a result of its influence had long been superseded in Europe. The developments that transpired, however, were far from immediate or tumultuous, a factor that may be related to the broader social mood. A lingering opposition presented obstacles to the ground swell, straining against the apparently evolutionary force of international fashion and occasionally giving way to latter-day imitations. And while the 1940s have been recognised as begetting the moment when Australian art became modern, the contemporary impulse was far from absolute, erupting, rather, in a sporadic and partial fashion.

In matters of national politics, 1939, the year the exhibition opened, presaged a long period of conservatism with the induction of Robert Menzies as United Australia Party Prime Minister. Menzies retained the leadership until 1941, when Labor took over power with John Curtin and then J. B. Chifley as Prime Minister. In 1949 Menzies regained power for the Liberal Party in coalition with the Country Party and held it for the next seventeen years.[5] On his resignation in 1966, a series of conservative governments followed, until Gough Whitlam gained power for the Labor Party in 1972. Art was significantly changed by the priority it was given and by the egalitarianism of the Whitlam and succeeding Labor years. It remains a matter of debate whether or not this has been a positive influence.

When Menzies made his first claim to the reins of power, Basil Burdett, modern art critic for the Melbourne *Herald* newspaper, had set sail for Europe to curate his exhibition of modern French and British painting. Academic Realism was losing its hold as the dominant style in favour of Australian 'Impressionism'. In 1938 Burdett wrote: '… there is very little, if any, modern art in this country. Surrealism is practically non-existent. Abstraction is practised very little by even our more advanced painters. Even Post Impressionism is in its infancy here …'[6]

PAGES 8-9
Yvonne Audette, *Chinese Poem,* 1963 (detail), oil on composition board, 122 x 91.5 cm

PAGE 10
Imants Tillers, *Izkliede,* 1994 (detail), synthetic polymer paint, oilstick and gouache on canvasboard, 292 panels, 304 x 914 cm overall. Private collection, Sydney

But when nine Picassos, eight Matisses, eight van Goghs, seven Cézannes, seven Gauguins, five Rouaults, four Braques and other works by Bonnard, Chagall, Dali, Derain and Modigliani were viewed by the 40,000 people who were said to have attended the 'French and British Contemporary Art' exhibition at the Melbourne Town Hall on 16 October 1939,[7] Van Gogh's *Sunflowers* was already fifty years old.

Just three years after this exhibition, the Angry Penguins group — Sidney Nolan, Albert Tucker, John Perceval and Arthur Boyd — began to produce their revolutionary scenes of urban Melbourne. While there is no doubt their work was radically conceived by comparison with prevailing styles, these artists were still setting their action in a reworked, recognisable Australian landscape, albeit according to precepts based more on the imaginative narrative of the dream than the measurable effects of the weather. Boyd placed the people he had seen among the terrace houses of South Melbourne. The cripple, an escapee from the circus, stage or film, struts his stunted strides, reaching out to embrace the evils issuing from the gargoyles that jut out menacingly to tempt him. In this allegory, entitled *The Gargoyles*, 1944 (Figure 1), in which humanity is distorted if not broken by life's difficulties, the cripple's disproportionately large head emphasises that this work tells of his state of mind.

But again an international comparison is salutary, as by this time the American Abstract Expressionists had already abandoned notions of figurative representation, producing instead work that depended more on the depiction of abstract metaphor and mood. As long as Australian art was presented in a language considered outdated by the international art world, it could not engage in the wider debate. A tangential problem involved difficulties in establishing a system that would nurture and incorporate the original in art. Since the audience that is receptive to the unusual is always small, and particularly so in Australia, there was not, until the 1980s and 1990s, a sufficiently viable audience to encourage entrepreneurial risk. The responsibility for this task had largely devolved to government, whose political and bureaucratic spheres are necessarily unwieldy and unresponsive to change. And only recently has the mainstream media begun to modify its antipathetic stance towards ideas in the arts, which on television have usually been side-lined in favour of fast-moving visual grabs that demonstrate the creativity of the producers rather than the artists they present.

Also functioning to maintain the status quo was a small and closed system which often dealt the fate of failure and anonymity to any who were not known to, or whose artistic profile was at variance with, those of the powerful in the art hierarchy. The fact that Boyd and Perceval were among those who led the 1940s Australian modern art revolution and that they also appear in the literature as principal artists of the 1950s may not, therefore, be testament merely to their ability.

The work that primarily characterised the 1950s was the allegorical and metaphorical landscape. Sometimes it was an urban landscape, at other times a scene from the bush fringe or the greater outback. It was a sombre and relatively intellectual art deriving from Melbourne that contrasted markedly with Sydney's interest in either

FIGURE 1
Arthur Boyd, *The Gargoyles*, 1944,
oil on cotton gauze on cardboard, 51 x 63.2 cm. Collection: National Gallery of Australia, Canberra. Reproduced with permission of Bundanon Trust

John Perceval, *Sulphur Smoke,* **1959,**
oil and tempera on composition board,
90.8 x 121 cm. Private collection, Melbourne

abstraction or the prettiness of the so-called 'charm school'.

Paintings by Perceval were a compromise between city and country. Painted from the pier at Williamstown, *Sulphur Smoke*, 1959 (Plate 1), showing boats bobbing in the water, might have been an affectionate afternoon study were it not for the massive pall of yellow smoke that discolours the sky and pollutes the water. A black swan is left marooned between the yellow sludge and the equally dangerous shore. The Australian-born international art critic Robert Hughes appeared not to notice the rotten side of many of the Williamstown paintings that typified the emerging complication confounding Australia's clichéd, pleasant scene. Hughes dismissed the series as 'Disney-fodder … tugs and ferries merrily bobbing like children's toys in the bath'.[8]

Hughes also expressed little confidence in the possibilities for Australian art when, in 1970, he wrote: 'One cannot imagine an Australian equivalent of David's *Death of Marat*, Goya's *Second of May*, or Delacroix's *Liberty Guiding the People*. The experiences that produce such paintings do not exist there. Neither does the genius.'[9] In making this comment Hughes set Australia an impossible task. It was indeed unlikely that an Australian would produce a monumental work in the style of nineteenth-century Europe (Goya's *Second of May* was painted in 1808) in the second half of the twentieth century, but comparisons between work from such different times and contexts are inevitably flawed. In a despotic fashion Hughes also negated the up-and-coming artists who were not noticed at his time of writing because either they were too young or they had not yet arrived in Australia. Was Hughes, one could ask, engaging in a little cultural cringeing himself?

The landscape had never been an important subject for John Brack, who in 1955 drove a car through and out of it, as if departing the bush once and for all to join the new subject matters of art. Beaming with the pride of ownership, Brack's occupants of *The Car*, 1955 (Figure 2) exemplify the new materialism that was a defining element of 1950s society. His subtle irony mocks the self-satisfaction this acquisition gives his subjects, who also seem to take some pleasure in leaving behind the discomforts of the countryside. With their neat, well-behaved, perfect-sized family of one girl and one boy, the couple are like the idealised subjects of advertisements at the time that were directed towards the ordinary wage-earner who was joining the new middle class.

Often focusing on the down-to-earth qualities of popular culture, art of the 1960s was striking and refreshingly uncomplicated after the sometimes weighty considerations of the 1950s. Australian insularity was breaking down and it looked to the United States rather than to Britain for stimulus. The result was an interest in a flat-surfaced, abstract minimalism and colour painting that contrasted with the painterly, impastoed layering of Melbourne's Antipodeans, and required an entirely different approach in comprehension. The new concept-laden, hard-edge abstraction could be read only by reference to its own unique code. The pattern in *Slippery Seal III*, 1967 (Plate 2), by Robert Rooney, for example, is based on a children's cut-out seal from a Kellogg's Corn Flakes packet and refers to Rooney's daily breakfast routine.[10] But despite its domestic origins, his pattern evokes no sense of homely wallpaper comfort.

International Pop art had introduced the notion of repetition through which it commented on the ephemeral nature of the new commercial culture. Andy Warhol's first silk-screen prints of photographs on canvas were made in 1962 and brought to 'fine art' the suggestion that it need not be handmade. But while Warhol included the

FIGURE 2
John Brack, *The Car*, 1955, oil on canvas, 41 x 101.8 cm. Collection: National Gallery of Victoria, Melbourne

PLATE 2

Robert Rooney, *Slippery Seal III,* **1967,**
synthetic polymer paint on canvas,
106.7 x 106.7 cm. Collection: Monash University,
Melbourne. Photograph: John Brash

element of chance which occurred when, for example, his ink faded, Rooney incorporated a deliberate, slight modification to his pattern. There was also an interest on Rooney's part in the application of the recurrent musical phrase from jazz compositions, as is indicated by the use of the word 'variations' in his title,[11] an idea Philip Glass developed to full effect in the 1980s.

An example of Rooney's serial works[12] was included in the 'The Field' exhibition, held in 1968 at the National Gallery of Victoria, which provided many with their introduction to so-called hard-edge painting. Another generation was familiarised with 'The Field' when the artists included in the exhibition were shown again in 1984 at Melbourne's Heide Park and Art Gallery, now the Heide Museum of Modern Art.[13] Titled 'The Field Now', it presented what has become an institutionalised gallery strategy of stimulating debate by reconstructing notable art events from the past.

Denounced at the time for its dependence on New York art, the original 'The Field', or at least Robert Rooney's part in it, may now allow for a more benign critique in which the work is found to comprise more innovation and less imitation when compared with the art to which it owes its genesis.[14] Once again, the value of the local contribution was diminished, if not underrated, in favour of that produced in the United States.

Locally inspired movements have variously and simultaneously directed Australian art away from and towards international trends. While both the Melbourne Antipodeans of 1959 and the Sydney Annandale Imitation Realists of 1962 wished to halt what they saw as the negative and overwhelming trend towards abstraction, the latter challenged standard notions of aesthetics by looking to Australian, New Zealand and Papua New Guinean indigenous art to create a Dada of the South Pacific. In Sydney in the early 1970s, the Yellow House artists and the group who showed at the Inhibodress gallery looked again to import features from the American avant-garde.

Acting as a harbinger of the performance artform in this country, as well as foreshadowing the increasing role of business in art patronage, the artist Christo, with assistance from the entrepreneur and collector John Kaldor, arrived in Sydney in 1969 to wrap up Little Bay. The work was important for the widespread and international press coverage it received (but there was no public or official acknowledgment of the environmental disturbance to native flora and fauna, including that caused to nesting birds). The expansion of private and government support that followed had the effect of increasing the numbers participating in the artistic process at all levels and, with other international influences, began the establishment of a new and more complex dynamic.

Isabel Davies, quipping on the female preoccupation with food preparation, as well as the artistic practice of paying homage to male art of the past, applied a sly irony in preparing and wrapping a *Lunch for Christo*, 1978–79 (Figure 4). From her series 'Masterpieces from the Kitchen', this meal proves that women as housekeepers daily turn out works of art with no hoopla and less thanks. Davies was a member of the collective that produced the independent magazine *Lip* in 1976, designed to present the case for art by, and about, women. The publication of other art journals,

FIGURE 3

The Annandale Imitation Realists: Mike Brown, Ross Crothall and Colin Lanceley with *Byzantium*, **1961**, oil and synthetic polymer paint, collage of found objects on wood on composition board. Collection: National Gallery of Australia, Canberra

FIGURE 4

Isabel Davies, *Lunch for Christo*, **1978–79,** from the 'Masterpieces from the Kitchen' series, mixed-media assemblage, 26 x 48 x 43 cm. Collection of the artist

including *Tension* and *Art + Text* in the 1980s, provided a forum for international art and ideas. More recently, *Artlink* and *Art Monthly* have presented a balance of all these influences in a lively local debate. *ART AsiaPacific* magazine, begun in 1994, extended the discourse to its sphere of interest, including articles by non-Australian specialist writers.

The artificiality of the art historical tendency to encapsulate styles within decades became increasingly clear as art in Australia expanded to reflect the stylistic admixtures that were infusing its character. Art techniques first seen in the 1970s, for example, were not only still being employed in the 1990s, they were continuing to receive critical recognition and acclaim. Without the same clear-cut, unified stylistic approach that had operated as the sole avant-garde until the 1960s, an artist might choose to follow trends from several periods and place them within one work. At the same time art had moved decisively out of the frame, off the wall, and beyond the studio and gallery. From the predominant oil on canvas with some sculpture, photography, and the various print forms, there was now a diverse idiom including video, environmental and performance art, installation and assemblage. Subjects had evolved through the narrative, the representational and the abstract to include the conceptual as well as the intentionally meaningless.

But there were still many artists whose first and only interest was to work with conventional oil on canvas. The era of the predominant style was passing in favour of an all-inclusive attitude, admitting one proviso: that the work have an intellectual component which could be as quirky as questioning whether there should indeed be an intellectual component! Art in the 1970s no longer had to look 'good', but it did have to stimulate.

In a number of ways, Paul Partos's work exemplifies some of the transitions in Australian painting between the 1960s and 1990s. Partos, who had exhibited in 'The Field', began in the late 1970s to incorporate lettering in his paintings with the use of Letraset stencils.[15] The incorporation of an epigraph was a technique taken up internationally in the 1980s and 1990s as a feature of postmodernism. In *Now Where Was I? No. 2*, 1991 (Figure 5), Partos draws the viewer into the complex levels of a dark secret. He begins to explicate the conundrum with scratches that insinuate but do not explain. There are letters from the alphabet but they do not amount to a word. The artist is lost in his narrative: Now where was I? The answer is a riddle, perhaps even to the artist. Despite what would be in conventional terms an unsatisfactory dialogue, there is no doubt that the desire to involve oneself in this work by Partos is compelling. The search for direct dialogue between artist and viewer is, however, thrown into question. There are no longer straightforward answers.

In the late 1970s, Peter Tyndall retitled all his works *detail/ A Person Looks At A Work Of Art/someone looks at something …*, which had the effect of directing his entire body of work towards the analysis and appreciation of cultural production.[16] In his quest to contemplate the problem from every possible angle, he utilised all (non-electronic) media. Often performing the viewing role is the 'stereotypically perfect viewing unit':[17] the same neatly dressed 1950s family who had amused John Brack. Tyndall's family subject is literally drawn into the image both to view the artwork and to consider the elements of the discourse. The main, ironic gist of the work is that rather than creating and then inviting the viewer to understand his intentions, Tyndall places the onus on the audience, which he renders largely responsible for its own cognitive and perceptive process. In removing the cues that might encourage a search for aesthetics, Tyndall rejects such matters as pretentious and largely dictated by fashion. Always present is his sign for the work of art — the frame, and the two strings that attach it to the wall. Together, these guide the viewer's attention back to the conceptual issue at hand without the distractions of colour, form and style. In *detail A Person Looks At A Work Of Art/someone looks at something …, –1974–1984–* (Figure 6), there are references to Mondrian's square, Minimalism and the Abstract Expressionist emphasis on brushstroke.[18] The challenge involved is the notion that a painting can be the repository of high ideals: 'a thing of beauty.' Tyndall suggests rather that it is merely descriptively adjectival in a system of constantly changing stylistic emphases.

As art of the 1970s to 1990s was no longer confined to the frame, Tyndall often showed frames within frames, so posing a dilemma as to where the artist's fiction begins and ends.

The early experiments with installation and assemblage of the 1970s generally took place at the expense of painting. It was a transition that again ensued from an international orientation inspired by a search to discover a new means appropriate for new times. The art historian Terry Smith has explained that it was felt the possibilities for painting had been exhausted: 'Its history seemed complete, its future bleak.'[19] Showcasing international artists of 1973, the Sydney Biennale lubricated dialogue with international trends, including the theoretical approach to art appreciation based on modern French philosophical discourse. As a consequence, Australian artists were encouraged to look more strenuously towards the production of an art involving an intellectual dimension.

Although not the earliest example of interest in semiotics in Australia, the first conference on the subject, 'The Foreign Bodies Conference: Semiotics in/and Australia', was held in February 1981 in Sydney, marking the formal beginnings of Australian reflections on theories deriving from structuralism, post-structuralism and postmodernism.[20] However, the influence of structuralist philosophies and the postmodern style was not felt in any wholesale or immediate way at the time of the introductory conference, but was a germinal development that was to change art and the analysis of it significantly, and continues to be evident in the work of Australian artists.

In the 1970s the French structuralist Roland Barthes pointed to the crucial role of context and convention in analysis, demystifying social myths associated with a wide variety of activities, from the wrestling match to the striptease.[21] In the latter, he showed how the tantalising gestures of the stripper act to make her more erotic while partly clothed than when she is naked. These gestures, which are superfluous to the business of undressing, are so well known that they have become signs of eroticism — as are the traditional stripper props of feathers, furs, gloves and fish-net stockings. All these objects and gesticulations, Barthes explained, are the structural components that coalesce to conjure a mood and create a successful and convincing performance.

In his essay 'The world of wrestling', Barthes examined again the process in which institutionalised and exaggerated behaviour is demanded by an audience, revealing that the wrestling match is no more than a ritualistic exhibition of primal and aggressive postures. The physique of the wrestlers signifies their type and the phoney gestures and rites they enact tell instantly of agony, victory, deception and cruelty.

FIGURE 6
Peter Tyndall
detail
A Person Looks At A Work Of Art/
someone looks at something …
–1974–1984–
CULTURAL CONSUMPTION PRODUCTION
131.5 x 246 cm

FIGURE 7
Linda Sproul, *Which Side Do You Dress?*, 1992,
installation and performance, Experimenta,
Theatre Works, Melbourne. Photograph:
Heidrun Lohr

In *Which Side Do You Dress?* (Figure 7), first performed in 1992, Linda Sproul worked with installation and performance to contrive a translation of Barthes to Australian circumstances of the 1990s. She wore male business attire, but since the cloth of her suit was transparent and she was naked underneath there was an ambiguity in the cues or signs embedded in and beneath her apparel. Her subject exemplified the female body as the object of male titillation and as a tool for commercial gain. It also referred to the history of the female nude in art and its reconsideration in the new gender discourse.

The central focus of Sproul's performance is the display of male gestures, from cricket and boxing to Australian Rules football. Out of context, the referee enacts an authoritarian, didactic and ludicrously convoluted gestural display. Paradoxically, his signals may also be mistaken for certain female gestures which, despite their similarity, are read differently when performed by a woman. The salute, for example, is close in execution to the action involved in signalling a swoon. But the hand resting on the forehead is entirely superfluous to the swooner's symptoms, functioning only to indicate the need for assistance, along with, perhaps, the quaint custom that she be caught as she falls. It becomes clear then that much of the responsibility for the communicative process lies with the reader.

As Sproul's performance proceeds, slides of advertisements for electric equipment are shown, all bearing the advertising blurb 'Sleep Wonderfully Warm With Linda', urging the purchase of sleeping-blankets and toasters, and involving the well-worn implication that some sexual gratification might accrue from their purchase and ownership.

It was the obstacles that beset female artists wishing to communicate modern women's issues to a contemporary audience in a fresh, original way that led them in the mid-1970s to circumvent the established system in favour of such media as performance art. Since performance was a fringe activity in the system from which women had been virtually denied access, they were released from the values it espoused and could work on a more equitable basis.[22] Such new non-painting media, calling for entirely different methods of assessment, led to a reduced interest in technique that spread from the new media to painting itself. The quest for beauty continued to recede, with a growing interest in issue-based material, allowing for art to be politicised and exploited in the presentation of marginal interests. Occurring simultaneously was the evolution of personal power so that the individual came to feel he or she could be a more active and influential participant in the political process. This attitude was first visible in anti-Vietnam War marches and through the feminist activism that had encouraged individual women to at least think about, if not act, to improve their circumstances.

Such changes on the wider scale were reflected in the art arena where the individual art viewer was now obliged to take a more participatory role. The artist's motivation and design concerns were no longer implicated in analysis, as the viewer, now liberated from the constraints of passivity, was licensed to engage in the imaginative process. Barthes's controversial proclamation that the author is dead, arising from his assertion that the writer does not write anything that can be defined or designated but just writes, was again involved.[23] The place of the dead author could equally be taken by the deceased artist or any other creator of material, however they wished to define their role. According to Barthes, meaning does not reside within the text, nor is it dependent on authorial intentions; rather, it exists in the 'intertextual' system or structure of the conventions which are woven together by the reader.

The production of the artwork was now considered neither a fixed process nor a static entity. Since it was not perceived to be wholly governed by the artist's intentions but influenced by anything and everything that constituted a viewer's life, it could include factors of which she or he may not be aware, such as prejudice, for example. Indeed, to read the image according to the artist's supposed intentions was to fall into the flaw-filled trap of intentionality. The reader–viewer had become a partner in the artistic arrangement, bringing a life of unique experience to the artwork and taking away perceptions that may be only partly shared with others.

Once confined to the examination of such formal techniques as composition, brushstroke, modelling and colour relationships, analysis of the artwork proceeded from the influences of structuralism to post-structuralism, the latter having its origins in literary deconstruction by Barthes and Jacques Derrida, Michel Foucault's work on knowledge and power, and the psychoanalysis of Jacques Lacan.[24] A major proponent in Australia throughout the 1980s was the journal *Art + Text*. Post-structural deconstruction — the analytical process in which elements are considered in isolation, independently of their known contexts — also involved the application of sociological, philosophical, anthropological and literary discourses to an artistic purpose. With the benefit of the post-structuralist insights and methodologies of Foucault and Derrida, it became clear that when the details and circumstances of a power relationship are separated from one another their origins are clarified and often revealed to exist on such baseless grounds as prejudice and convention. The influence of these theoretical approaches was gradually to infuse the art debate so that an artist often encountered the ideas of these philosophers second-hand, without undertaking detailed study.

Thematically, David Wadelton's *The Mirror*, 1993 (Figure 8), aptly defines the moment between structuralism and post-structuralism, although the birth of *Art + Text* in 1981 marks its introduction to Australia's avant-garde. Lacan's so-called 'mirror stage' of development represents a critical moment of discovery for the child as he or she views himself or herself for the first time. In so doing, maturation is advanced and identity is more clearly defined. But since the image in the mirror is reversed, this moment foreshadows the imperfection that characterises the formation of the ego, resulting in an illusionistic misunderstanding of the self.[25] (Interestingly, experiments have shown that the process of self-awareness is inaccessible to the young chimpanzee because, rather than looking into the mirror, it searches behind it to find the other chimpanzee, with no understanding that the image is of itself.)[26]

The look of astonishment on the subject's face in Wadelton's painting parodies art's long history of solemn portraiture. The apparently slick style, based on a found cartoon,[27] contrasts with a studied painterliness, a combination rarely found within one work. Wadelton tantalises and amuses, directing his statement towards the viewer, who is required to unravel the layers that have among their themes the history of art. While the subject is captured discovering something startling about himself in the mirror, the viewer sees two sides of him via both the reflection and the original view. On another plane, an old, sculpted hand holds a mirror which should, according to the laws of

FIGURE 8
David Wadelton, *The Mirror*, 1993,
oil on canvas, 183 x 122 cm

physics, show the image of the viewer. This, however, is left blank, perhaps allowing every viewer to imagine it is his or her own physiognomy that fills the space. Does Wadelton ask his audience to enhance its understanding of its own identity by looking in his mirror? Does he, at the same time, challenge it to an improved understanding of the painter as well as his work?

A general interest in self-awareness directed the artistic attention towards an internal, psychological concern with identity and away from description of the objective world. Early moves towards this understanding in Australia were advanced by the radical artist-run Inhibodress gallery that opened in Sydney in 1970.

When art was viewed 'laterally' with the influence of intellectual rigour, the concept of the 'good eye' was revealed for its immeasurability, and the role of judgment was questioned. Specifically involved in this development was Barthes's definition of the new active — as opposed to the conventionally passive — reader.[28] The problem of exactly whose eyes are best able to judge the quality of a work of art was revealed as problematic, along with the convention that art was comprehensible only to a few select members of a cultured class rather than by anyone in an ideal, ever-expanding, classless society. How did we know that the experts were dependable? How does one acquire such an exceptional 'gaze'? Among the answers was that coined by Lacan, who unveiled the process of looking to show that the type of sight and perception directed towards the reading of a book, for example, is quite different from that engaged in the viewing of an artwork.[29] But paradoxically Lacan's influence proved no deterrent to the critic who remains an integral member of the gallery system, interpreting current offerings for the readership of newspapers and journals. Prompted by John Berger in *Ways of Seeing*, feminists pointed out that there was something distinctly male in the determination of who possessed the ability to 'gaze' and what constituted art worth gazing at.

The matter of who is accepted as an artist has also undergone considerable change through a number of influences, the most important of which has been the worldwide movement for political emancipation that has in turn expanded the perception of the artistic identity. This evolution of the artistic character, from its fixed and narrow parameters of selected race and gender, has also served to abrade the extravagant claims associated with the notion of genius. As a consequence, the de facto qualifications required to become an artist have been redefined to include a different range of qualities. With the influence of trade unionism, the artist could be called an artworker, so retrieving artistic status from dilettantism to that of a form of employment as valid and open to membership as any other occupation.

Although social realism was present in Australia in the 1940s, political commentary became more overt, as well as more concerned with the rights of the individual. An artist might include in his or her art a political component that also involved the disclosure of personal detail: that the artist's preference was for same-sex partners, for example. This aspect of personality may be highlighted, while other aspects — such as the fact that the artist is a member of a racial minority — may be omitted, for a time at least, in order to direct attention towards the area for which social and attitudinal change is sought.

Hackneyed comments about the camera having superseded anything that could be done in paint were to seem particularly nonsensical when figuration took centre-stage again in the early 1980s. Now in the form of Neo-Expressionism, it was a development partly stimulated by the adaptability of representational art to the portrayal of a home-grown sense of identity. It was also driven, however, by its antithesis: an international impulse with which Australian artists grappled to present a regional and personal variant. After the 1970s' avoidance of what could be called conventional media, paint on canvas and the traditional skills involved in careful representation were once

Dennis Passalick,
Myself Portrait/Hostile Landscape, 1991,
oil on canvas, 170 x 274 cm

FIGURE 9A

Peter Corrigan and Maggie Edmond,
Belconnen Community Centre, Canberra,
1985–88, Youth Centre entrance, corner
Chandler Street and Swanston Court

FIGURE 9B

Peter Corrigan and Maggie Edmond,
Belconnen Community Centre, Canberra,
1985–88

FIGURE 9C

Peter Corrigan and Maggie Edmond,
Belconnen Community Centre, Canberra,
1985–88 (detail)

again highly prized. Art historian Richard Haese has noted that the post-conceptualist, new figuration received a form of official blessing by art journal writers with the opening of the 'Tall Poppies' exhibition in 1984 at the Melbourne University Gallery, which included work by Imants Tillers, Mike Parr, John Nixon, Dale Frank and John Dunkley-Smith.[30] The exhibition also received substantial praise from Memory Holloway, then art critic for the *Age* newspaper.

Pre-dating the widespread adoption of the figurative mode was work by Peter Booth, who was one of the first Australians to take up neo-figuration as a vehicle for self-exploration. His well-known *Painting 1977 (Man on the Road)* brings the bizarre to a dream landscape which does not identify a recognisable place. Rather, the solitary subject of the painting finds himself in an impastoed, imaginary, post-nuclear night that allows both icy wind and burning sun. In *Myself Portrait/Hostile Landscape*, 1991 (Plate 3) Dennis Passalick, who has been a racing cyclist, paints himself riding out of a surreal nightmare. As he travels across a nowhereland, urged to speed up by the train travelling behind him, horrific personalised associations appear. Passalick's dream in vermilion accents acknowledges those of Booth with whom he shared accommodation in Melbourne in 1968.[31] His coded narrative was a disturbing discovery even for the artist as he created it, and is discomforting to the viewer for whom coherent understanding is precluded. The apparently dissociated, deformed and disembodied animal parts have a real-life basis, however, in that in this work Passalick recalls experiences of cruelty to animals.[32]

The arrival of figuration in the 1980s also met a need among the community in general to participate more actively, not just in the shaping of events but in their designation to history. Diluting the exclusive character of the art system was the widespread motivation of so-called community art projects. These teams, working together without the sanction or support of the gallery system but often with financial assistance from local governments, worked to produce public art for the enjoyment and education of their community. Similarly functioning to expand the artistic community are the prizes, traditionally awarded to male painters of male subjects, that are now also open to women and younger artists. The Moët & Chandon art prize, awarded each year to an artist under the age of twenty-five, is rich in prestige, beneficial in its $50,000 grant and, with no gender limitation or subject specifications other than that it be contemporary, exemplifies the new climate of encouragement that has prevailed since its inception in 1987.

A most significant influence in the shaping of art and the art system over the 1980s was the espousal of postmodernism. In its purest form, the postmodern building, painting, poem or film is said to mark the end of the era in which individual experiments introduce new expressions and variations that change the genre in which they work. There is a belief and acceptance that there can be no more experimentation and no further originality because all possibilities have been exhausted.

The term 'postmodern', although first used in architectural analysis, is by no means limited to it.[33] Indeed, the earliest example often given is James Joyce's novel, *Ulysses*, published in 1922. Nevertheless, it finds its most lucid explication in the architectural form. A postmodern building will present the reassembly of historical and other features in a discontinuous, dislocated fashion, creating metonymics or signs that refer to other architectural styles, as well as objects other than buildings, that in total give the construction a wholly new character that it alone possesses.

The practice of quotation from various periods of architecture began in Australia in the mid-1970s when, as well as performing a functional purpose, buildings presented analyses on the art of architecture. Another typical feature was the presentation of ambivalent signs as to their use.

The Belconnen Community Centre (Figures 9A, 9B and 9C), designed by the architects Maggie Edmond and Peter Corrigan from 1985 to 1988, includes the quintessential characteristics of postmodern architecture. Although intended for youth recreation in the centre of a newly extended Canberra suburb, it suggests a former existence as a warehouse, as if it had undergone refurbishment in the inner cities of Melbourne or Sydney after seeing a century of industrial sweat and toil. Blind arches, with a respected past that leads back to the renaissance, here imply bricked-in windows as part of the renovation. Relentless brick along the sides of the building is also evocative of a factory. Architectural historian Conrad Hamann has described the Belconnen Community Centre as 'part corner pub, part milk-bar, part railway ramp … with forms that are older than Canberra itself'.[34] He has also observed the window over the entrance to be 'vaguely Saracenic',[35] exemplifying the postmodern practice of quotation from earlier styles. This Saracenic window is placed immediately above two circular windows in a discontinuous, 'irrational' and playful arrangement that illustrates the absence in postmodernism of the uniformity and functionalism which had guided earlier styles. Here the windows perform a largely decorative role, as substantial light is accessed through the glassed roof.

By the 1990s, 'postmodern' had become a word descriptive of Australia itself, now that nearly one in four Australians had been born elsewhere.[36] This eclectic character added both complexity and a transavantgarde quality to culture and the arts. One might drive a Japanese car to an Italian restaurant, wearing clothes made in China, meet a friend from Lebanon who has a partner from Germany and, after dinner, see an American film. Although the national character of each of these is identifiable they have been modified by provision, use and consumption in Australia. Indeed, it is difficult to conceive of a social activity that is entirely all-Australian.

Imants Tillers has the diaspora or *Izkliede* — the title of his major 1994 work (Plate 4) — in his blood, having been born of Latvian parents who settled in Australia. Within the work are events, symbols and conclusions which are important to Tillers's personal autobiography. But the style of the work also reflects an international diaspora since its fragmented ideas and motifs derive from around the world. There is no chronology in the way elements are arranged; ideas migrate, clash and then settle, appearing as if this is where they had always been. Tillers's crossword puzzle with local allusions, that might once have extended logically as a narrative across the work, deals rather with the meta-narrative that involves a search for the deepest universal truths that transcend continents. Work by Tillers may be classed as international also for its exhibition in prestigious art venues abroad. In 1986 Tillers represented Australia at the Venice Biennale and in 1993 received the Grand Prize at the Osaka Painting Triennial.[37]

In a lower-left panel of *Izkliede* an innocent prayer is written to God the Master while in a central panel the swastika is signal enough to stir recollections of the call to a master race. In the art context, the master narrative or traditional historical view is also disrupted. Classical German text is contrasted with the blocked 'I' of New Zealand's Colin McCahon who, Tillers has said, 'dares to quote from God'.[38] But acts of courage are part of the character of this work since Tillers dares to challenge the constraints of provincial interests; New Zealand dares to be noticed in the interna-

tional art discourse; Latvia dared to survive under a series of colonial rulers, including the Polish, the Swedish and, most momentously, the Germanic. To assist him, Tillers called on the modus operandi of the 1960s Fluxus movement, exploiting anarchy, humour and cooperation between people of different cultures in an attempt to destroy boundaries between artforms, as well as nationalities. Stimulating Tillers's production of the work[39] was a 1974 article by art historian Terry Smith, titled 'The provincialism problem', which summed up the dilemma for Australian artists as the 'provincial bind' from which they could not break free.[40] However, Australians, he argued, found themselves in the same position as artists working anywhere else in the world that was not New York. They could only follow or fail. But they would fail also if they followed, for, ipso facto, they would fall short in originality.

Changes undreamt of in 1974 when Smith was writing have since loosened the 'provincial bind'. In the 1980s and 1990s attention has been drawn to Asia and the South Pacific, with the Eurocentric view of art history being recast. The development of a flourishing contemporary art culture in Asia and the sale to the world of traditional Aboriginal art have been major factors in this redirection. The conventional wisdom that art began with cave painting in France is now challenged by those discovered in northern and Western Australia. Performance artists have recognised they must look to antecedents among the body painters of Aboriginal Australia and Papua New Guinea. Artists wishing to actively engage in the contemporary discourse must now consider work produced in China and Japan.

Australia has begun to play a significant role in the Asia-Pacific region, fostering artistic endeavours and providing professional guidance.[41] But whereas the United States was once the dominant cultural imperialist, Australia is now in a position to be accused of attempting to adopt a similar position in its relations with the countries of the Asia-Pacific in a new post-colonial age.

The relative ease of international travel has encouraged artists to extend their fields of interest and influence and to rethink prejudices and preconceptions. Along with the rest of the community, artists are now more likely to choose to live away from their places of birth and among people of other racial origins, a development which has produced art with cross-cultural dimensions.

Technological change, although providing channels of communication for the relatively rich, has had a democratising, as well as an internationalising, influence, in that anyone can become a published artist via a homepage on the Internet. While there is a language difficulty for non-English speakers — as English is the Internet language — national boundaries which would normally confine communication and experience of other cultures no longer exist.

With the dissolution of the conventional view that art evolved in a linear fashion as one movement makes way for the next, either in a hereditary genealogy or as a result of opposing motivations, the new pluralism has given rise to discussions about more than one type of postmodernism, about many styles of artist, about several sexualities,[42] blurred nationalities and innumerable contexts. These changes have occurred in synchrony with the realisation that in a multifaceted system, as Australia has now become, influences operate side by side and affect each other as cross-currents.

A Continuing Romance: The Biography of the Tree

In the late 1990s attention was drawn to the urban landscape, in recognition of the fact that many Australians live city lives with little or no connection to the land that has long been a heroic subject of art.[1] Nevertheless, an attachment to naturalism has persisted, despite the pressure for change to which Australian art has been subjected over the second half of the twentieth century, both from external forces and those within. The biography of the tree in Australian art is a microcosm of its larger art history. ➤

FIGURE 10
Banduk Marika, *Sacred Palm (Gulwirri)*,
1987, colour linocut, 56.5 x 36 cm.
Photograph courtesy Lyttleton Gallery,
Melbourne

This historical loyalty to the landscape may be related in part to Australians having formed their perceptions of what is appropriate as an art subject from their links with Britain and its art, which also retained naturalistic allegiances well into the mid-twentieth century.[2] Another influence is the rural subject of peasants at work, an artistic lineage begun in France in the 1850s.[3] It is often argued that much of this affiliation is motivated by a sentimental, ersatz identification with a lost age for which Australia's literary and artistic traditions have been the medium.[4]

The continuing appeal of work by the so-called Heidelberg School painters may be encapsulated in the same terms as those that art historian Leigh Astbury applied to describe the motivations of the painters themselves, who, he argues, turned to the bush for its capacity to represent the liberating qualities of dreams rather than real aspirations.[5] However, the veracity of this assertion should not negate the fact that there is often an authentic component to the Australian experience that operates to sustain the myth. Unlike the situation in much of the United States or Britain, for example, the natural environment still plays a significant role in the lives of Australians who cut their identities from raw bushland on city fringes, as well as in the greater outback.

The infatuation with the landscape's undisciplined rawness continues, despite much of the country's population deriving from other corners of the world. Indeed, it can be the very lack of acquaintance with Australian natural history that stimulates a fresh appreciation. The pioneer persona, with its real threat of bushfire and snakebite, is adopted over and again, even if the struggle is moderated by the supportive infrastructure of a nearby middle-class suburbia. Even so, this experience has a validity unknown to those in other parts of the country where such an existence survives only as a literary cliché. The landscape has always been and continues as the main theme for non-urban Aboriginal artists whose methods and media were, until the 1970s, too foreign for acceptance in a predominantly figurative, oil and watercolour culture.

Put simplistically, the ramifications for art have been that when the landscape was the dominant mode it was expressed as the painted scene rather than in the relatively avant-garde modes of installation or art performance. Consequently, it was via the techniques involved in applying oil to canvas — and achieving either a 'perfect' fidelity to the subject or a new interpretation — that experimentation took place. When paint and representation were the preferred media, criticism and debate necessarily centred on matters of good or bad aesthetics and the degree of 'artfulness' in the illustration. When painters of the landscape in oils were pronounced the best in art, exploration in other media was inevitably discouraged.

More specific than the general landscape is that signifier of it, the tree, which delineates this artistic and personal connection with the land and the earliest art in Australia.

Banduk Marika, from Yirrkala on the Gulf of Carpentaria coast in north-east Arnhem Land, chose a 'spirit' tree, the *Sacred Palm (Gulwirri)*, 1987 (Figure 10), as a subject for a linocut. It is less a descriptive tree of the area than a mythical emblem signifying the domain of the Ancestor Creators who existed in a place somewhere near the morning star. Stylistically, the tree is sited in a hatching stroke pattern that is a common feature of the Aboriginal work of the region.

Tom Roberts's 1880s depictions of the bush just beyond suburban Melbourne were among the first recognisable portrayals of the Australian countryside and have remained favourites. But the grounds on which they are so affectionately perceived may not be as secure as is generally thought, since there is a degree of formularisation and artifice employed that is not well recognised or understood. At times the same approach is also followed by Frederick McCubbin and Arthur Streeton and coincides with the compositional structure adopted by Cézanne for a number of his Mount Sainte-Victoire paintings,

PAGE 28
Godfrey Miller, *Blue Unity*, 1954–55 (detail),
oil, pen and ink on canvas, 69.8 x 88.2 cm.
Collection: National Gallery of Australia,
Canberra

PLATE 5
Tom Roberts, *A Summer Morning Tiff,* **1886,** oil on canvas
on board, 76.5 x 51.2 cm. Collection: Ballarat Fine Art Gallery,
Victoria, Martha K. Pinkerton Bequest Fund, 1943

occurring, for example, in *Montagne Sante-Victoire*, 1885–87.[6] This compositional design involves the placement of a straight-trunked tree — in Cézanne's case a cedar and in the Australian bush setting a eucalypt sapling — in the foreground to unite it with the middle and distant spheres. Where Cézanne's mountain forms the background, for Roberts and others, the wider forest acts as a background 'curtain'. This curtain technique that blocks off the distant view is not accurately descriptive of the bush scene and weakens the resolution of the works which, contradictorily, have faithfully painted leaves and tree shapes in the foreground. The curtain effect may be seen in Tom Roberts's well-known paintings *A Summer Morning Tiff*, 1886 (Plate 5) and *The Artists' Camp*, c. 1886.

A main feature of the Heidelberg School bush — which presumably extended to Box Hill, then on the outskirts of Melbourne — where *A Summer Morning Tiff* and *The Artists' Camp* were painted, was the *Eucalyptus polyanthemos* or, as it is commonly known, the red box, which is often included in the foreground of the work, and is recognisable from its blue-green circular leaf. In correspondence, Roberts often referred to these eucalypts as 'blue gum(s)', and they form the title of a work, but the red box is no Tasmanian blue gum.[7]

The roundness of the red box leaf, as it is seen in the middle distance, produces a dappled effect which lends itself to a French Impressionist pointillist brushstroke, but this was not adopted by the Heidelberg artists. They did not develop this technique, even though they had before them the perfect subject matter, but neither did they attempt to show botanical detail unless a tree is shown as a foreground specimen. Although the Heidelberg painters took the trouble to make their legendary camps and paint *en plein air*, they appear not to have looked closely enough at their subjects, or were not sufficiently inspired to render them either accurately or with spirited invention.

Indeed, this problem appears to have infected the entire discourse regarding the Heidelberg painters in that the eminent art historian Bernard Smith has attributed the blue-grey tones of the Heidelberg works to the teaching of the Australian portraitist James Quinn. Quinn, Smith explains, spent nine years in Paris, developing 'a richly colourful style in which greys were skilfully deployed', thereby influencing the later work of Roberts.[8] But, however much Quinn may have been an influence, the inherent grey tones of Roberts's *Eucalyptus polyanthemos* subjects must have been at least as significant a guide to his palette, especially when it was so changed for the different eucalypt species of Sirius Cove in New South Wales. In *A Summer Morning Tiff*, even the atmosphere radiates the same blue-grey of the *Eucalyptus polyanthemos*, and it occurs in shadows and encircles tufts of grass that are of a quite different hue.

The tree has continued to be an important subject of painting in high and low art, as it was early in the twentieth century when Hans Heysen created his grandfather of gnarled trees that presided over the misted, red-brown views of rural Adelaide. It is the Heysen rendition of the *Eucalyptus camaldulensis*, both in its original and much reworked form, that has been the model for so many newcomers to art in their early attempts in oil or watercolour, and it is these same imitation Heysens that inspire the novice collector to acquire.

Heysen's affection for the landscape was accompanied by an unusual commitment to natural conservation for the early 1920s, which he expressed in terms both sentimental and anthropomorphic. In various communications made at this time, trees are referred to with the masculine pronouns 'he' and 'him',[9] and they are personified in a letter written after a period of bad weather as: 'The poor old trees must be feeling quite bruised and sore.'[10]

The Sydney-based photographer Harold Cazneaux, although working more than ten years later, continued in this manner with his portrait, *The Spirit of Endurance (Flinders Ranges, South Australia)*, c. 1936 (Figure 11). Here, the tree is shown as at

FIGURE 11

Harold Cazneaux, *The Spirit of Endurance (Flinders Ranges, South Australia)*, c. 1936, gelatin silver photograph, 29.3 x 24.4 cm. Collection: National Gallery of Australia, Canberra

once protective of the wider landscape and its human population, and as the personification of the best in the human spirit, taking up what has become the clichéd position of the struggle against the severity of Australian conditions.

Epitomising the change in Australian society as urbanisation took on a post-war determination to renew and improve, the Melbourne Angry Penguins artists produced an art that combined a relative intellectual complexity with a technical simplicity that has been characterised as modernism. Their nonconformist approach, however, now celebrated as innovative, left art institutions of the time generally unmoved. It was not until 1962, when their work was presented in the exhibition 'Rebels and Precursors: Aspects of Painting in Melbourne 1937–1947', at the National Gallery of Victoria, that it reached a wide audience. Similarly, in the 1980s and 1990s, examples shown at this landmark exhibition were still unlikely to realise auction prices comparable to those paid for 1950s paintings by these same artists. The market still preferred the pristine landscape.

In his analysis of 1950s interest in the urban landscape that occurred in tune with developing urbanisation, Chris McAuliffe portrays the Antipodean group of 1959 as purveyors of an aesthetic that conveyed an urban Australian experience as an alternative to the landscape version of Australian art history.[11] But this claim is most accurately applied to only three of the group — Robert Dickerson, Charles Blackman and John Brack — while three of the four remaining artist members — Arthur Boyd, Clifton Pugh and John Perceval — still believed, according to the work they showed in the 'Antipodeans' exhibition of 1959, that their preferred medium was the bushscape. Even Dickerson's alienated people in dark, indeterminate spaces demonstrate the ambivalence of the group towards committing themselves to urban subjects, as his scenes are often defined as city-sited only by their titles, by the absence of bush, and by the office clothes of the main characters. Dickerson included a landscape in the 'Antipodeans' exhibition, titled *Children in the Bush*, c. 1959.

Albert Tucker, although not a member of the Antipodean group, also abandoned the dark metaphor of his 1945 series, 'Images of Modern Evil', to depict totemic heads whose cragged facial features stood simultaneously as landscapes or aspects of topography. These were followed in the 1960s by straightforward picturesque landscapes showing birds flying through treed settings.

Sidney Nolan had discovered the fundamental features of a distinctive artistic landscape when experimenting in the Victorian Wimmera, where he was posted after being conscripted into the army in 1942. In 1944 he arrived at supply depots in Dimboola and then moved on to Horsham where he adapted the reductive technique developed for the radically spare St Kilda and Luna Park paintings of the early 1940s to the landscape.[12] His method involved the synthesis of a simple Wimmera landscape with the two-dimensional quality he had seen in Cézanne's works in the *Herald* exhibition of 'French and British Contemporary Art'.[13] This fusion led to a flattened scene in which the land rose vertically towards the sky. But more important to the biography of the tree in Australian art than Nolan could possibly have imagined were those before his canvas as he surveyed the pale dryness of the Wimmera. Rather than making the generalised, interpreted tree his sole concern, Nolan also recorded the botanical characteristics of the region. Common to the area is the *Allocasuarina lehmannii*, which has a tall, straight, dark trunk and a spherical, grey-green crown. When grouped, they occur as scattered trees in an open, grassy understorey, just as Nolan described.

The 'Kelly' series of 1946–47, Nolan's next major works and arguably the most significant of his oeuvre, although primarily mythological, still depend for much of their atmosphere on a landscape with conventional painting interests, such as the colour

PLATE 6
Sidney Nolan, *Wimmera River,* c. 1942,
ripolin enamel on cotton gauze on cardboard,
51.3 x 63.7 cm. Collection: National Gallery
of Victoria, Melbourne, presented by
Sir Sidney and Lady Nolan, 1983

PLATE 7
Sidney Nolan, *Landscape*, 1944,
ripolin enamel on cotton gauze on pulpboard,
51 x 63.4 cm. Collection: National Gallery of
Victoria, Melbourne, presented by Sir Sidney
and Lady Nolan, 1983

and fall of the setting sun. The landscape is not just a backdrop but a three-dimensional stage on which characters are engaged in an unfolding narrative.

Exemplifying the abiding Australian search for identity and place in the international art discourse was the proclamation in 1967 by collector, patron and president of the Contemporary Art Society, John Reed, that Nolan's 'Kelly' series had provided an 'authentic national vision'.[14]

Following this series, Nolan painted the empty expanses of the Australian outback as seen from a high point above the mountains. Rather than serving metaphorical or allegorical ends, a work such as *Musgrave Ranges*, 1949, is purely descriptive of the landscape, which continued to feature in a similarly one-dimensional fashion in later works.

Although Nolan, Arthur Boyd and Fred Williams are credited with significantly advancing the depiction of the landscape with the introduction of metaphor, allegory and the technical displacements of time and space, there have been other eloquent transformations that have received less consideration. From 1945, Godfrey Miller, also referring to Cézanne,[15] began to lose the figurative image by analysing it to the point of refraction. Whereas Cézanne showed the object from two or three simultaneous vantage points, Miller intensified this process so that his object was divided into an infinite number of separate and differently viewed elements. But oddly, with the use of what has been described as a mathematical, formulaic approach,[16] Miller produced an effect that is as aesthetically emotive as those interpretations, usually expressionistic, that are said to emerge from the soul. Miller explained that his process was governed by a 'logic basis or framework onto which intuition or personality can be placed'.[17] Using this system, he paid regard to symmetry and precision but still achieved a marriage of these with an intellectual dimension, as well as concerns for the spiritual and the aesthetic.

As unlikely as it may seem from his diagrammatic approach, Miller worked from life with just as much affection for the environment as Heysen, for example, given his reclusive years in the Yarra bushland at Warrandyte on the outskirts of Melbourne.[18] Elucidating his tree painting method, Miller explained how he applied the observed, natural scene to a rigorous geometric analysis. He wrote: 'the sense of perpendicularity is the dominant note, there is too the break from geometricised parallels by the standing trees as these often cluster in groups perhaps on an incline — where their roots slant into the ground the pattern gets relief from monotony.'[19] Through the

FIGURE 12
Lloyd Rees, _Gentle Morning Sydney Cove_, 1981, oil on canvas, 121 x 151 cm

'latticed' (Miller's word)[20] intersecting lines which define his forms but which also allow them to radiate beyond their delineated edges, one can argue that he created a greater sense of his subject than is normally apprehended in figurative painting. The blue of the _Eucalyptus polyanthemos_, the same species that charmed the Heidelberg painters, also appears to infuse this work. The technique of extending colour beyond the edges of the image may have derived from Miller's study of Hinduism.[21] Through Hindu philosophy he would have learned that beyond and surrounding the tree is an energy that connects it to universal forces, a phenomenon that is known in New Age terms as an aura and is referred to in Christian painting as a halo.

Deborah Edwards has written on Miller's interest in directing the philosophical ideals of Krishnamurti through his own art and applying them to a twentieth-century existence.[22] Again, perhaps from Hinduism and his interest in the interpretation of it by the German theosophist and anthroposophist Rudolf Steiner, there is the visual representation of the essential cell on which life depends, as well as the repetition of it, that constitutes the whole object. There is also, in the multitudinous elements created by the dissection of his subjects, a sense of the vibrational quality that living organisms possess, as theorised and described by Steiner. Miller died in 1964 before he could appreciate that he must have been among the first western artists to so ably represent the association between the Hindu understanding that detailed characteristics of plants and organisms are visible again on a larger scale within those same plants and organisms, as well as elsewhere in nature. The same phenomenon is given a 'scientific' interpretation in the Mandelbrot Set from the fractal geometry branch of chaos theory.

Miller's disdain for the career-artist life, the complexity of his work and its superficial hard edge have meant that his art has taken a subordinate place to that of many other more facile landscapists, including the acclaimed Lloyd Rees. In Rees's case, a diffuse surface, reminiscent of that used by Turner to capture the delicate prettiness of an English sunrise or the stillness of a frosty morning,[23] was applied to bring an indistinct quality to aspects of the Australian landscape and to create, as Rees put it, 'a gentle light'.[24] To achieve this, his oil, when already on the canvas, was sometimes thinned by a drenching with turpentine to create a flat underpainting in the watercolour manner.[25]

PLATE 9
Brett Whiteley, *The Jacaranda Tree (on
Sydney Harbour)*, **1977**, oil on canvas,
208 x 456 cm. Private collection

38 • CROSS-CURRENTS

A cloth was sometimes used to blur any demarcation,[26] while a brushstroke texture was added later (sometimes with a brush in each hand, as Rees was ambidextrous)[27] to give objects solidity and to highlight. Another Rees hallmark: the preference for minimal, tonal variation, prevalent in work from 1973, is often produced in light-keyed pastel interpretations. This proto-impressionist manner, when used for the landscapes of Sydney Harbour, combined romance with sentimentality and could not fail.

For Brett Whiteley, memories of Rees's landscapes, as well as recollections of childhood holidays spent on beaches and harbours near Sydney, were evoked when he painted the view from his window on taking up residence in a house overlooking the harbour at Lavender Bay.[28] Whiteley's landforms, much as those by Rees, protrude like elbows into the waveless sea of Sydney Harbour. But the light-keyed harbour paintings that possess a Rees-like gentle touch are rare. More characteristic is Whiteley's dramatic sea of ultramarine with white highlight dashes, such as that shown in *The Jacaranda Tree (on Sydney Harbour)*, 1977 (Plate 9), which has a theatricality that accords with his time, his noisy, speedy life and the energetic city that was rapidly advancing around it. At the same time, Whiteley captured the curious quietude that descends over the harbour and shields it from whatever cacophony erupts around it. Indeed, Whiteley's water is so still that when seen in panorama it reveals curious and naturalistic changes in depth and mood. The two boats near the Sydney Harbour Bridge in the upper left corner, for example, appear to lie on a lower plane than those to the right of the painting that are moored near the jetty.

This same attention to shadow modulates landscapes by Fred Williams and adds to their significance as important contributions to the artistic view of Australia.

Whiteley's interest in the work of the English painter Francis Bacon, and his subsequent friendship with him, may have stimulated the formulation of the large, open scene on which the occasional boat is dotted, in a manner quite unlike the traditional maritime convention which has boats shown either in close up as the main subject of the work, or clustered in a side or central setting.

Whiteley's jacaranda tree is a psychedelic affair in which the play of artificial light at night is exaggerated. Taking a cartoonist's licence, Whiteley has his tree contain an oversized bird's nest to which the stork hastily returns. The enormous eggs, the apparent source of the bird's anxiety, represented a fascination for Whiteley since childhood,[29] and may symbolise some fragile hope in a lonely sea. But it is to Williams and Nolan that Whiteley pays homage in setting his scene on a horizontal plane with the jetty rising in a direct vertical line.

In the prosperous late 1980s, after the turmoil of the financial boom had swept up art and the world that managed and packaged it, creating a chaotic whirlwind that dislodged forgotten artists and old art, some artistic taste-makers still placed the landscape first. Throughout the 1980s numerous exhibitions and a number of travelling retrospectives presented the Fred Williams landscape to local and international audiences. Two large-scale books by high-profile authors were produced on his work, an honour rarely bestowed.[30]

As Patrick McCaughey first pointed out, Williams was influenced by Cézanne,[31] carving his terrain into segments which could be viewed from various angles as if walked across and photographed at various points and from various perspectives. The results that were later manipulated and melded together in works from the mid-1960s show how the distant landscape would appear from the seated position and, within the same painting, as it would be seen from above. This same technique shows each tree as it swirls to reveal itself from various viewpoints. The thick globules of paint that suggest trees on the distant scene were not often shown in the singular, or in the small-group configuration, but usually as an entire stand. Again, as McCaughey clarified, there was no desire on the artist's part for a diffused image but rather one of objective linearity.[32] Williams's approach is generally regarded as unemotional, in direct contrast to the romantic manner of Rees, for example, but nevertheless the later dot forms are indistinct, with no attempt to describe foliage or generalised tree shape. The argument follows therefore that lack of definition is not a reliable gauge of emotional involvement.

For Williams, it appears, colours were adapted and experimented with as they related to each other, rather than as seen. A Williams signature, the brow of the hill, is made spectacular with exaggerated hues that are then veiled by repeated straight-trunked trees. Colloquially, in the 1980s, everyone saw the Australian landscape through Williams's eyes.

The Williams career serves to refute the argument sometimes raised to explain why it was not until the 1980s that Australia occupied a place in the international art discourse. The suggestion that Australia's preoccupation with the landscape resulted in the production of work that appeared too foreign to appeal to those unfamiliar with it other than as items of exotica is invalidated by the Williams example at least, if not by the 1961 'Recent Australian Painting' exhibition at the Whitechapel Gallery in London, which introduced Australian art to the United Kingdom, including highly praised landscape paintings.[33] Fred Williams was chosen to exhibit at the Museum of Modern Art in New York in 1977, where he introduced the Australian landscape to American and other international audiences.

The issue of whether or not Nolan is an influence for Williams was raised by art

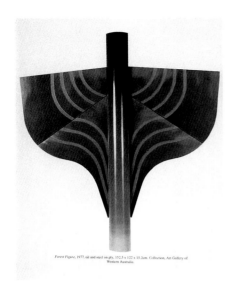

FIGURE 13
Howard Taylor, *Forest Figure*, 1977,
oil and steel on ply, 152.5 x 122 x 15.2 cm.
Collection: Art Gallery of Western Australia,
Perth

historian Richard Haese, who argued that Williams's engagement in 1958 as restorer of Nolan's 'Kelly' series brought him into close and incontestable contact with the Nolan style.[34] It is, of course, possible that Williams had made himself familiar with Nolan's work, apart from the 'Kelly' series, given their associations within the same city, let alone the small coterie that could call themselves Australian artists in the 1950s and 1960s. As the argument stands, Patrick McCaughey's citing of Cézanne as the direct source for Williams's verticality does not account for the repeated circular representations of trees and the similarly striated trunks that are seen in his early 1957–61 phase and which also occur in Nolan's Wimmera paintings. While comparable features in Williams and Nolan include these simplified stick and circle trees, and a flattened, upward perspective, some similarity might be attributed to their subject matter, if it were not that each was standing before a different, albeit Australian, landscape.

In retrospect, it appears Nolan provided a rough, topographical framework upon which Williams applied a more sophisticated composition and finish, transforming the former's loose and relatively uncontrolled picture. It seems Nolan was primarily concerned to meld composition and other descriptive techniques with the vegetation and topography he actually saw. Williams's works, however, suggest that although he often travelled to bush locations for first-hand study he was more interested in experimentation that was at a remove from his surroundings.

Some of the differences evident in work by the two may be explained by the contrary materials and procedures employed. Williams used painstaking methods, such as turning the painting upside down to check for the balance and symmetry of his composition and sometimes using wires to create diagonals from corner to corner.[35] Although Williams's result often has a look of ease, his task was deliberate and considered. His concern for compositional balances meant that all parts of the painting should cohere; one section of the painting was not accomplished until another was intellectually, as well as visually, resolved. Lyn Williams, the artist's wife, has summarised his approach as: 'You paint your way out of it … you do it and do it, and if you do it enough it'll come right.'[36]

By contrast, Nolan's approach was far more spontaneous, at least partly because he chose to work with ripolin whose fluid and quick-drying properties, when compared with oil, necessitated a rapid technique that involved on-the-spot decision-making that left little time for reworking and reconsideration.

The relative lack of appreciation of the early Nolan landscapes — until reincarnated as Williams presented them — may be related also to a more decorative, stylish handling of paint and colour by Williams who presented the modern, painted landscape as more appealing and agreeable. Ian Burn suggested that the application of postmodern analysis may have adjusted our vision of Nolan, facilitating a more positive re-evaluation.[37] Burn stressed that this new perception is not simply due to the passage of time but rather that a postmodern understanding is more receptive to artistic experimentation of the kind employed by Nolan. Burn wrote: 'The "look" he reproduces is no longer an end in itself but a means towards destabilising the conventionality of our relation to that "look".'[38]

The Western Australian artist Howard Taylor was concerned, throughout a career begun in 1935, to find new interpretations of the landscape by means of the Karri forests near which he has lived for many years. With an early interest in British natural realism he worked to release his dependence on figuration, moving to create shapes with a schematic inclination[39] until, paradoxically, he discovered a means whereby he could portray the unrepresentable. In *Forest Figure*, 1977 (Figure 13), there is a vague, generalised reference to a human figure with outstretched arms, but there is also a suggestion of the energy that rises with the sap, up the trunk of the tree and out along its branches.

In *Tree Line with Green Paddock*, 1993 (Plate 11), Taylor manages a rare feat by giving an impression of trees without recourse to the general tree format of trunk topped with foliage. This is achieved in a way that appears, again contradictorily, to cross Op art with Abstract Expressionism. The figurative image is insinuated by the use of green and the conventional division of the picture plane into foreground, middle ground and distance. With the memory of landscape representation, the eye fills in the detail that it knows so well. The main aim of Op art — the production of optical effects to induce a kind of mesmerism in the viewer — is softened by Taylor's blurred edges, and sentiments are aroused as they were by work of the American Abstract Expressionists.

Dale Hickey, having come to prominence with the National Gallery of Victoria's 'Field' show of 1968 and, following this, by devoting periods to hard-edge painting and installation, would seem among the least likely to look at the old faithful tree subject. But in 1980, and just metres away from Clifton Pugh's home, Hickey painted *Cottlesbridge Landscape*, 1980 (Plate 12). Hickey's incidental choice of location is ironic in that so much landscape art was produced at Cottlesbridge, both by Pugh and those he invited to work there, that it seemed at the time to be the unofficial headquarters of Australian oil-on-canvas landscapism. Hickey's painting was the only treed landscape in the prestigious 'Field to Figuration' exhibition held in 1986 at the National Gallery of Victoria, and was purchased by the gallery. In retrospect, it seems the landscape subject was acceptable provided it was given a new interpretation and was painted by an artist whose interests went beyond it. Hickey's relatively objective, patterned and linear landscape was hung with photographic images of *Bleeding Trees No. 2*, 1979 (Figure 14), originally presented as a conservationist performance by Jill Orr. In this performance, the artist wraps herself around the tree, thus implying that both are vulnerable. As we look up the length of the naked tree we are reminded of female physiological dynamics and the requirement to bleed.

Rather than appealing to the beauty of nature in order to save it, Jan Senbergs paints its desolation in a composite of real and imagined location.[40] The exposed rock

PLATE 11
Howard Taylor, *Tree Line with Green Paddock*, 1993, oil on marine ply panel, 61 x 122 cm. Private collection. Photograph: Victor France

FIGURE 14
Jill Orr, *Images from Bleeding Trees No. 2*, 1979, performance at the 1979 Sydney Biennale, Art Gallery of New South Wales, Sydney. Photograph: Elizabeth Campbell

Dale Hickey, *Cottlesbridge Landscape*, 1980,
oil on canvas, 244 x 198.6 cm. Collection:
National Gallery of Victoria, Melbourne

of the Davis Base at Antarctica is clothed, not with topsoil and vegetation, but with ice and human spoilage. In the predominant tradition of Australian landscapism, Senberg's scenes are uninhabited. In *Davis*, 1987 (Figure 15), the scientists have abandoned their encampment. Unemotionally and without value judgment, Senbergs picks over the detritus that remains, like an archaeologist inspecting a site. Through his microscope he finds old packing cases and used food cans in a natural, eternal fridge that enables the identification and dating of each encampment. At the same time, these articles provide an opportunity to site a characteristic Senbergs sculptural configuration. The limited natural colour range of Antarctica must here, as is almost always the case in a Senbergs landscape, take second place to three-dimensional form.

FIGURE 15
Jan Senbergs, *Davis*, 1987,
acrylic on linen canvas, 213 x 289 cm.
The Bourne Griffiths Collection, Melbourne

This settlement, located on the fringe of the greater continent, mirrors Australian history at the frontier and is examined with an attitude of benign fascination as well as a little humour. As Senbergs knows that the rubbish is soon to be removed,[41] his work veers towards a parody of pure conservationism as applied both practically to the environment and as an art subject.

The landscape takes on a purely conceptual cast in Ian Burn's carefully amateurish 'Value Added Landscapes' of 1993 (see Figure 16). Worked as if following a 'how to paint in oils' manual, with obvious and corny experiments in brushstroke and shadow, they take on profound dimensions that go beyond a satirical joke at painfully serious attempts to capture the landscape Heysen-fashion, and involve the whole art system. The aphorism, 'This painting is better than the next one', followed by 'This painting is better than those on either side' and 'This painting is better than the last one' — all titles from the 1993 'Value Added' series — asserts the notion that discrimination between these works in the search for quality or for the purposes of sale is clearly absurd. And in putting forward such images as ideas the landscape is no longer presented in a solely representative way, but as a conceptual subject also.

Postmodernism's dismissal of the landscape from its primary position in the art hierarchy was accompanied by a shattering of its conventional reading and rendition.

Such fragmentation is exemplified in Elizabeth Kruger's *The Last of the Cool Skies*, 1988 (Plate 13). Kruger's painting, which won her a Moët & Chandon fellowship in 1989, assumes that we are all acquainted with the landscape tradition, including that paramount nineteenth-century purveyor of the rural scene complete with stratocumulus cloud: John Constable. Kruger seems to say that in the Constable tradition each square centimetre of cloud is worth millions of dollars and that any one of these

FIGURE 16
Ian Burn, *This painting is better ...*, 1993,
oil, card, wood, three parts,
each 29 x 39 x 4.5 cm

sections is enough to signify the entire landscape. Accordingly, she takes a fragment of sky, and frames and hangs it on the living-room wall where it must compete with the wallpaper to serve a decorative purpose. As she confirms in her title, much as its subject, the landscape tradition is under threat. But, at the same time, Kruger presages the return to technique that typifies art of the 1990s and exemplifies the postmodern tenet that art may be as concerned with itself as with anything else.

Not just in the boom time of the 1980s but on into the new century the Sydney painter and commercial artist Ken Done sells a painting on most days of the year.[42] Since the majority of these works are held by collectors in Asia, Europe and the United States, they relay an image of Australian culture to the rest of the world, both in their description of Sydney life and as sketch summaries of Australian landscape painting. Done's scenes, both as formal paintings and as decoration on objects as disparate as beer cans and tea-towels, involve Pop versions of the harbour for which it appears he had landscapes by Whiteley, Williams and Nolan in mind.

Done often paints the view from his studio, called the 'Cabin', located at Chinamans Beach near Sydney. As Whiteley did in the 1970s with reference to Matisse, Done has the frame of the window and objects inside the house act as a border. The Cabin is shown as a casual place where spontaneity prevails. In *Postcard from the Cabin*, 1981 (Plate 14) a carefree day is helped along by music on the record player, still playing although its audience is out of sight. The vase has a twisted neck and leans as if stirred by the same wind that propels the flotilla of sailboats. The champagne has been drunk. For Done the vegetation speaks of luxuriant decadence; palm trees and the giant hibiscus flowers picked for the artist's decorative pleasure are just ripe for thick paint.

Figures on Done's densely populated beach owe their amorphous shapes, their placement and paint application of highlight and shadow, at least in part, to the landscapes of Fred Williams. Referring to a painting of beach-goers seen from the distance as dots on the beach, much as trees are scattered over a Williams canvas, Done has written: 'I'm sure I could never have painted a picture like this if I hadn't seen Fred Williams's paintings of the bush. It's the same kind of pattern, the same use of the vertical picture plane, only with people.'[43] In converting the Williams method for the description of trees to figures, Done may have translated them back to their original language: the French Impressionist representation of figures. And, however unwittingly, it is possible that Williams derived his 'dot' method from the same French Impressionist technique of applying a loaded mixed-colour brush to the painting of the figure.

By involving the figure in the landscape, Done is among the exceptions in Australian art who include the Heidelberg painters and Russell Drysdale. Although

PLATE 14
Ken Done, *Postcard from the Cabin*, 1981,
oil on canvas, 95 x 125 cm.
Private collection, Sydney

people are present in Done's paintings, they are nominally rather than personally present, as if the artist is removed from, and even above, the throng. But, again, this is very much an Australian tradition, in which the painter travels to a location and, *en plein air*, works up a composition. Historically, the landscape has been separate or Other to the painter and viewer — a place for paintings but not for life.

The vertical picture plane device in Done's work is seen in the vertically placed palette that could just as simply have been angled to one side to create perspective. Although a minor vignette, this example is one of many that serves to re-direct the eye back to Nolan's Wimmera.

Rather than producing a timeless scene in the style of Nolan and Williams, Done shows Australia at the turn of the century. When such a work as this is obtained by the tourist it represents the same romantic, if somewhat shallow, notion which has characteristically defined the Australian identity and is the kind of stereotype with which visitors are familiar before they have even arrived. Done provides an update on the man-versus-the-land relationship adopted earlier in the century. But now, rather than struggling against it, Australians are seen to be the idle beneficiaries of its bounty. Australia is a land of sun, surf and leisure; life is styled as a public relations movie. It is a place of plenty and play. From good weather to prawns on barbies, there is a never-ending supply.

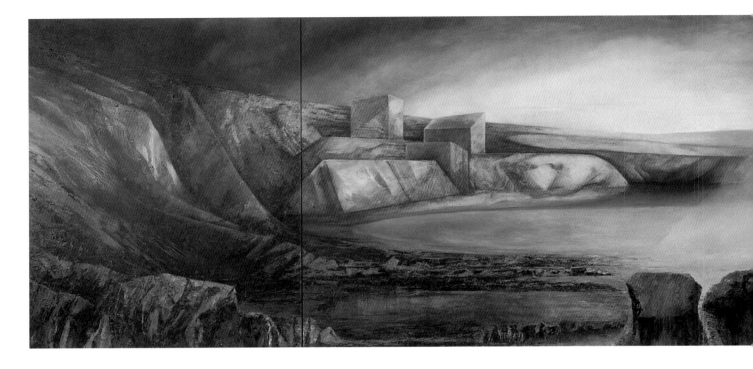

Even though Done may be painting from personal experience, his perspective of the world is privileged. It stands in the historical tradition of the landscape which, for many Australians whose orbit is less aesthetic, is irrelevant. Whether artist or viewer, their focus is less on an escapist art than on one that documents details from their own experience. Interest in the landscape may not be a priority and their circumstances may not include a gum tree.

It was increasingly believed in the 1970s and 1980s that descriptive representations of the landscape, however innovative, are inadequate presenters of ideas beyond it. The pressing need arose for a plural method that could express the dynamics of an international society with a complexity of cultures. With this recognition, a break was made from an enslavement to representation and material effects that made way for ideas and left behind criticism couched in the formalist terms of style, technique and quality.

Mandy Martin's construction of a mythical landscape with an allegorical narrative based on a complex mélange of artistic and literary sources proves, however, that there are new possibilities for the traditional landscape that are as original as the switch to representative permutations on the urbanscape, such as Jenny Watson's houses that suggest there is so much more going on behind their neat exteriors, or Howard Arkley's poetic, Synthetist reworkings of Antipodean decorative kitsch. Mandy Martin's approach answers the post-colonial need for a statement that refers to place but is not merely descriptive, purely technically adept, or playfully postmodern, but all of these and more.

Because *Red Ochre Cove*, 1987 (Plate 15), was commissioned for Parliament House, Martin devised a means by which to reflect aspects of the Tom Roberts painting that also hangs there, titled *The Opening of the 1st Parliament of the Commonwealth of Australia May the 9th 1901 by HRH the Duke of Cornwall & York, Exhibition Buildings*, 1901–03. Her treeless location was based on a section of the South Australian coast, near Rapid Bay, south of Adelaide, and was intended as a commentary

on the destructive effects of mining which denudes the land and discolours the water.[44] The red ochre pigment found in the area was collected by Aborigines and later excavated by mining companies whose schematic buildings are shown to the left of the work.[45] Each played their part in draining life from the land and are cited within the one 'snapshot' caught as if through the elliptical eye of the camera lens.

Another reading of the painting derives from the novel *The Volcano Lover* by Susan Sontag.[46] Set in seventeenth-century Italy, the narrative relates a heroic love affair — into which Martin's landscape is metamorphosed with rock forms shaped as gargantuan genitalia. On a narrative level, the tension of the lovers increases as the reverberating volcano threatens to erupt. Diagrammatically, the love affair is described by reference to the circular composition that delineates the crowd in the Tom Roberts painting, and acts in Martin's work as the receiving female genitalia that are enclosed in a tunnel. The shaft of light, also from the Roberts work, provides the imagery for the penetrating male aspect.

Since it hangs in the Parliamentary Committee Room, Martin's narrative is often shown on television and forms the background to reports on decisions made there. From another realm entirely, Martin's engrossing layers of metaphor suggest that the landscape in Australian art is not so much a dull subject of the past as an absorbing and continuing romance.

Managing Modernism: Australian Artistic Movements since 1940

Artistic movements conceived to advance the artist's cause in Australia have sometimes sought to curb the influence of overseas trends and at other times to graft local interests onto the international Zeitgeist. Despite their disparate and even opposing concerns and the variation in their impact, these groups have a number of common characteristics. They were established primarily to influence prevailing stylistic trends in order to develop an Australian art; in all cases their association was brief and their membership was almost exclusively male. Pivotally, an associated art historian has interpreted and presented these groups' art and aims. ➤

The Angry Penguins 1941–49

The formation of the Angry Penguins was to a minor degree attributable to the art historian Bernard Smith, who is most readily identified as the organising member of the Antipodeans of 1959. In 1943 he reviewed contributions by John Perceval, Arthur Boyd, Yosl Bergner and the Sydney artist Nan Hortin to the avant-garde Contemporary Art Society exhibition of 1942, describing them as 'the most vital movement in Australian art today'.[1]

In Smith's *Australian Painting 1788–1960*, first published in 1962, the Angry Penguins are referred to as a cooperative group associated with the art patron and collector John Reed, the Adelaide poet and publisher Max Harris and their *Angry Penguins* journal. The artists nominated as involved are Sidney Nolan, Albert Tucker, Arthur Boyd and John Perceval.[2] In 1973 the historian Geoffrey Serle wrote of the John Reed 'school' of art in his cultural history of Australia, *From Deserts the Prophets Come*, and cited the major artists concerned as Nolan, Tucker and Boyd.[3] The main art history on the 1940s period, *Rebels and Precursors*, by art historian Richard Haese, has the group consisting of artists and writers: 'Albert Tucker, Max Harris, Harry Roskolenko, Neil Douglas, John Yule, Tony Underhill, Max Dunn and many more.'[4] At the core of Haese's text are Nolan, Tucker, Perceval and Boyd, with Yosl Bergner and Danila Vassilieff shadowing them as significantly influential. The revision involved in writer Janine Burke's biography of Joy Hester, published in 1983, resulted in Hester being added as a central member.[5]

Nolan and Boyd were already household names when major reinvestigations of their 1940s work, as well as that of their colleagues, were undertaken in the 1980s and 1990s. Further concentrating public attention on them was the donation of the John and Sunday Reed collection in which they were represented, and the opening of the Reed house in Melbourne to the public as Heide Park and Art Gallery in 1981. Through the associated publicity, the art of the Angry Penguins became synonymous with radical, expressionist modernism in Melbourne in the 1940s; indeed, it came to epitomise Australian modernism itself. By 1988, the year of Australia's bicentennial celebrations, when they were shown at the Hayward Gallery in London, the group had assumed a cohesive character, but one that relates only questionably to the artists' original intentions.[6] In the foreword to the exhibition they are referred to as: 'the group associated with the Reeds (Boyd, Nolan, Tucker, Hester and Perceval) …'[7] But, unlike the Antipodeans and other Australian art movements, their association was formed by external sources rather than personal membership. Questions remain therefore as to whether or not their alliance originally possessed the resolute solidarity consequently attributed to it.

Nevertheless, these artists are forever united, at least as the painters who exhibited with the Contemporary Art Society under the presidency of John Reed in the early 1940s, even though to some extent they have found their united personae by what they are not in relation to other groups of the period. The excitement and daring of their early 1940s Melbourne work revealed an energy and freedom that contrasted dramatically with the comparative genteel pallor that had characterised much of the work by the so-called Heidelberg artists who are traditionally viewed as the previous great Australian art movement. The Heidelberg painters' depiction of the natural landscape and its narratives had maintained an emotional control, but now it was human experience at an intense pitch, located in a brash, city landscape that engaged these young painters who looked to literary, artistic and mythological sources to create a personal symbolism.

The general artistic make-up of Melbourne at the time is said to have fallen into three significant groups: that deriving from the restrained Australian academy and the

Angry Penguins, as well as the documentary-style commentary of the Social Realists. The latter, who included Noel Counihan, Vic O'Connor and Yosl Bergner, have never received the recognition accorded their rival Angry Penguins associates, even though, as has been acknowledged, there were times when the interests of the two groups overlapped. Bernard Smith has argued that:

> a fair-minded assessment will reveal that their [the Social Realists] wartime work was every bit as personal and passionate, as much involved with the terror and contradictions of those times, as their colleagues who turned for inspiration to French literature, child and primitive art, [and] psychoanalysis … to become the heroes of the post-war Australian art establishment.[8]

What the Social Realist work lacks by comparison with that of the Angry Penguins is symbolism, abstraction, dislocation and reference to sources beyond the surface subject; what it possesses is a touching sensibility. The clothes of the old woman portrayed by Noel Counihan in *In the Waiting Room*, 1943 (Figure 17), indicate, in a more accurately descriptive and technically refined way than an Angry Penguins painting would, aspects of her character and such details as when she was painted and that she was poor. The old woman's hands may be arthritic, she has no teeth and the dark circles under her eyes attest to a life of hardship and perhaps pain.

The relationship of the Angry Penguins artists to John and Sunday Reed and their attitude towards the support given them is also worthy of analysis, since the general representation of a thoroughly harmonious relationship with assistance warmly welcomed is not necessarily accurate. Besides deriving benefit from John Reed's selection of work for Contemporary Art Society exhibitions and his direct purchases, there is the matter of his provision of financial support, along with artistic encouragement and patronage, and the ongoing invitation to participate in an intellectual milieu. Not all of these, however, were sought by the artists. While the stipend paid to Albert Tucker[9] and the support given to Joy Hester were substantial, Arthur Boyd, for example, is not mentioned as having received any such assistance, although there is evidence that he did experience hardship. This is exemplified by his circumstances in 1946–47 when he, his wife Yvonne, and their daughter lived in a simple cottage on his father's land at Murrumbeena with only an external cold water supply.[10] There remains a query, however, as to whether or not Boyd would have accepted such an offer had one been made. John Perceval had been given an important promotion by John Reed in an introductory article for the September 1943 edition of the *Angry Penguins* journal. Apparently more significant, but in retrospect less so, was the Reeds' extension of one pound per week to him for about eighteen months, from 1943 to 1944.[11] Although unquestionably generous, this amount was hardly enough to make a significant difference. When converted to today's dollar value it amounts to about $40 per week or $2000 a year.

Perceval had met Boyd in 1941 and joined the Boyd household on marrying Arthur's sister, Mary, in 1944. As is well known, most members of the extended Boyd family were involved in artistic activities and their rural home at Murrumbeena, called 'Open Country', was a literary and philosophical focus for intellectuals. Both, therefore, had already felt and continued to experience the influence of the extended Boyd household when they became part of the Reed circle.[12] An emphatic defence of Murrumbeena as a comparable cultural centre was made by Peter Herbst, who was for many years professor of philosophy at the Australian National University. He had been a partner at the Arthur Merric Boyd pottery, begun in 1944, and a close friend of the Boyd family. Herbst wrote: 'The Reeds, Tucker and Harris did not set up a

FIGURE 17
Noel Counihan, *In the Waiting Room*, 1943, oil on hardboard, 62 x 43.5 cm. Collection: Art Gallery of New South Wales, Sydney

paradigm, to which all the modern painters of that society did or should have aspired. They made taste at Heide but not for us all.'[13] Herbst went on to argue that the Boyd inclination towards traditional literary and religious themes was of equal value to what he saw as the self-conscious Reed preference for the avant-garde, which was at least partly motivated, he argued, by 'the projection of the personalities of its protagonists' and whose position at the centre of progressive art in Melbourne had gained notoriety by its access to publicity.[14]

By 1945 the stylistic changes and new interests that were absorbing Boyd were deemed, according to art historian Richard Haese, 'a betrayal of the values which all had appeared to espouse and express between 1943 and 1945'.[15] Since the 1945 religious works by Boyd are so different from his 1943–44 paintings, it appears the earlier innovation is attributable, at least in part, to the Reeds' influence, or to others in the Angry Penguins cohort. His later and continuing development of literary and religious themes is therefore attributable to dialogue at Murrumbeena and is sufficiently profound to argue ultimately for the superiority of this influence, as well as for Boyd's decision to distance himself from the inner circle. Of his attitude towards the Reeds and their interests and aspirations, Boyd explained:

> I found that it was best to keep a fair distance because you could get eaten up and I didn't like that … you could be absorbed in a world in which you would be too inhibited to break out of [and] I didn't need the stimulation of the emotional involvement. I felt that I had enough and that it was all I could do actually to paint.[16]

FIGURE 18
Joy Hester, *Drawing from the 'Love' series,*
c. 1949, ink on paper, 75.3 x 55.5 cm. Collection: National Gallery of Australia, Canberra

Another aspect of the group that has received little consideration is the number of women associated with it who also painted but who, for various reasons, have not been equally acclaimed. Yvonne Boyd (née Lennie) studied art and produced work of a similarly figurative expressionist style to that produced by others of the group, but very little of her work remains extant. *Children, Fitzroy,* 1944 (Plate 17), could be placed into either the Social Realist or the Angry Penguins category. Its subject matter has been considered by Yosl Bergner, and it is rendered with the fluidity of a work by Arthur Boyd or John Perceval. It was painted when Yvonne and Arthur lived at 2 Henry Street, Fitzroy, the inner Melbourne suburb which housed a large Aboriginal population at the time.[17] Many of Arthur Boyd's 1943 works were painted in this flat, situated above a workshop, when he returned from daily army duties. Arthur's sister, Mary Boyd, also painted but, sadly and similarly, very little of her work has survived.[18] For both women, the tasks of mother and artist's wife, as well as the social proprieties of the time, were enough to force them to relinquish their practical artistic interests.

Although larger than that of Yvonne and Mary Boyd, Joy Hester's oeuvre was regarded as secondary to that of her male associates for nearly forty years, again for its incompleteness, but also because it consists almost entirely of drawings and watercolour sketches, media which generally have been classified as secondary to the painted form. Despite this history — indeed, in part because of it — Hester, as wife of Albert Tucker, friend of the Reeds and artist in her own right, acquired a cult-like following in the 1980s and 1990s for her token female presence in a male story of angry, masculine art that had neglected her contribution. But in an attempt to redress the situation, her followers produced another mythology. Rather than focusing on Hester's work, accounts of her achievements have invariably focused on the tragic and eccentric aspects of her life — a modus operandum long rejected as specious and clichéd in the analysis of work by male artists. These largely biographical considerations of Hester's contribution also tend to place emphasis on her emotional and circumstantial difficulties rather than on her art. Typically, considerations that purport

to consider her work devote considerable attention to her struggle to make time for art, her beauty and sexual relationships, and her untimely death at the age of forty from Hodgkins disease. Such accounts also fail to note the extraordinarily fortunate path Hester's career (as distinct from her personal life) took by virtue of her marriage to Albert Tucker, which automatically brought her to the attention of his artistic connections. Similarly, the support of John and Sunday Reed could hardly have been greater, since they provided the gift of a house, some financial assistance and took on the full-time care of her son, Sweeney.[19]

Ultimately, the notion still propounded, of Hester having been overlooked by the established art system[20] founders on the matter of her commemorative exhibition at the National Gallery of Victoria in 1981, an honour she was granted some ten years before retrospectives were held for her colleagues Tucker, Perceval and Boyd. Contemporary critiques of her art therefore tend not to denigrate it for its repetition and lack of intellectual scope, however pleasing and original the free, sweeping lines, as exemplified in what may be one of her most successful works, *The Lovers*, c. 1949. The love theme, central for Hester, is here shown as lovers melting into each other in a locale beyond place that exists within the psyche alone.

Indeed, when a postmodern laterality is applied to the collective Angry Penguins as pre-eminent banner-carriers for modernism, they may be drawn back from their elevated position. The Sydney artists Roy de Maistre and Roland Wakelin, for example, had experimented with a 'purer' form of abstraction some twenty years earlier. This work was shown in 1919 in an exhibition entitled 'Colour in Art' that included de Maistre's well-known *Rhythmic Composition in Yellow Green Minor*, 1919.[21] Despite the precedence of work by de Maistre and Wakelin, assessments made contemporaneously with their exhibition, as well as many since, have omitted their significant role as innovative abstractionists. Art historian Heather Johnson puts forward the suggestion that a continuing preference for the dark, tonal approach of the influential teacher Max Meldrum may have been a factor. Also operating, she argues, was a generalised fear of 'bolshevism' associated with anything new and especially applicable to what was seen as a decadent breakdown in figurative art, an attitude not only seen in Australia in the 1920s.[22]

The role of de Maistre and Wakelin as pre-empting modernists may also have failed to gain currency for reasons that relate to the perceived attributes of modernism. For audiences attuned to an art centred on the figure or the landscape, de Maistre's abstract images were devoid of meaning and therefore lacking in validity. His careful, calculated approach to abstraction — based on colour–tone principles and the relationships between colours and musical notes — was not seen to convey the same emotional intensity as the Angry Penguins' depictions of the human figure, made with a free, apparently careless, expressionist brushstroke. This was a brushstroke thought to suggest not just an abandonment on the part of the characters portrayed — such as Perceval's gyrating jazz musicians — but an unrestrained artistic method, and a similar uninhibited personality on the part of the artists.

Challenges to the Angry Penguins as modernists have also been levelled on behalf of Margaret Preston by historian and writer Humphrey McQueen and art historian Jeanette Hoorn.[23] Their argument was taken further by art historian Helen Topliss, who suggested that not only Margaret Preston but also Thea Proctor, Ethel Spowers, Eveline Syme and Grace Cossington Smith may all be regarded as early modernists if it is understood that modernism can take many forms.[24] The basis of the claim that these women artists of the 1920s and 1930s had broken new ground, is their introduction of bold, flat planes of colour and their modification of natural shapes to create a stylised patterning. Working against these women as avant-garde modernists was the connotation of revolt as tumultuous rather than subtle. Coincident is the belief that anger resides within the male character rather than the female, in whom rebellion is conventionally perceived as neurosis.

The *Angry Penguins*'s status as the revolutionary voice of modern Australian culture has grown to such proportions that the original irony of the journal's title is often lost — another thread among the influences that led to the primacy of the literal notion of 'anger' and revolt. Despite its intellectual origins, the name of the journal now evokes little more than the ludicrous image of pompous, strutting penguins. The poem by writer and journalist Max Harris, from which the phrase is taken, was, however, a good deal more metaphoric and concerned the Spanish Civil War, with the Angry Penguins image descriptive of drunken, dinner-suited young men. It was titled 'Progress of Defeat':

> *We know no mithridatum of despair*
> *as drunks, the angry penguins of the night,*
> *straddling the cobbles of the square,*
> *Tying a shoelace by fogged lamplight.*[25]

The easy 'angry' tag became a pun on the group name that helped to reinforce and propel the notion of impatience with the status quo. It was the stuff of journalistic headlines and advertising one-liners, and was taken up as such in the early 1980s when the media responded to the call of public relations consultants employed to acquaint Melburnians with their latest public gallery — the erstwhile home of the late John and Sunday Reed.

The tale of the fictitious writer Ern Malley, contrived by the poets James McAuley and Harold Stewart, had also grown mythically extraordinary, and for a time stimulated an interest that threatened to surpass the country's most enjoyed 'authentic' poetry. The poems were put forward as evidence of Malley's ability but, having been compiled from unrelated quotations that were intended to read incoherently, they were actually a hoax devised to entrap the journal's publishers, Max Harris and John Reed. Intended to reveal Harris and Reed as pretentiously and mistakenly mesmerised by anything new and complex, they were ultimately designed to sabotage the credibility of the *Angry Penguins* journal.[26] Deepening the legend was the decision by the South Australian police to charge the publishers of the broadsheet with indecency for their publication of these Ern Malley poems, and several other short stories and poems published in the Ern Malley edition of 1944.

But responsibility for initiating an alignment between the art produced and the rage of the artists involved ultimately devolves to Harris and Reed. It falls to Harris for his use of 'Angry Penguins' to title the journal he began in 1940 in Adelaide that preceded the better known Melbourne journal, and to Reed for retaining the same name for the broadsheet they both hoped would simultaneously signal the modernist revolution in Australia and advance the cause of a local artistic identity. Writing in 1988, Max Harris referred to the Melbourne Social Realist painters as having 'an anger in common with the

FIGURE 19
Bill Moseley, *Angry Penguins*, 1994, photograph

PLATE 18
Albert Tucker, *Tram Stop (Image of Modern Evil # 26)*, 1945–46, oil on hardboard, 80 x 120 cm. Collection: ICI Australia, Melbourne

Angry Penguins',[27] but when he wrote the poem from which the name derives, it was unlikely he was thinking of the particular modernist painters whose work it came to represent.

Regardless of the way the group is styled, and as innovative as its diviners thought the movement to be, ultimately the very notion of a modernist revolt is a transplantation of a European development. The sum total of Reed's 'authentic national vision', as identified in the work of Nolan, is much diminished by the simple association with rebellion that has prevailed in the Eurocentric discourse since the birth of Dada. Overlooked is the fact that work by the group is far more constructed, contrived and thoughtful than is permitted by such a reductive appraisal. Even on an emotional level, there is greater complexity than simple ire. Albert Tucker, for example, finds offensive the ritual allurement he considers in the well-known *The Pick Up*, 1941. The women involved, dressed in luminescent, transparent clothes, serve like neon lights to attract their mates for an inelegant sexual engagement, an episode that appears to arouse a moralistic displeasure in the artist. More blatant still is his disgust with the soldiers on leave who are reduced to animal types, grasping at the flesh of their equally bestial girlfriends in *Victory Girls*, 1943. Despite the intensity of Tucker's reaction, his response to such sexual displays is more accurately described as indignation or revulsion than anger.

In Tucker's *Tram Stop*, 1945–46 (Plate 18), the travellers' efforts to avoid each other's gaze, apart from their indulgence in discreet, sexual glances, have a humorous edge. But there are also stylistic variations that argue against generalisation to any one emotion. There is a marked difference in these loosely painted works compared with the study and relative restraint evident in some of Tucker's other 'Images of Modern Evil' paintings, with their ornate street lamps and carefully considered light-plays of the city night. Such intricacies reveal that the association between a loose brushstroke and emotional outrage is more appropriately applied to Hester, Perceval and Boyd, and to a lesser degree to Nolan, but even then the expressionism concerned does not equate with hostility. The fluidity of Hester's work, for example, is concerned with love and perhaps fear rather than anger.

Perceval is in some senses the most and least angry Penguin. His stroke carries a recklessness but his subject is not as precisely politically directed as is that of Tucker. When related to autobiography, such as is the case in his well-known *Boy with Cat*, 1943, his subject is emotional, but when concerned with documentary it reaches out to universal rather than local themes. The main street in *Exodus from a Bombed City*, 1942, is set in a fictitious purgatory in which heaven and hell coexist as warlike domains of winners and losers, rats, sinners and the saved. The hard outlines and contrasting flat-planed areas indicate an apparent interest in the German woodcuts of Emil Nolde, with whose work this painting shares a sense of ominous despair. Perceval slips into superficial documentary in *Child Drawing in a Carlton Street*, 1943. Hostility is nowhere to be found in this affectionate study of the child engrossed with the city street that is his drawing board.

For Boyd the early 1940s period marked his first time away from family life. Artistic, literary and religious interests, as well as distance, shielded him from the brash, ugly and threatening aspects of urban humanity. In some ways he and his colleagues led a privileged existence in these war years, during which they produced some of the most important work of their careers. Boyd and Perceval experienced no risk to life in South Melbourne where they carried out their daily office duties in the Army's cartographic section. Albert Tucker was discharged from the Wangaratta army training camp after what he has described as 'a few harrowing months until the Army decided I was no good to them, and threw me out',[28] and Nolan went Absent Without Leave from his base at Melbourne's Watsonia Army Barracks in 1944.[29] Christmas 1945 at Heide, showing Nolan, John Sinclair and John and Sunday Reed captured in a photograph[30] often used to illustrate articles concerning the Reeds and their legacy, suggests the casual air of a social occasion. It is one well catered for, with no shortage of wine bottles on the table. A pretty puppy has its photograph taken along with the small gathering and there is no sense whatever of the horrors taking place elsewhere.

Although the disdain for wholesale slaughter can be appreciated, these young men and women had little to be angry about by comparison with others who had no choice but to go to war, as well as others still who underwent serious hardships for what they saw as an appropriate duty.

Definitions aside, the strength of the Angry Penguins group was to switch direction to a new objective that involved considering subjects hitherto unseen in Australian art and expressing these sometimes complicated issues in the most simple terms. The surrealist influence was applied to elements of life that were already disturbing, producing the unexpected and contradictory around every corner. Matters usually concealed by night's refuge were also their material. Perceval's naked couple in the graveyard in *Lovers Surprised by the Dawn*, 1944, are surprised that daylight has revealed them for all to see. Boyd's disabled and dysfunctional people have personalities that extend them physically and take them to the edge of sanity as repressed psychological extremes are brought to the surface. Elements of the postmodern have also been identified in their work. In *Image of Modern Evil No. 19*, 1945, Tucker touches at the edges of postmodernism by building a shrine to the pleasures of the flesh from bathing bodies, ignoring naturalistic matters of perspective, but his symbolic tale has a consistent coherency that does not accord with postmodernism. Perceval takes things further in *Negroes at Night*, 1944, in which a discontinuous array of references is spread across a night sky with little concern for such conventional matters as perspective or continuous narrative.[31]

But for all the myths that have proliferated around the group one need only imagine discovering this work for the first time to agree with John Reed that its freshness and innovation is astonishing indeed.

The Antipodeans 1959

Its impact aside, the activities of the Antipodeans may be summed up as consisting of several meetings (which wives were not allowed to attend),[32] the production of a manifesto,[33] and the mounting of an exhibition at the Victorian Artists Society's gallery in Albert Street, East Melbourne, from 4 to 15 August 1959. Antipodeans members were John Brack, Clifton Pugh, Arthur Boyd, John Perceval, Robert Dickerson, Charles Blackman, David Boyd and the art historian Bernard Smith.

It is probably fair to suggest that without Bernard Smith's organisational guidance the group would never have formed as effectively as it did, its objectives instead remaining confined to talk, however impassioned, over drinks at the end of a day's painting. Furthermore, without his imprimatur this brotherhood was unlikely to have entered the history books and there may not have been a manifesto. Each of the artists was already known in his own right, but Perceval and Boyd at least were not much given to putting their attitudes in writing.[34] Pugh was a frequent letter-writer but not as competent in matters of art history as Bernard Smith. John Brack acted as group secretary and, as Smith has explained, took a somewhat sardonic attitude to the proceedings.[35]

Smith has written that the group had its genesis in the idea for an exhibition, stimulated by a day Perceval, Blackman and Pugh spent painting together. It was thought of interest to demonstrate the different interpretations that resulted when the three worked before the same landscape.[36] This experiment coincided with Smith's concern that international abstraction was becoming increasingly popular in Australia and, most importantly, that a monopolistic critical attitude towards it existed, disallowing any other aesthetic. According to Smith, the next crucial step was a meeting with David Boyd on 15 February 1959 at which the possibility of holding an exhibition in defence of figuration was discussed and agreed upon.[37] Following this, and after contributions and discussions were put forward by all members, a manifesto was drawn up. But, as might be expected in a document formulated by six people, there are moments in the final document that appear contradictory. It is argued, for example, that 'It is natural therefore that we should see and experience nature differently in some degree from the artists of the northern hemisphere', while in a later paragraph it is stated that 'Nevertheless our final obligation is neither to place nor nation'. In a later summary of events, Smith stresses the self-parody on the part of members regarding the whole subject of the group's formation, while at the same time arguing for an impassioned basis to its motivation.[38]

In the light of post-colonial discourse, such apparent contradictions may be interpreted as reflecting an early stage in the acquisition of a post-colonial status. Typically, the model demonstrates that a nation having undergone a period of colonial rule will emphasise its regional identity at the termination of such domination. Given that Australia has been a de facto colony — in that it is a self-governing country of the Commonwealth, as opposed to a nation that has experienced coercive control — its expression of its independence is not precisely true to form.

All meetings of the Antipodeans were held at John Perceval's Canterbury house, but as Professor Margaret Plant has pointed out, paintings by him at the time, although still figurative, were most like the American Abstract Expressionists against whom the group railed.[39] Backgrounds by Pugh, laid down before the details of bush interior and a feature animal or bird, are either coincidentally like Jackson Pollock works or influenced by them. A Pollock, however, would not constitute acceptable art to a member of the Antipodeans because it does not communicate 'life experiences'. Indeed, it appears there was an esoteric meaning to the definition of abstraction and figuration among the group. Writing in 1988, Bernard Smith suggested: 'If you want to see abstraction working at its best in painting, don't look at the work of an artist like Jackson Pollock, look at the work of an artist like Jan Vermeer.'[40]

In his essay 'The truth about the Antipodeans'[41] Smith included a number of quotes from the artists, all of which assert with John Brack that: 'Our experience must be our material.'[42] In their contributions and in the final manifesto, the artists give no brook to the notion that life may be captured other than literally. Furthermore, they appear to have rejected art that did not render the figure a dominant characteristic and, although not said in so many words, there is an inference of this in the manifesto, in such lines as: 'People, their surroundings and the past that made them are still subjects, we should like to point out, worthy of the consideration of the artist.' Similarly: 'we accept the image as representing some form of acceptance of and involvement in life.' But the proposition that the Antipodeans preferred to paint the figure, as well as figuratively, is a line of argument dismissed by Smith.[43]

Perceval showed six of his Williamstown scenes at the 'Antipodeans' exhibition, none of which involved the figure, and nine of his ceramic sculptured angels, all of which did. In the 'Williamstown' series, he virtually ignored the extremities of artificial and night light that he had been instrumental in introducing to the Australian discourse. It is clear that he and Arthur Boyd undertook to hone their techniques according to precepts that by comparison appeared less risky, less freely expressive and more decorative and 'finished' than those applied to works they had produced ten years before, and one might speculate on the role of Smith, as significant critic at the time, in this regard.

Abandoning to some degree what appears to have been a natural inclination to innovation, Boyd and Perceval avoided the dramatic subject, as well as their apparently hasty brushstroke. The dreamlike dissonance of narrative and mood that had distinguished their earlier work was also relinquished as they opted for a more carefully considered approach. Adaptations included a more logical, although still allegorical narrative and an adherence to such technical matters as conventional perspective, modelling, and relatively careful figure description. Boyd's 'Bride' series of 1957–58, for example, shown at the 'Antipodeans' exhibition, is generally thought to have been his most significant work of that decade. But however poignant, these works do not involve radical experiments with states of mind as had preoccupied him in the South Melbourne paintings, such as *The Gargoyles* (Figure 1) and *The Seasons*, both of 1944. Instead, albeit with the involvement of details as symbol and metaphor, his subjects were orientated further to the narrative, with the 'Bride' series relating the courtship and marriage of the gigantic but nevertheless vulnerable Aborigine to his diminutive, mixed-race bride. The art historian Ursula Hoff has mentioned that when Boyd was in Alice Springs he saw Aboriginal women wearing delicate, white bridal dresses and travelling to church in trucks that were more suitable for transporting animals.[44]

Clifton Pugh showed six landscapes, a portrait and a landscape-portrait of Charles Blackman titled *Charles Blackman and the Black Birds*, 1959. *A Feral Cat*, 1957, showing the animal with a captured bird, set against the bush, was included in the exhibition,

Clifton Pugh, *Cat in a Rabbit Trap*, 1957,
oil on composition board, 91.4 x 137.1 cm

FIGURE 20
Robert Dickerson, *The Bank Clerk*, 1959,
oil on composition board, 153.2 x 138 cm.
The Holmes à Court Collection, Heytesbury

but more interesting is his *Cat in a Rabbit Trap*, 1957 (Plate 19), in which a cat with numerous heads and limbs, as if recorded on film, struggles frenetically to release itself from the trap. The flat, two-dimensional cat is outlined in white to look as if it were etched onto the landscape like an Aboriginal rock painting.[45]

Charles Blackman showed eight paintings, including *Girl with Flowers*, c. 1959, David Boyd his 'Tasmanians' series, and John Brack his distinctive children with their amusing personalities in *The Girls at School*, c. 1959. Robert Dickerson showed his solitary figures, such as the intense, neatly attired bank clerk (Figure 20) who grips what one assumes is his desk, as if his entire security and identity were contained within it. The critical response to the exhibition, according to Smith, was generally negative,[46] despite the reported exuberant patronage at its opening.[47]

Terry Smith's 'provincialist bind' here operated exactly according to form.[48] The group wished to find an alternative expression to American abstraction but were bound to fail, if for no other reason than because they were not in New York and therefore would not be perceived to be associated with the experimental vanguard. Ironically, this was the case, even though Clement Greenberg, the main advocate of Abstract Expressionism, lavished praise on Pugh nine years later, saying: 'Nolan tries to be visionary. Pugh potentially wrestling with the visionary is a talent I admire.'[49] Greenberg made this statement at a press conference in which he is reported as saying that he was impressed by the high level of competence in Australian painting compared with American. He went on to qualify his praise, however, by saying that he considered this to be the case in a technical sense only because he felt Australian painting lacked the 'visionary streak' of American art.

Towards the end of the group's existence it had been agreed to allow new members to join. Among those considered were Jon Molvig, Albert Tucker, Sidney Nolan and Fred Williams, but by then bad reviews acted to splinter opinion as to the value of the alliance.[50] The last formal meeting of the group was held on 29 January 1960.[51]

As Bernard Smith has pointed out, an important adjunct of proceedings had been preparations for an Antipodeans show at the Whitechapel Gallery in London, which eventuated in 1961 as 'Recent Australian Painting'. The exhibition showed the work of some who had equivocated about joining the formal Antipodeans movement, including Albert Tucker, Fred Williams and Sidney Nolan but, as events transpired and the group disintegrated, they were included in the London exhibition along with the Antipodeans proper, and were able to avoid the risk of losing face by becoming official members of an unfashionable movement.[52] The embarrassment of taking this figurative stand has continued to dog the group's heritage, as, anecdotally, members have sought to alter their position vis-à-vis it ever since. It must be said, however, that all the original members, with the exception of Brack, agreed to participate in a reconstruction of the 'Antipodeans' exhibition in 1988.[53]

Regardless of the uneven quality of the original Antipodeans' work, they were a group out of their time whose motivations might satisfy a more thoroughly postcolonial audience more effectively. The earnest, unselfish element that stimulated their formation — the production of an Australian art — has perhaps been too hastily lost to the image of a King Canute-like refusal to accept the incoming tide.

The Annandale Imitation Realists 1961–62

The embarrassment felt by the Antipodeans in not being taken particularly seriously was not helped by the fact that, despite their protestation in the manifesto that 'Dada is as dead as the Dodo', within the year a group of Sydney artists were finding it very interesting indeed, so much so that they went on to form a movement with Dada as a guiding principle. Mike Brown and Ross Crothall, who were joined in 1961 by Colin Lanceley, were drawn to the Dada approaches first employed in the 1920s by its best-known advocate, Marcel Duchamp. When, like the Angry Penguins, the group adopted surrealist strategies it added to them visual references to the assembled figures of Dubuffet.[54] It was the absurdity and the confidence of Dadaist assertions, made without regard to viewer expectation, that were a main influence. But disrupting the search for influences, with a contrariness typical of Annandale Imitation Realism, is a statement by Mike Brown who once said that the group was subject to absolutely any influence at all.[55]

The principal aim of the Annandale Imitation Realists, according to Brown, was to achieve no less than 'the virtual demolition of modernism'.[56] The fact that they were no more than art students, fleeing what they considered an oppressively conservative system may, it seems, have been a useful qualification in the projection of such an immense ambition. The specific ruination they sought to wreak was directed towards ego-driven individualism, the prevailing monopolistic hold of abstraction and the attendant pretensions of both. Another characteristic to be countered was art's fashionability, as one preferred mode is characteristically taken up and discarded to make way for the next.

Among the approaches through which such change was to be effected was collaborative production. Brown has described a difficult, preferred situation, in which ego is dissolved by cooperative effort while authorship is retained. He wrote: 'I. R. was emphatically *not* a "collectivist" group in which individualism and legitimate ego aspirations were suppressed or submerged in a group identity. Rather, it was an individualist *and* communalist group whose energy derived from an additive blending of personal and communal interests.'[57] Coincident with the negatives of individualism, and with abstraction, they believed, went an élitist, 'heartless cleverness' and the cult of the superhero.[58] This latter concern, usually involving use of the word 'genius', was to gather pace and be taken up widely in the 1980s.

But attempts to clarify Annandale Imitation Realist precepts are invariably met with contradiction. According to Mike Brown's accounts of the group's formation and development, élitism of any kind was denounced. But the new art was to be the best and, as such, by definition must fall victim to the narrowing parameters of élitism. To avoid this eventuality, Annandale Imitation Realism was to be a more ethically sound best art, the development of which was to exclude no-one. Associated with attempts to engender an attitude of egalitarianism was the choice of group name. Although Crothall and Brown had shared a studio at 28 Rose Street, Annandale, the appeal of identification with their suburb was almost entirely subversive. Anti-heroic in its poverty, blandness and apparently limited prospects, Annandale was to have not fifteen minutes of fame but the ultimate reward. Like a latter-day Heidelberg School, it was to have its place in Australian art history. And more than a mere nominal or even visual reference, bits and pieces of Annandale itself were to be embedded in the work. Items of domestic and industrial rubbish thrown into back streets were collected for later use and judiciously placed in works as required. Oddly shaped scraps of wood may be traced to a furniture factory located near the Annandale studio. Similarly, the concepts of imitation and, in the cultural climate of Sydney at the time, realism, were taken up because they were either anything but de rigueur or, better still, downright taboo.

In a rejection of most art styles and their accompanying commitment to material practice, the Annandale Imitation Realists opposed the Antipodeans but shared their misgivings about the prevalence of abstraction as the only acceptable form. In

PLATE 20
Mike Brown and Ross Crothall,
Sailing to Byzantium, 1961,
pencil, oil crayon and enamel on
composition board, 91.5 x 122.1 cm.
Collection: National Gallery of Australia,
Canberra

accordance with them, and with the Angry Penguins, one of the primary motivations of the Annandale Imitation Realists was the establishment of an art that would express an Australian rather than a European identity. But as distinct from both groups, the Annandale Imitation Realists found the language of homage to European classicism or myth anathema. To counter deference to Europe and artistic fashion they dug for the roots of art and harvested that of the so-called fourth world (undeveloped, as opposed to developing countries) with a 'style' which could undermine western artistic superiority.[59] But, then again, a methodology such as this was inadvertently to involve support for western modernism since it followed Picasso's appropriation of the indigenous image. The Imitation Realists' version of this procedure was to adopt images from Australian Aboriginal art, that of the New Zealand Maori and Sepik art of New Guinea. The Polynesian influence is evident in Mike Brown's *Mr Hodge*, c. 1961 (Figure 21), which depicts a character whose face is covered with a striated pattern that appears to mimic ceremonial body painting, or the all-over tattooing practice of the region, the facial lines appearing sometimes as tattoos and at others as facial wrinkles or imperfections.

Important to Annandale Imitation Realist artists was the synthesis of certain apparently opposing approaches. Their art was to be simultaneously intellectually stimulating and universally accessible; it was to be carefully considered, as well as open to chance. Both Brown and Lanceley have mentioned the invention of the aesthetic chess game played early in the group's formation. In Annandale Imitation Realist chess, participants would sit opposite each other, in keeping with the game from which their title derives, but move whatever was to hand in place of chess pieces to see how they looked.[60] The game highlights another paradoxical characteristic of the group's aims in that aesthetics were rejected — according to Brown's explanation of the group's objectives — and yet nominated as a minor but elemental, precursory influence. A similar contradiction occurs in their stated reference to a Dadaist dependence on anarchy and accident and yet their apparent visual pull towards the aesthetic, as if it was a struggle to make an unattractive or purely unaesthetic work. It must be said, however, that changes in taste since these works were made, and the exposure to wider and alternative sources, may render Annandale Imitation Realist work more visually agreeable now than it was in the early 1960s. In this regard, Mike Brown once made the point that he was aware when making the work that anti-art inevitably becomes art and, conversely, that no art will prove successful and lasting unless it goes through a period of radicalism and unpopularity.[61]

Contradictions abound when the group's objectives are related to analysis of the works. *Byzantium*, 1961, is said to be the only work contributed to by all three artists, and *Sailing to Byzantium*, 1961 (Plate 20), was made by Brown and Crothall, who, it is claimed, produced most of the collaborative images.[62] At first acquaintance, these collage and painting works strike a European connection, since *Sailing to Byzantium* is the title of a poem by the Irish poet William Butler Yeats. But the European association is brought to an abrupt halt as, it seems, is the journey depicted, by hands that reach out of the would-be sea, as if to say 'halt'! Journeying references include a canoe and the painted label: 'fragile archaeological Xpress freight to Byzantium.' Again cutting across the European associations are Polynesian-styled circular, striped and diamond patterns that traverse much of the work. Added to this oil-painted ornamentation are a variety of buttons, shells, screws and milk-bottle tops, among a

FIGURE 21
Mike Brown, *Mr Hodge*, c. 1961,
enamel and gouache on composition board, 45.8 x 31.4 cm (irregular). Collection: National Gallery of Australia, Canberra

plethora of eclectic materials that are to be found throughout Annandale Imitation Realist works.

The art historian Richard Haese has acted as the main voice for the Annandale Imitation Realists, arguing the case for their role in the introduction of postmodernism to Australia.[63] Their anti-modernist motivation fulfils a first prerequisite of post-modernism, and recourse to the combined tools of chance plus assemblage to create a discontinuity, form a second. A crucial further indication of postmodernism involves their presentation of assembled sculptures and paintings, as seen at the 1962 Annandale Imitation Realists exhibitions, to form a unified three-dimensional image in the manner of an installation. There is also the collapse of high or intellectual, and low or unworked, spontaneous and purely decorative art methodologies. Playfulness and humour, minor by-products of their chance and anti-aesthetic methods, are other characteristics typifying postmodernism. Discordant with it, however, is the sexism intended as humorous that has the artists titling their works *Woman Driver*, 1962, *Gross Debutante*, c. 1961, and *Stupidly Inhibited Woman*, c. 1961, among others. As if to correct this approach, Mike Brown wrote in the 1990s of the appreciation in which female members were held — even though their contribution has not been documented, taken up by the art system, or no longer exists. The female members of the group were Magda Kohn, Leonora Howlett, Peggy Purple and Julie Nicholson.

Important to the group's progress was John Reed, who, as director of Melbourne's Museum of Modern Art, mounted the exhibition in 1962 which served to mark its public formation. Like the Antipodeans, the Annandale Imitation Realists' association was brief, beginning in 1960 and ending shortly after a second 1962 exhibition at the Rudy Komon Gallery in Sydney when they titled themselves The Subterranean Imitation Realists — formerly of Annandale.[64]

Unintentionally, but in parallel with the great collaborations of history, the group became involved in a spectacular public quarrel about its historical program and procedures. Following Colin Lanceley's outline of the group for *Art and Australia* in 1994,[65] Brown wrote a two-part rejoinder for *Art Monthly*, the first part of which was provocatively titled 'What on earth are you saying, Colin?',[66] putting paid to any higher motives that might have emerged at this stage regarding a cooperative historical reconstruction. (Crothall had disappeared in 1968 on release from a mental institution and is thought to have committed suicide.)

The avowed egalitarian ethic was similarly dispensed with, in its purest sense and in the long term, as Brown was to give his consent for a solo retrospective exhibition at the National Gallery of Victoria in 1995, shortly before he died. But that is exactly the point, as Brown once said: 'at the heart of Imitation Realism is paradox.'[67]

The Yellow House 1970–72

The Antipodean collective of 1970–72, named and styled after Van Gogh's tragedy-bound 'Yellow House', aligned itself with a romanticised vision of art and the artist that belonged to another time. The story of the original house and the lives and careers of van Gogh and Gauguin that devolved to a 1970s world was as much idealised and media-sponsored as it was historiographic. Van Gogh's simple but moving description of the solace he found at the 'Yellow House', after a long period of being beholden to hotel-keepers, has provided a basis for identification on the part of many artists who have served out apprenticeships with minimal financial resources. And while there have been a number of late twentieth-century artistic communities around the world with precursory, cooperative influences deriving from that founded by

FIGURE 22

Greg Weight, Yellow House, photocollage, top row (left to right): Brett Whiteley, *Rembrandt* (detail); poetry recital; 'Rembrandt to Magritte' room. Second row: Brett Whiteley, Karen, Sebastian Jorgensen; Tim Burns, Mary in the bathroom; Brett Whiteley and Peter Wright. Third row: Peter Kingston and the geodesic tent; George Gittoes's puppet theatre; Martin Sharp and Tim Burns with Chris and Bruce Goold in the distance. Fourth row: Greg Weight and Albie Thoms reflected in the crystal ball; Peter Kingston; Martin Sharp in 'Magritte's Remembered Journey'. Fifth row: Brett Whiteley and bottom half of *Rembrandt* seen in top panel; Jam in the 'Cloud Room'; Martin Sharp; Moth of the White Company (mime)

van Gogh and Gauguin in 1888, the Australian version took homage about as far as it could go. In the Australian Yellow House there was an identification that, as well as including the name of van Gogh's house, involved the appropriation of his well-known imagery and the arrogation of his purported values.

Van Gogh wrote:

> My house here is painted the yellow color of fresh butter on the outside with glaringly green shutters; it stands in the full sunlight in a square which has a green garden with plane trees, oleanders and acacias. And it is completely white-washed inside, and the floor is made of red bricks. And over it there is the intensely blue sky. In this I can really live and breathe, meditate and paint.[68]

Interestingly, van Gogh himself conspired in a form of homage in that he was aware, in wishing to transform his home into a studio to be shared with others, that the area in which he had chosen to live was already distinguished by its association with artists. He greatly admired the work of the Provencal artist Adolphe Monticelli (1824–86), as well as that of the American, Dodge MacKnight, who lived near Arles. He also knew of Degas's visit there in 1855.[69]

The establishment of the Sydney Yellow House was the most overt homage to van Gogh Australia had or has since seen, but other significant Australian artists, including Arthur Boyd and John Perceval, who were not involved with the Yellow House experiment, have also cited van Gogh as having an important and almost mystical influence on their careers. Both, as well as Brett Whiteley, whose involvement with the Yellow House stemmed from an enduring interest in van Gogh, have narratives that relate to him in their artistic biographies. All discovered illustrations by him when in their teens and were affected by his technique.[70] Whiteley's first acquaintance with van Gogh was in the often mentioned form of a book discovered in a church in Bathurst — a tale bearing the hallmarks of an epiphany-style, divine direction. What became an abiding interest led to participation in an exhibition at the Yellow House, although Whiteley was not a founding member and never worked there.

Whiteley's fascination with van Gogh led to a series devoted entirely to portraits of him, with associated imagery, but this influence appears in other important works in a more subtle and perhaps more satisfying way. The ultramarine harbour, for example, a key feature of his well-known Sydney paintings, may derive from study of Van Gogh letters. Van Gogh wrote to his brother Theo: 'The sea was very deep ultramarine — the shore a sort of violet and russet as I saw it, and on the dunes … some bushes of Prussian blue.'[71] Whiteley's ink-coloured harbour pours over through the open window to stain the forms in his studio. Among several examples, a faded blue tint influences all the hues in *Blue Naked Studio*, 1981.

In 1969 Whiteley returned to Australia from London via the United States and Fiji and caught up with his old friend Martin Sharp — best known as joint publisher with Richard Neville of the radical, 1960s *Oz* magazine — who had also recently returned from the United Kingdom.[72] Martin Sharp is another mentioned as having had an influential childhood van Gogh episode, in that he saw a reproduction in his father's surgery that 'shaped' his personal and artistic vision.[73]

Sharp's search for a building that would provide accommodation, studio and gallery space, and also act as a stimulus for broader social and intellectual interaction among artists, found its first foothold with the vacation of 59 Macleay Street, Potts Point by Clune Galleries. The building had its share of romance, with Russell Drysdale and Donald Friend reputedly having set up studios there. Sharp's idea had been to mount a last exhibition in the building before its demolition, but as events proceeded the sympathies of the owner were sufficiently aroused to stave off this eventuality.[74] (The future of this same building still stands in limbo at the time of writing; it is now a rooming house and subject to a preservation order proposed by original Yellow House member George Gittoes to prevent its demolition.[75] A plane tree still stands outside the building, as van Gogh mentions several did at his Yellow House.)

Fused with visual concerns at the Sydney Yellow House were 1960s flower-power aspirations of love and beauty which had also influenced the van Gogh mythology. In associating themselves with this irresistibly popular legend, the artists hoped for inspiration on a broad scale; if not to experiment with modifications to conventional painting, then to try other artforms; if not to make, then to participate in the viewing of them. The visual arts were not to be the exclusive focus of the endeavour but were to cohabit within a mélange of theatrical, musical, literary and video interests — a notion that equates with 1990s artistic hybridity.

At the Yellow House there was no close association with an art historian who monitored the formation and events of the group (although founding member Greg Weight recorded the proceedings photographically) until the 'happenings' at the house were reconstructed in 1990 by Joanna Mendelssohn for the Art Gallery of New South Wales. Nevertheless, both phases of the Yellow House received widespread publicity in the press and on television, and featured in magazines as unlikely to run art stories as *Dolly* and *Woman's Day*.[76] The point of such broad media coverage was to encourage a wider participation in the art system and it appears the Yellow House was successful in arousing interest, at least. But however noble such egalitarian ideals, the cacophony of noise, colour and absurdity, coupled with the experimental, the risqué and the drugged, must have seemed a bit much for the mostly middle-class readers and viewers at whom the publicity was directed. Contrarily, for the art cognoscenti, the association with art and values of another century was unpalatable, given that 1970s trends involved the abandonment of both the painting medium and notions of the heroic artist.

Other than the pursuit of the van Gogh legend, the desire to unite was motivated on a practical level by the need for a base in which to work and exhibit, and the desire to share with like-minded others. On a comprehensive scale there was, once again, a wish to locate Australian art within the greater international movements, now propelled by a frustration that this had not yet occurred.[77] This was to be an Australian translation, however, as is clear from an early mooted name for the establishment — The Ginger Meggs Memorial School of Art — that was chosen for the red-headed likeness between the C. J. Dennis character and van Gogh.[78] A low-brow connection of this kind signalled that the school was to be on street level rather than among the higher planes of the avant-garde, but even so it managed to bridge the two. Indeed, this was part of the Yellow House program, since, according to Gittoes, there had been discussion regarding the comparative aims and procedures of the German expressionist group Die Brücke, or the bridge, as well as those of the Bauhaus.[79]

Gittoes was another who is reputed to have developed a particular admiration for van Gogh. Conceived when he was an art student, the van Gogh influence took the form of an artists' code of ethics rather than any stylistic direction.[80] This influence was applied to his involvement at the Yellow House, but just as important was Gittoes's meeting with Clement Greenberg and subsequent travel to the United States.[81] Gittoes's return coincided with that of Whiteley and Sharp and all brought to their contributions elements that had been developed internationally.

What may now be seen as somewhat undigested postmodern ideas of appropriation as they were employed at the Yellow House, involved the allocation of a particular room to a past master who was referred to in the works produced. These included a

'Rembrandt to Magritte Room' by Sharp and Whiteley, and a yellow room with wall paintings and an installation by Peter Powditch, Sharp, Philippe Mora, Peter Wright, Vivienne Pengilley and Tim Lewis. There was an ultraviolet and kinetic light-installation room, and a 'Footprints on the Road to the Yellow House Room', by Sharp, whose pen-and-ink cross-hatched drawings alluded to van Gogh, Magritte and Mickey Mouse, among others; the latter a reference more palatable to an audience of the late 1990s. Albie Thoms showed some of his films and created a 'Caterpillar Room' which consisted of a caterpillar-shaped tunnel that was to act as a birth-canal enabling rebirthing experiences. In the 'Cloud Room' and 'Puppet Theatre', run by Gittoes, performances and readings were held that often involved adaptations from the Sufi poets.[82] Whiteley's main contribution was the Bonsai Show, for which all the Yellow House artists were asked to paint their interpretations of a bonsai tree that Whiteley owned and was particularly charmed by. Whiteley painted his space for the bonsai exhibition an all-over white, while everyone else was decorating the house in lurid colours.[83]

The cluttered, part-random, part-related style that characterised art at the Yellow house prefigured the widespread interest in installation that was to take hold in the 1980s. Authentic innovation such as this was as much determined by the youth of its mostly male membership, and their frustration with both the limitation of accepted styles current at the time, and the need to gain the imprimatur of the established system in order to launch an art career. Equally influential were the international social movements that redefined youth as having its own culture, expressed largely through pop music's communal and democratic principles. An adjunct was the licence, if granted only by example, that gave vent to the collective youth voice and its desire for change through affirmative action, such as anti-Vietnam War street marches. Gittoes was arrested for performing street theatre outside the Yellow House and has summarised the motivations in the establishment of it as the desire to produce 'an outrageous eyesore in a very stuffy city'.[84]

Inhibodress 1970–72

Also in 1970, and within a kilometre from the Yellow House, an avant-garde experiment of quite another kind was evolving. Conceived by Mike Parr, Inhibodress opened on 7 November 1970 on the second floor of 38–40 Charles Street, Woolloomooloo, and like the Yellow House was significant for being non-profit-orientated and artist-run. Inhibodress's unconditionally conceptual and intellectual interests, however, were directed towards those at the other end of the art audience from the majority of those attracted to the Yellow House. Nonetheless, there was some cross-fertilisation in the areas of theatre, music and poetry, as well as in performance and the videotaping of

it, despite differing ideas as to what constituted appropriate subject matter.[85] Perhaps recalling the Annandale Imitation Realists amusement with an art marriage between the absurd and the unpretentious, the name for the new group derived from the Hibodress Blouse Company that had previously occupied the Inhibodress space.[86] Not surprisingly, given Mike Parr's fascination with Freudian symbology, psychoanalytic jargon is hinted at by the similarity between Inhibodress and the word 'inhibited', even though the group style was entirely antithetical to this notion.[87] An Inhibodress opening 'manifesto', a press release sent to media and critics, laid down its aims.[88] Added to the break away from the commercial gallery system, in itself radical for its time, was the dissociation from any existing school of art,[89] a facet that remains exceptional among artist collectives.

Although elements of the revolutionary characterised both the Yellow House and Inhibodress, at their extremes one group was dedicated to visual fun and frivolity while the other granted little or no importance to visual appeal. At Inhibodress conventional media such as painting were all but dispensed with and efforts were dedicated to a serious-minded attack on the artistic status quo. The chasm between the two groups' artistic approach was reinforced by divergent attitudes towards promotional and personal style. The 'psychedelic' drug culture that influenced the Yellow House contrasted, for example, with Parr's decision to serve non-alcoholic beverages at openings in order to concentrate audience attention on the art in question. Inhibodress was at the forefront of galleries in Australia in concerning itself with the idea of involving the audience in the process of artmaking and, historically, may remain the most convincing in this regard. The art historian David Bromfield has explained that Parr wished the space to be one in which artists had some control over the character of their audience, and with whose participation art could evolve.[90] Parr went so far as to suggest that art events might approximate group therapy sessions, once again simultaneously paralleling and dramatically contrasting his Woolloomooloo collective with the party atmosphere a few minutes away at the Potts Point Yellow House.[91]

A principal concern for both cooperatives was to connect Australian art to the international debate, but while the Yellow House dedicated its 1 April 1971 exhibition — a spectacle of mixed art media called the 'Incredible Shrinking Exhibition' — to the eccentric American ukulele-playing warbler, Tiny Tim,[92] just two weeks later, on 13 April 1971, Inhibodress wrote to the American critic Lucy Lippard and asked for her assistance with an exhibition of overseas artists.[93] One of Lippard's main texts, *Six Years: The Dematerialization of the Art Object from 1966 to 1972*, published in 1973, centred on, as its title suggests, the dissolution of the material quality of art, a concept that formed a major plank in the Inhibodress platform. Lippard made reference in the book to Parr, Peter Kennedy and Tim Johnson, the three most involved with the Inhibodress experiment.[94] Along with an anti-materialist stance that rejected all formal aesthetic modes current at the time, including figurative expressionism and minimalism, Inhibodress artists wished to devise a medium devoid of symbol and illusion that emphasised fact rather than fiction. Art was to be an enquiry into life experience rather than a descriptive contrivance of it, as had been the case for the Antipodeans, for example, a position exemplified throughout the group's existence. An exhibition titled 'Processes, Activities and Participation in Time' by Terry English commented on the regulated life of the factory worker. The audience was required to clock in and out during its visit while the artist documented attendance by means of a graph.[95]

Self-management at both galleries allowed for artistic experimentation, the combination of exhibition and studio space, and opportunities for new artists whose work was not easily incorporated within the extant system, given the profit-making pressures that tie galleries to market tastes. The separation of the avant-garde from commercial methods and values was also marked at both the Yellow House and Inhibodress by the utilisation of the installation form.

In line with its predecessor, but with no reference or homage in mind, Inhibodress followed the Angry Penguins in publishing a broadsheet. Entitled *Inhibodress Information*, it ran to three issues in which work produced was elucidated, along with the presentation and analysis of international trends.[96]

An exhibition which demonstrably broke new ground was titled 'word situations' and involved a combined display–performance opening. Words previously typed by Parr had been hung on the wall, and in the presence of the audience he pressed the keys of a typewriter. Parr's point was to present neither a visual exhibition nor a poetic performance but a conceptual, environmental offering concerning the relationship between the typewriter and the word. At the same time, it was intended that this same relationship also resonate that between humanity and the machine, with the quality of the word as the main focus. The visual conception of each word was to match its meaning in a visual form of onomatopoeia. When the word 'sneeze' is spelled it makes the sound it describes; when Parr typed 'zig-zag' he configured it to the shape it describes. Later performances were to highlight senses other than the visual.

The multimedia series, 'Idea Demonstrations', from 1972 by Mike Parr and Peter Kennedy (Figure 23) involved a number of performances, some of which were sited on the body and linked by their title to the notion of political, anti-bourgeois street demonstrations. These performances were sometimes filmed and at other times photographed with sound recordings that comprised actual and contrived distortions to form a sound art, the subsequent vision and recordings then compiled to form an exhibition. At the core of the exhibition were masochistic performances, including ones in which Kennedy would bite Parr or put steel clips onto his own bare chest until the wounds were too painful to continue. Conceptually, they were designed to highlight both the involvement of the artist — after the objective distance of 1960s minimalism and the intellectuality of post-structuralism[97] — and to alter the similarly distant and passive role of the audience who in this case, it has been argued, were culpable in allowing the violence to continue.[98]

It was through the ensuing international interactions that Inhibodress evolved to produce work that Parr's biographer, David Bromfield, has described as heralding a 'new internationalism in which all participants were equally able to give and receive ideas'.[99] It also led the art lecturer and critic Donald Brook to describe Inhibodress artists at the time as 'the first adults of the global village, who do not think of themselves as inferior to their contemporaries in London and New York ...'.[100] According to these reactions Inhibodress had made the supreme leap, breaking through the so-called cultural cringe and the provincial bind!

Donald Brook was to continue to act as chief advocate for Inhibodress, along with the critic and curator Daniel Thomas, who was also an important supporter of the Yellow House. In his review of work at the Yellow House, Terry Smith concluded that, although it 'succeeded unequivocally on its primary level of entertainment', it did not go far enough, lacking 'bite' and failing to 'take one out of oneself as great art does'. Smith noted the work promised significant possibilities as a multimedia experiment but did not go beyond an indefinite 'good intention'.[101]

While both movements included elements that ensured them significant places in Australian art history, Inhibodress is generally considered to have made the more substantial contribution in expanding the discourse. It must be said, however, that there were moments in both experiments that asked much of their audiences in terms of unreserved, open-minded acceptance. How, for example, could crawling through a plastic tunnel shaped to suggest a birth canal at the Yellow House promote any benefit, humorous or otherwise, other than to stimulate laughter at the work of art itself? Similarly, fair-mindedness was taken to the brink at Inhibodress when an international visiting artist did not actually arrive but sent instead an instruction requiring that the viewer: 'Put A Paper Bag On Your Head And Over Your Eyes And Keep It On 5 Minutes and Think … Absence Of Ben Is Ben Too.'[102] The question arises as to whether or not anyone who needs assistance to discover such truisms could actually benefit from acquaintance with this art.

Commitment to the collective identity at both cooperatives was short-lived. Although there were eleven original members at Inhibodress, most had fallen away by late 1971, leaving only Mike Parr and Peter Kennedy.[103] Through these organisations the collaboration seen in work by the Annandale Imitation Realists was given no particular boost in Sydney in the early 1970s. The group ethos survived in the 1980s, however, to the extent that the *Artlink* journal devoted a whole issue to art collectives operating around the country.[104] There had also been concurrent groups, among them those that flourished at the Sydney Tin Sheds.[105] Most important was the Boomalli Aboriginal Artists Co-operative, established in 1987 in Chippendale, Sydney.[106]

Roar 1982–83

The Roar 2 Studios cooperative operating until the late 1990s in Melbourne owed its philosophical origins and its address to the founding Roar group of artists who made their mark in the early 1980s. Best known among those involved in its instigation were David Larwill, Mark Schaller, Sarah Faulkner, Jill Noble, Andrew Ferguson, Karan Hayman, Stephen McCarthy, Mark Howson, Mike Nicholls, Pasquali Giardino, Peter Ferguson, Richard Birmingham and Judi Singleton.[107] As its name suggests, Roar Studios was run on a dual-purpose studio and gallery basis to function as an alternative career conduit to the existing gallery system. The limitations it attempted to counter involved the perception that even in boom times there were still disadvantaged groups whose art, no matter how innovative, was refused acceptance on the grounds of gender, age and race. Accordingly, women, who were represented among the organisers, were to be granted equal opportunity and status. Those of non-Anglo-Australian backgrounds (again, with members included in the group itself) were seen to suffer undue obstacles in their efforts to win recognition. Aboriginal art, at this stage emerging from its classification as ethnography, was to be given space in the gallery schedule. But the trait

FIGURE 24
Roar Gallery sign and logo

FIGURE 25
Judi Singleton with Mark Howson (left) and
Pasquali Giardino, working on a joint painting for
the National Gallery of Australia cafe, 1986.
Photograph: John Gollings

regarded as the greatest impediment was youth. Without a track record, the artist was dismissed as a novice unworthy of risk. This inexperience, however, first understood as a disadvantage, was transformed by the Roar artists to become the greatest of assets.

The youthful energy that characterised the Roar personae found a heroic precedent in past Australian masters, or at least in the popular presentation of them. Heide Park and Art Gallery was opened in 1981 in Melbourne with attendant fanfare. Its recently packaged history was fresh in the minds of the Roar Studios artists when they opened in June 1982 at 115A Brunswick Street (at the corner of James Street), Fitzroy, Melbourne. To Roar, the Angry Penguins possessed a power particularly worthy of imitation since it was similarly seen to spring from an unruly energy tinged with youthful impatience. As well, there was the eagerly received Angry Penguins legacy that proclaimed an Australian tradition sited in the city rather than the bush. Such an alliance was preferable also to those who felt no relationship with what they saw as the unquestioning fashion for American Pop art and its veneration of consumerism. Thus, the angry brush began to roar, reinterpreting Melbourne in the 1980s. The crass rawness of Punk had arrived, and grunge was around the corner. Each embedded itself in the collective Roar psyche, and coincidentally and oddly were melded with similar aims to those adopted by the Antipodeans. Rather than 1940s American abstraction, it was Melbourne conceptualism that for Roar paraded as the naked emperor. In the seat of power was John Nixon with his own artist-run gallery, Art Projects, begun in 1979.[108]

Art Projects 1979–84

The Art Projects gallery was established in Melbourne's central Lonsdale Street as a venue for 'New Art with conceptual overtones',[109] since the gallery system was thought to have become complacent and inadequate in its representation of the avant-garde.[110] Budgetary constraints were presented as part of the gallery's radical profile to contrast with the increasing emphasis on conspicuous opulence, and therefore commercialism, among the established alternatives. As Inhibodress did, Art Projects produced its own publications, most of which concerned the art of its cohorts, and especially that of John Nixon. With the demolition of the Lonsdale Street building in 1984, Art

FIGURE 26
John Nixon, *Self Portrait (Non-Objective Composition)* 79, installation view, seventy-nine paintings, Art Projects, Melbourne, 1982

Projects moved to a warehouse in Crombie Lane, but was soon closed — after a total of seventy-eight solo and group exhibitions — owing to a failure to recoup costs.[111] Although assistance was received from government arts bodies, this was insufficient to sustain activities. A greater concern, however, was the lack of patronage by public galleries which, it was hoped, would grow to recognise their policy of neglect. Besides Nixon, contributing artists were colleagues from Melbourne and Sydney, including many who have become significant names in art history: Peter Tyndall, Jenny Watson, Imants Tillers, Virginia Coventry, John Dunkley-Smith, Ti Parks. Emphasis was placed on originality and conceptualism, with no mention in the scant literature concerning the venture — other than that produced by the gallery itself — of any desire to produce a home-grown art.

Nixon's work has its basis in that of the Russian Suprematist Kasimir Malevich (1878–1935), whose white square on a white ground was said to be a purer form of cubism. From this stimulus, Nixon developed his own opus, comprising endless variations on the basic cross. As Terry Smith has explained, in maintaining that these images were self-portraits Nixon challenged established ideas regarding the exact nature of abstract, non-objective art and its relationship to figurative representation.[112] Whose reading is correct? Is it that of the artist who claims his image is within the work, or that of the viewer who may, or may not, find it there? Nixon clarifies both question and answer by his cool objectivism. The art is as you find it. The sign and the referent here, and always, are arbitrarily related.

Like the Roar artists to follow, Nixon was antipathetic to postmodernism and, as they did, he looked to past art for inspiration.[113] The main difference between the two was the role assigned to figuration: entirely absent in one and crucial to the other. For Roar the pre-eminence of the visual and tactile, involving such traditional interests as colour relationships and surface texture, ruled their methodology despite their often simplified forms. David Larwill's dripping stick figures and Judi Singleton's animistic amorphous patterns did not cater for intellectual conceptual analysis; indeed, the procedure of providing a lengthy essay for explanation at the exhibition was loudly scorned.[114] Conceptual work, such as that by Nixon, was rejected by them as inferior for its visual limitations. The Roar group in turn was dismissed by Paul Taylor, the influential critic and editor of *Art + Text*, who in his sneeringly titled article, 'Angst in my pants', decried the work as consumerist, lacking in intellectual depth and suitable only for decorative purposes.[115]

As much as these groups worked against the trends of their times and had some success in redirecting them, they all suffered from internal disagreement as to their primary purpose, a factor that worked to restrict their life spans and reduce their impact. Also working against these movements was the critical reaction to their propositions, even though it is now clear that some of those who berated local art for its provincialism were constrained by the very same syndrome. 'The Field' show, for example, is almost universally dismissed in the literature as derivative, this generalist approach concealing the validity that resided within the group, so that Robert Rooney's interesting serial works became categorised as insignificant.[116]

Begun in the 1950s, the tradition that argues for two mutually exclusive conceptual and figurative schools, along with the notion of either intellectual or non-intellectual art practices, continued. Figurative art, unlike the ostensibly purer and intellectually demanding conceptualist form, was construed as catering to commercial or decorative interests. For the conceptualists, government assistance was acceptable, but private sale was not. Critical responses to the Antipodeans sent them scattering for cover, but without their resolve we may not have the poetic work produced from 1959 on by Arthur Boyd. There were very few reviews of the Yellow House, even though it acquainted Australian art audiences with the installation form. The Roar group, mocked as juvenile, re-emphasised the Art Brut notion that not all satisfying art must be finely worked. Merely in their existence there was a small supplementary resonance to Melbourne life, in that their roaring dog sign symbolised a group of young people who were devoting considerable energy to the exploration of art and its channels to other interests. Although enthusiasm occasionally took the place of contemplation, their resultant productions were not all bad, and some artists of note, such as Peter Ferguson, Judi Singleton, David Larwill and Stephen McCarthy, have emerged.

The 1990s acceptance of what was once the realist bogey may signal the end of the conceptual–figurative dichotomy in Australian art and give rise to a consequent appreciation of diversity in artistic expression.

3

A Female Space: Australian Women's Art

The French writer Simone de Beauvoir remains as well known for her relationship with the philosopher Jean-Paul Sartre as for her contributions to literature and cultural debate. In her book *The Second Sex* she wrote: 'humanity is male and man defines woman not as herself but as relative to him … He is the Subject, he is the Absolute — she is the Other.'[1] Although de Beauvoir's motivation was to define the male–female relationship in order to release women from its limitations, she was unable to free herself completely from the enduring perception of woman as secondary to man. ➤

The biblical tale of Adam and the spare rib from which God made Eve has a long and pervasive mythology. Indeed, it is remarkable that such assumptions should find modern permutations in the face of scientific evidence that all humans spend the first few months of their existence *in utero* as females, acquiring male characteristics only later, and producing a male child approximateley only half the time.

When she was a life-class student in Adelaide in the 1890s, Margaret Preston was criticised by Hans Heysen, who described her as a 'shameless hussy' for sitting too close to the nude model.[2] Preston had already demonstrated an atypical individuality in choosing to paint onions, rabbits and eggs, rather than landscapes at sunset and the elegant figures considered appropriate subjects for young female artists at the end of the nineteenth century.[3]

But, far from perceiving her gender to be an obstacle, Preston worked confidently to establish her own artistic career, as well as to proselytise the concept of a new Australian, regional style.[4] In doing so, she proved herself a founding feminist, but one who appears not to have adopted the suffragette rhetoric or procedures. (By 1908, the so-called first-wave feminist movement had dissipated, and female suffrage had been achieved in Australia.)[5] Rather than working within a group to achieve gender reform, Preston undertook to promote her own artistic advancement and simultaneously, as she saw it, the art of the nation.

Preston found herself in unusually supportive circumstances and, far from being constrained by marriage, she is represented in the literature as finding liberation through it. Having been the beneficiary of gratuities, and later experiencing the security that followed marriage to W. G. Preston in 1919, she was free to pursue her career.[6] Art curator Ian North has argued that gender roles were less of a hindrance — not just for Preston, but for many other women of her 'class' and period — than they were for men. He mentions Dorrit Black, Grace Crowley and Grace Cossington Smith as women whose careers were advanced by such assistance. Would-be male artists, North suggests, without the financial assistance accorded their female counterparts, were obliged to spend their lives pursuing money-making careers, rather than devoting themselves to artistic professions and concomitant financial risks.[7]

But the suggestion that women were often financially advantaged does not allow for the still dominant male order, when the mere idea of the female artist was, if not a foreign notion, then a discomforting one to the general male consciousness. J. S. MacDonald, a former director of the Art Gallery of New South Wales, for example, is said to have declared that there had never been a good female artist.[8] Compounding the problem, according to art historian Helen Topliss, was the female inclination to act as accessory in the 'crime', in also believing that men and women were born with different artistic skills. It was thought that male artists were best suited to representing form, for example, while women possessed a particular competence in the treatment of colour.[9] This complicit attitude was neither new nor peculiar to Australia, and was only an expression of what Simone de Beauvoir identified in 1949 when *The Second Sex* was first published. She wrote: 'To decline to be the Other, to refuse to be a party to the deal — this would be for women to renounce all the advantages conferred upon them by their alliance with the superior caste.'[10]

Running counter to such prevailing beliefs was Preston's talent for self-promotion, a skill which enabled her to acquire a wide public profile.[11] It would be another half-century before it was generally acknowledged that a woman's life involves issues, subjects and events worthy of illustration as fine art. But as early as 1927, when Margaret Preston was fifty-two years old, she explained her decision to change her artistic subject matter in order to represent aspects of her life, in an autobiographical narrative called *From Eggs to Electrolux*.

She wrote:

> *She knows that the time has come to express her surroundings in her work. All around her in the simple domestic life is machinery — patent ice-chests that need no ice, machinery does it; irons heated by invisible heat; washing-up machines; electric sweepers and so on. They all surround her and influence her mind, and her mind is expressed in her work she has produced.*[12]

Preston's historic declaration, that women's lives contained minor detail as well as major events that were worthy of representation, has a 1985 counterpart in the theoretical discourse. This was the coinage of the term 'gynocritics' by Elaine Showalter, an American literary theorist, to denote women who were separating the female experience from that of men and celebrating it in their 'texts' or creative products.[13] Innocent of such complicated contrivances, Preston had little in her art to compare with the commonly 'appropriate' female subject of her time other than the still-life flower arrangement. Upon these she imposed adaptations that transformed them from the usual delicate, velvet subjectivity to depictions that were loud and direct. Ian North has described Preston's woodcuts, made from 1923, as relatively free when compared with the detail and control of work by Lionel Lindsay, who was particularly popular at the time.[14]

FIGURE 27
Margaret Preston, *Flying Over the Shoalhaven River*, 1942, oil on canvas, 50.6 x 50.6 cm. Collection: National Gallery of Australia, Canberra

As far as the reception to Preston is concerned, it would be false to portray her as having received inadequate recognition when the sum of recent analysis is taken into account; as well she received many commendations in her lifetime, such as being the first female artist to be commissioned by the Art Gallery of New South Wales to paint a self-portrait.[15] At the same time, her technical innovations were only partially acknowledged. Features seen in Preston's paintings were granted greater acclaim when they appeared in work by Fred Williams, Sidney Nolan and Clifton Pugh, even though hers predated theirs. While Preston is not suggested as the influence in this regard, her dotted trees, as observed in an aerial view of the landscape in *Flying Over the Shoalhaven River*, 1942 (Figure 27), coincide with Nolan's earliest explorations of the perpendicular. Similarly, her 1940s adaptations of Aboriginal designs and craggy close-up scenes of the bush interior are similar to those that became Clifton Pugh's signature style a decade later.

Clarice Beckett is another female painter who provided a distinctive interpretation of the landscape. Her appealing views of Melbourne's bayside suburbs, painted in the 1920s, link the female watercolour tradition with painting in oil. Her diluted oil paint has the

FIGURE 28
Clarice Beckett, *Bay Road, Foggy Morning*, c. 1926, oil on hardboard, 29 x 37 cm. Private collection

look of watercolour, linearity is reduced and features are blurred, as would occur with a watercolour wash. Belonging to no Australian school of painting, Beckett's work is precursory in its atmospheric renditions of otherwise mundane scenes. What might have been considered unattractive subjects, 'inappropriate' for artistic depiction, such as telegraph poles, are transformed to become picturesque (see Figure 28).

Writing in 1962, Bernard Smith argued that the introduction of Post-Impressionism to Australia in the 1920s owed much to women. He cited Norah Simpson, Grace Cossington Smith, Thea Proctor, Margaret Preston, Isabel Tweddle, Dorrit Black, Ada Plante, Aletta Lewis, Vida Lahey and Mildred Lovett as 'only the more prominent'.[16] Recent enquiry has reinforced Smith's assertion, with an added emphasis on the extensive contribution made by women printmakers in the 1920s and 1930s.[17] Helen Topliss refers to the historically high representation of women as art students in Australia and notes that as early as the 1890s more women were attending the National Gallery of Victoria Art School than men.[18] On completion of their courses, however, social constraints acted to preclude these women from taking the next crucial step to professionalism.

The maintenance of the traditional role of women as the painted rather than the painter depended to some degree on the notion that certain forms of art are superior to others (another assumption that was to be rejected as élitist in the egalitarian sweep that characterised art politics of the late twentieth century). Until then, decorative or functional art made by women as part of their domestic duties was identified as folk art or domestic craft, and therefore inferior to that produced by men for patrons and museums. This was the case even if the skills applied to creating the craft object were equal, or more demanding, than those required for work defined as art. The utilitarian designs of the De Stijl (Holland, 1917–28), Bauhaus (Germany, 1919–33) and Purism movements (France, 1918) exemplify the initial breakdown of this attitude in the male domain.

Being of the 'wrong' gender, women invariably found themselves in the wrong class, as well. Art produced by 'upper-class' women in the early twentieth century was dismissed as a mere manifestation of their womanhood and, consequently, once again regarded as substandard. And while artistic pursuits remained a hobby for aristocratic women, they were unavailable to those of the working class, partly for lack of finance but more importantly because expectations, ambitions and opportunities were circumscribed so that women did not even aspire to such activities.

Indeed, prior to so-called second-wave feminism,[19] which began in the 1960s, the designation of objects made by women as secondary art was universal, whether the work was conceived in modern, urban circumstances or among people of indigenous tribes where the practices employed had been handed down from woman to woman for millennia. Tribal art objects made by men were received no more favourably and were similarly categorised, often as items of ethnographic curiosity. The failure to value such objects, whether made by men or women, has compounded the global influence of contemporary art in developing countries resulting in the loss of traditional skills as modern art adds further pressure to the drive for westernisation and perceived commercial advantage.

Whatever the grounds for the repudiation of women as artists, fundamental to this rejection, it is argued, has been the perception that a female brain is less able than that of a male to engage in abstract reasoning.[20] To explain the phenomenon of the woman who is unaware of her constraints, modern feminists coined the phrase 'consciousness-raising'. Taken from revolutionary Chinese theory, the practice known as 'speaking bitterness' involved the sharing of reliable information regarding domination by 'the system'.[21] In the same way that Communism disallowed questioning to the degree that an individual could lose sight of the fact that he or she was inculcated into its ways, so a woman's view of her circumstances, if formed through social conditioning, would not accurately reflect her situation. Her frame of reference would be derived from the extant patriarchal society that either did not wish to admit to the fact or did not itself recognise that she was oppressed. Once she became acquainted with the limitations of her existence, it was argued, a woman's consciousness was raised.[22] However, the capacity of white, middle class, and usually academic, women to argue the part of those whose circumstances are so different from their own has been questioned,[23] and is a particularly important tenet of post-colonial theory and its application to the circumstances of women in developing countries.

Deep-rooted attitudes against women's art have generally placed it, according to the term popularised by Simone de Beauvoir and elaborated upon by numerous subsequent theorists, as 'Other' to the conventional. De Beauvoir's observation precipitated a shift of vision so that it became clear there was nothing inherently inferior either in the way women made their art or in the subjects they chose to consider.

Historically, in the 'fine' art arena, subjects depicted have only questionably related to a woman's life: the nude portrait for which she has been the model is less descriptive of her character than suited to an artistic genre. Similarly, the domestic genre piece referred to a woman's circumstances but was an artificial portrayal, concerned more to create an appearance in accordance with others in its category than with the life of its subject.

The traditional landscape, which began to dominate in the nineteenth century, became the main form through which artistic facility was demonstrated but arguably had less 'meaning' for a woman given its association with the apparently instinctive male motivation to possess territory and to show off the ability to capture it. Similarly, women do not have the same inclination to show off the trophy head of game hung on the wall to signify the prowess of the shooter.

But while de Beauvoir's analysis has been beneficial to the course of female art, the theoretical discourse and its application to art appreciation which rose to pre-eminence in the 1980s was not always sympathetic to the female cause. De Beauvoir's view that women found themselves at a disadvantage through faulty male under-standing may equally apply to the theories devised by prestigious male experts. Sigmund Freud, for example, categorised women as secondary for congenital reasons, believing them to be a lesser version of the whole male due to their physiological state of existence without a penis and their consequent powerlessness. If they wish to escape their constraints, he argued, and express themselves fully as a man does, they demonstrate 'penis envy'.

The Freudian-influenced theory of Jacques Lacan, put forward in the 1940s, also involved the construction of a model in which women found themselves at a disadvantage. According to Lacan, all individuals in their early years inhabit a psychological 'imaginary' in which their world and identity is mother-dominated. When speech is acquired, a transition occurs, in that the maternal identity is sup-planted by that of the father. At this stage, the maternal identity is repressed, creating the unconscious from which it can never be retrieved, except through the dream state and in artistic production. Men are equipped to leave the imaginary and enter the 'symbolic order' or the social and cultural world, the theory goes, because language is male. This is a language foreign to women, who cannot emerge from their imaginary into this same symbolic order and are thereby, according to Lacan, condemned to an existence as 'Other'.[24]

Lacan's is an intractable scenario in which the female cannot negotiate an improve-ment in her circumstances. This situation, as expressed in theory, is also sufficiently abstract that it does not translate easily to a sociological framework.[25] One feminist approach, therefore, is to advance the female cause by attempting to overthrow the patriarchal order via the expression of the repressed in art and literature.

Contradicting the feminist position, which argues that the difference between the sexes is the fundamental prize and problem for femaleness, the French philosopher Michel Foucault argued that the individual is not born with a persona but must create one. But problematic for feminists is Foucault's premise that sufficient freedom and resources exist to enable this process to occur. The argument follows that such an ideal world does not exist for many women who have devoted themselves, or continue to commit themselves, to household, wifely and maternal duties, and who have therefore foregone the financial remuneration and/or the opportunity to acquire the requisite qualifications to achieve personal and professional fulfilment.[26]

Under investigation by Karl Marx, women often found themselves external once again to the main argument. Although Marx recognised that women were alienated because they were precluded from reaching their full potential, he categorised them in a wider group, this generalisation resulting in the failure to allow for their specific circumstances. The point at which Marxist theory is said to fail to meet women's needs is in its application of the idea of productive work. Since Marxism rests on the relationship between power and class, between productive labour and the means of production (in which the bourgeoisie owns the means of production by virtue of the entrenched class system), the only negotiable item in the equation for the proletariat is productive work. Given that productive work is defined as wage labour, domestic work is classified as non-labour and non-means-orientated. As most domestic workers are women, their interests are positioned outside the work system, where they remain classless and second even to the working class.[27] This largely male alignment still leaves women as domestic slaves who are unrewarded, unpaid and unrecognised for their work in the home.

With the rise of the so-called proletariat and the redistribution of wealth that resulted in the first half of the twentieth century, rigid class distinctions were no longer relevant to either artmaking or public success. But middle-class women of the 1950s, who had adhered to the idea that their fulfilment lay solely in motherhood and wifely duties, were also, according to the women's movement, in need of assistance to obtain work outside the home, or at least to accept they were permitted such options.

It took one hundred years from the time Margaret Preston was rebuked for over-acquainting herself with the nude in the life class, for women to advance from the role of model and painter to recognised artist. Art historian Sandy Kirby has pointed out that between 1968 and 1973 there were five key exhibitions in Australia that presented the work of one hundred and thirty artists, only five of whom were women.[28] She refers in particular to the prestigious 'Recent Australian Painting' exhibition held in 1961 at the London Whitechapel Gallery, which introduced Australian work to Britain. On this occasion, the work of fifty-four male artists was shown, as well as that of Elizabeth Durack, the only woman whose work was exhibited.[29]

With the pendulum swing following the recognition that women had not been granted equal opportunity, the battle for redress saw second-wave feminists conscripting artists to their cause simply because they were women, regardless of the ideological positions they held or the subjects considered in their art. It was sufficient that the artist be discovered, usually long after her prime, in an era that was more predisposed towards the female as artist, and that historical records be corrected to include her contribution.

An artist whose history exemplifies this approach is Joy Hester. Hester's biography and oeuvre have been well documented and treated as if feminist, although it seems she knew little of feminism or its adherents, considering the subject neither in her life nor art. Her attitude towards her artistic career is similarly contradictory for a model feminist given that it is portrayed as equivocal, as well as characterised by a constant struggle to find sufficient peace of mind to enable its pursuit.[30] At the same time, a desire to recuperate and receive Hester's work into the canon was at least partly motivated by a desire to pay her the recognition accorded male members of the Angry Penguins group. As a result, twenty years after her death in 1960, and forty years after she produced her main body of work, Hester acquired the role of cult figure among young Australian feminists interested in the rise of art by women in the twentieth century.

Heritage: The National Women's Art Book, edited by Joan Kerr and published in 1995, contains many examples of work by women in all media, including fine portraiture that is as worthy of awards as the best of the same by men.[31] And as is clear from the scope of the work reproduced, often for the first time, much of it has remained hidden until researched to exemplify the tenet of the book: that a great proportion of our art history consists of work by women, some of which survives, while much has been lost to it.

Yvonne Audette is just one non-feminist artist whose substantial work, in both volume and content, was largely overlooked until collected by major public galleries in the 1990s, by which time she was aged in her sixties. A major exhibition of her work opened on her seventieth birthday in 1999 at the Queensland Art Gallery in Brisbane. Affecting recognition of her contribution has been the debate regarding the exact role of John Passmore, who, while officially her teacher, is said to have absorbed her finely tuned Abstract Expressionist style of the 1950s and early 1960s, committing a similar form to his own work and advancing his career accordingly.[32] Despite evidence arguing for Audette's influence on Passmore, he remains the authority in the literature, presumably on the natural assumption that teacher would mould student, but also on the understanding that female painter could not possibly inform master male. Whatever Passmore lent to Audette as teacher, the Abstract Expressionist influence in her work must, at least in part, have been formed by her experience in the United States in 1952 on winning a scholarship to the New York National Academy where she met Willem de Kooning and Franz Kline among others, and saw work by Jackson Pollock.[33]

Audette has referred to a journey made in 1958 to Turkey and Iran where she saw the intertwining patterns that decorate the interior of the minarets.[34] The most striking feature, she has explained, was the effect of the spirals that flowed as if there were a central focus that was never touched, and a final point never attained, much as the reverberation of sound made in these edifices loses any clarity of origin or completion. This lyrically resonant poetic metaphor, with its clues as to compositional approach, is affirmed by the visual allusion to the graffitist. Although not associated with Audette's methodology, their crass, esoteric inscriptions, made next to and over each other on an accreted, ageing surface, are transposed by her into a visual poetry.

While an interest in feminist principles developed around the country in the 1970s, the specific Women's Art Movement is said to have begun in 1974 in Sydney, twelve months before International Women's Year, when the American critic Lucy Lippard gave the Power Lecture for the University of Sydney's Power Institute, and went on to travel around Australia.[35] The Lippard connection had initially been made in 1971 through the Sydney artist-run collective, Inhibodress.[36] (Lippard's book, *From the Center: Feminist Essays on Women's Art*, was first published in 1976.)[37]

Feminist author Hester Eisenstein has highlighted the theoretical variations that comprised second-wave feminism by tracing what is referred to as essentialist attitudes towards differences between the sexes.[38] The female body had been compared negatively with that of the male, and the female persona was taken to derive from her biological capacities and weaknesses. These differences were seen to be channelled into appropriate sex roles that best utilised the affection and passivity of the female, for example, and the decisiveness and activity in the male, a process thought 'natural' and reinforced through social beliefs. Women were limited by their gender to a persona as sex object and/or carer, expressed as wife, prostitute, assistant, nurse or secretary, for example. Men were similarly confined, in general terms, to roles that befitted their biologically prescribed characteristics, but they were permitted the option of transcending such definitions through rational capabilities.

Eisenstein refers to de Beauvoir and other writers, including Betty Friedan, Shulamith Firestone and Kate Millett, having taken the early second-wave position that differences between the genders, still the source of male domination, should be eliminated to allow 'androgyny' to prevail.[39] Following intense scrutiny and analysis of the female experience, this same difference underwent a shift of perception, so that in the mid-1970s the woman-centred view was given preference.[40] In this model, female qualities, such as the capacity to nurture and express compassion, were perceived as superior abilities, worthy of celebration, and ones which men, and therefore society as a whole, should strive to acquire. Along with this argument, which Eisenstein explains was also problematic, went the assertion that female sexuality, with its capacity for multiple orgasm, should be a source of pride, so advancing women to a position of superiority and arguing for the female as the norm with the male as the deviation from it.[41] In the 1970s, Anne Koedt wrote 'The myth of the vaginal orgasm', an essay which, among others on the same topic, became a subject for widespread public discussion.[42] The entrenched view that 'true' orgasm was achieved by vaginal penetration was questioned and identified as a crucial part of a woman's oppression, because in this practice power rests with the male.

In art, expressions of the new confidence that sprang from any and all varieties of feminism took the form of dissertations on women's lives, feelings and sexuality. Vivienne Binns, a feminist artist who was an important member of the Sydney Women's Art Movement in the late 1970s, drew attention to female sexuality in no uncertain terms in *Suggon*, 1966 (Plate 23), combining 1960s hard-edge abstraction with the new gender debate.[43] Her mechanically operated, pulsating vagina made of polymer mesh was the quintessential, sexual, artistic shock for the viewing public, as well as art critics male and female. The critic John Henshaw described it as 'a work of monumental repulsion' and Helen Sweeney wrote of Binns's 'ungirlish impulse to shock'.[44]

Binns's radical *Suggon* was worked with paint and collage, but the painting medium generally came to be accepted among feminist artists as that co-opted by the male system. It was believed that a greater impact would be achieved if alternative means were found through which women could express themselves, define the female identity and describe their lives.[45] Performance art became an attractive alternative, since it generally involves minimal financial outlay and is not dependent on space in a venue for several weeks, as is the case for a conventional painting exhibition. At the same time, the introduction of domestic chores to the gallery was another kind of

PLATE 23
Vivienne Binns, *Suggon*, 1966,
enamel on composition board, electric motor,
synthetic polymer mesh, steel wire, 122.2 x 92 cm.
Collection: National Gallery of Australia,
Canberra

PLATE 24
Judy Normand, 'Normally I'd get a nurse to
thread the needle, but with their strike on ...',
1986, tapestry wools, embroidery cottons,
theatre suture silk on canvas, 30 x 40 cm.
Photograph: John Brash

shock for its audience, when Jude Adams presented her *Washing Performance* of 1979. In this work, the artist washed for three days, aligning the mundane with the sophisticated and intellectual, documenting her task as it proceeded through the stages from soiled to clean and folded nappies. The process was conducted in keeping with scientific method and, as art historian Anne Marsh has outlined, provided a critique of the procedural and presentation methods of conceptual art.[46] Along with performance art, other media adapted in the 1970s to a feminist, subversive language included political posters, photography and needlework. In the 1980s, the return to painting was embraced as much by women as by men, and in the 1990s, with the assurance that many battles had been won and options for women artists in Australia had been expanded, the strict feminist subject was considered a less urgent issue.

American initiatives, such as slide collections of women's artwork, were taken up in Australia with sustained success. The Melbourne Women's Art Register, situated within the Richmond Library, for example, now possesses research materials that document the art of thousands of women artists. In 1996 its holdings stood at 20,000 slides, as well as books, films, videos and catalogues of work by 2000 Australian-based women.[47] These materials are available for loan by joining the register for a small annual fee. The Melbourne Women's Art Register has a precursor in Sydney that dates back to 1974. It was begun by founding feminist in Australia and associate at Inhibodress, Barbara Hall, with the Women's Art Movement group at the Sydney Tin Sheds Art Workshop.[48] A counterpart has also existed in Adelaide, with various materials, such as slides, remaining extant, but neither this nor the Sydney organisation is currently operating.

Important exhibitions of work by unrecognised artists, acknowledged women and new artists, 'Australian Women Artists 1840–1940' travelled Australia in 1975 and 1976, and an exhibition of women's needlework called 'The D'Oyley Show' was first seen in 1979 at Watters Gallery in Sydney, after which it toured New South Wales regional galleries. Work included had been developed by women who had organised themselves three years before as the Domestic Needlework Collective that met regularly at the Tin Sheds.[49]

An exhibition celebrating the twentieth anniversary of the establishment of the Women's Art Register was held in 1995 at the VicHealth Access gallery at the National Gallery of Victoria. It is significant that this exhibition was not held in what might be called the gallery proper but, rather, was relegated to the space set aside to give voice to those not yet accorded the standing of accepted artists. Once again, honouring women's art and its domestic origins, the exhibition was titled 'Bias Binding', with the reference from dressmaking and the obvious puns on prejudice and joint effort. Another such initiative, 'The Art of Nursing' exhibition of 1994, celebrated, with a humorous and biting edge, the work of women whose identities are hidden and whose creative personae are lost to the caring cause that fills their lives. In keeping with the overt re-acceptance by women in the 1980s and 1990s of traditional 'feminine'[50] materials, Judy Normand exploited the needle and thread to a political purpose by embroidering a tapestry that is not just about the nurse's life but of it (Plate 24). With standard tapestry wools, embroidery cottons and numerous tapestry techniques she signifies 'hospital' by her choice of colours and the use of theatre suture-silk. Based on a *Herald* newspaper cartoon by WEG, her depiction stresses the importance of the nurse's role, not only through humour but in the transformation of the ephemeral cartoon to the permanent and 'female' tapestry form.[51]

Two galleries that opened in the 1980s are noteworthy as specific proponents of women's art. They are the Australian Girls Own Gallery (aGOG), located in the suburb of Kingston in Canberra, and the Women's Gallery in Brunswick Street,

FIGURE 29

Marie McMahon, *D'Oyley Disco*, **c. 1978**, screenprint. Reproduced courtesy Tin Sheds Gallery, Sydney

Mona Ryder, *Mother, Other Lover,* **1995,**
sculptural installation, mixed-media,
Queensland Art Gallery, Brisbane

Fitzroy, Melbourne, both of which have since closed, arguably because women have been substantially supported by the general non-gender-specific gallery system.

At the beginning of the twenty-first century, it can be proclaimed that women compete equally for places in art schools, and for art grants, art prizes and inclusion in national collections and histories. But still there are exceptions: women who fall into the subgroups of lesbian, disabled, chronically ill and aged, all of whom are less able than the young, white, able-bodied middle-class to fit the Hollywood and now generalised advertising stereotype to which most women aspire. Such semi-outcasts are considered by Mona Ryder in a sculptural installation that mimics and satirises the contortions and contrivances used by women to secure their success in almost every sphere, from personal relationships to professional careers.

In *Mother, Other Lover*, 1995 (Plates 25A, 25B and 25C), a Mother's Army, standing in formation with banner held high, is battle-ready to take up the cause of recognition for tasks performed and to secure liberation. The ironing board, a repeated skeletal symbol of womanhood for Ryder, stands with the perfume bottle to personify the stereotyped aspects of woman: Mother and her Other, lover self.

Although opportunities have been won for young women, the world has changed less for those whose lives are already half-lived. Ryder has the wounds to her sculptured creatures reveal past experience of such violence that a rib cage protrudes, piercing through a blood-drenched heart. But from this damaged, skewered organ grows a fine, bloodied spear, warning of revenge. The heart, the seat of passion and the life-driver, becomes a shield, its protective character indicating that she will survive. Then this strange cohort becomes a primitive tribe with barbarous, perhaps retaliatory intent.

The gigantic perfume bottle signals Mother's social self, while recorded sounds of mechanically driven water suggest the paraphernalia with which a middle-class domestic life is circumscribed: the washing machine, dishwasher and tumble drier. As the water surges it fills the perfume bottle with red dye, like a silent blood-rush or blush. A flush and swish sanitise the toilet, while another such gesture, equally efficiently performed, produces a puff of perfume, transforming Mother to the desired. To be loved the woman must slave, says Ryder; to be lovable she must labour to groom and ornament herself. There is a hint of romance, but one that holds false promise. This romance denies the mess of menstruation, the prolific flux of childbirth and the umbilical cord that is never fully severed, to hang painfully, forever attached in recollection. And always Mother provides the blood transfusion — if only by mobile phone — for the family in its eternal search for succour.

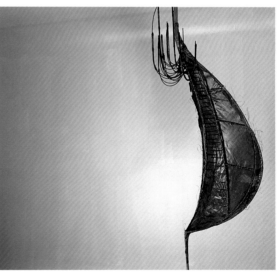

Making oblique reference to the traditional figure-in-water sculptures set in topographical scenes, female fingers, so often immersed, drip continuously in Ryder's work, like water circulating through a woman's life. The marriage of housework, surrealism and social commentary creates a confrontational dimension urging that women not dedicate their lives to such trivialities. It reiterates also a protest against the sole responsibility for such tasks devolving upon the woman who chooses the homemaker role. This re-contextualisation of the ironing board renders profound all of its mundanity.

PLATE 25B
Mona Ryder, *Mother, Other Lover*, 1995 (detail), steel, leather, drumhide, hair

PLATE 25C
Mona Ryder, *Mother, Other Lover*, 1995 (detail), steel, leather, drumhide, hair

Annette Bezor, NO, 1991,
acrylic and oil on galvanised iron,
two pieces: 120 x 150 x 10 cm

Ryder's earliest sculptural discoveries were through Old Master reproductions, but rather than attempting a homage in materials such as marble, with which she felt no familiarity, and in styles and images that were equally alien, she turned to the banal, and subtly and ceremonially raised them to icon status.[52] Ryder renders in mock heroic form the endlessness of repetitive domestic tasks with imagery that bears visual relationships to work by Georgia O'Keeffe and Frida Kahlo.[53]

The hide that is stretched over the skeletal form has the clear, medical connotation of the plastic surgeon at work, tightening the skin over the ageing face. Once it was an expansive, youthful grin that extended the skin; now, it is a grimace. The smile that signifies 'Happiness' — the necessary emotional condition for the would-be beauty — is an alternative or simultaneous suggestion of the rib-cage protrusion that pierces the heart-sculpture. At the same time, a *vagina dentata* reading is evoked, and, then again, teeth are an integral part of a comb, the all-important tool always carried by every woman who wishes to establish and reconfirm her attractiveness. The woman of this sculptural installation is universal but has experienced life and bears its marks.

The body as the object of control is important to the post-structuralist philosophy of Michel Foucault, who considered it as the focus of institutional practice in the prison.[54] Foucault refers to the body as 'the inscribed surface of events … totally imprinted by history and the processes of history's destruction of the body'.[55]

Annette Bezor makes a resolute *NO* sign to ageing in a galvanised iron sculpture more than a metre high (Figure 30).[56] But her *NO* is decorated with roses that soften and make ambivalent her determination. Nevertheless, there can be few words with as much political connotation for women who, through social conditioning of the old school, were taught agreeableness in all circumstances, including sexual, that made the mere utterance of the word 'no' a challenge. 'No' made headlines in the 1990s when, in a verdict of a rape case, a distinguished judge proclaimed that, if spoken by a woman, the word 'no' can sometimes mean yes. Such an incident was unlikely to have made news a decade before, but it does indicate that female equality has not been fully achieved. Added to such relatively isolated attitudes are more consequential, unresolved issues, such as non-payment for housework and child-care, for example. There are also the institutionalised forms of sexism of which many women are unaware. In this regard, the feminist philosopher Mary Daly has referred to 'sado-rituals', which include psychotherapeutic methods and the sometimes unnecessary gynaecological practices, such as hysterectomies, as exemplifying a sophisticated means of oppression.[57] They are 'scientific' and therefore accepted as appropriate. They are also covert.

More severe still are the extremes suffered by women elsewhere in the world. These include enforced prostitution, paedophilia, polygamy, infanticide, clitoridectomy, the bride price and the strictures of religious convention, among a litany of crimes now exposed to worldwide scrutiny and being considered by artists. But it seems a great deal more suffering will be endured and much art on these subjects will be created before such cruelties are erased from the map.

4

Take Away or Eat Here? Decisions on the Digestion of Asian Images

It could justifiably be argued that there has been no more perfect symbol for Australia's assimilation of the exotic place across the northern waters called Asia than that strange cross-cultural creature, the dim sim. The Australian dim sim is not very Chinese; the pastry is too thick, perhaps closer to that of a pie. The subtle flavours that typify Chinese cuisine are obscured by oil that is used primarily for fish and chips. But this has been the attitude to delicacy in Australia's 'steak-and-two-veg' culture. ➤

Olive Crane, *Design for the 'Gum Tree Pattern' Plate*, c. 1920, watercolour

Rupert Bunny, *Geisha Girl*, c. 1901, oil on canvas, 160 x 118.2 cm. On loan to Stuartholme-Behan collection, University Art Museum, University of Queensland, Brisbane

Yukinori Yanagi, *Asia-Pacific Ant Farm*, 1996 (detail), installation, ants, coloured sand, plastic box, plastic tube, plastic pipe and video documentation on LCD monitor, dimensions variable, Queensland Art Gallery, Brisbane

Australia has demonstrated a chauvinism that has led it in suspicious ignorance to wish to obliterate references to the 'Orient', as Asian countries were once collectively known, in a conglomerate difference. It was an Australian version of the western attitude, often promulgated through study, that the academic, Edward Said, defined as racist, giving new meaning to the term 'Orientalism' in his book of the same name. Said has argued that enquiry may merely reinforce the authority of the investigator over the investigated, further slanting entrenched prejudice.

Australians have been very selective about what they consider worthy in Asian culture. Aspects of dress, such as a Chinese collar, periodically become fashionable; they are in for a season to lend an air of exoticism, and decidedly out the next. In the 1950s the quintessential Australian shoe was designed bearing a resemblance to the Japanese *geta*. The *geta*, the traditional wooden thonged shoe supported by two struts, is now seen as the more casual rubber thong. Less elegant but more practical, the thong is suited to the long, confident stride of the late twentieth century rather than the stereotyped, diminutive shuffle of petite Japanese.

A dinner service decorated with the willow pattern implied a creative stylishness in opting for a foreign design. This fantasy on a Chinese theme, however, is far removed from the Chinese psyche. Olive Crane's *Design for the 'Gum Tree Pattern' Plate*, c. 1920 (Plate 26), places the narrative another degree further away from its source, as hers is an Australian version of the English Staffordshire design. This very Australian suburbia, complete with gum tree and washing line, is described by the artist in what reads now as an excruciatingly unfunny pseudo-Chinese language. A man called Doo-Ti owns a bungalow called 'See Vu'. He has a daughter called Loo See who elopes with Jon Sun.[1]

There was an interest in Orientalism in Australia in the 1880s, but it was a second-hand appreciation that arrived via Europe, on which, for the most part, Australians have fixed their strained gaze and from whose people they have adopted their attitude towards the East. Rupert Bunny's attempt to portray the *Geisha Girl*, c. 1901 (Figure 31), illustrates just how foreign Asian peoples were.[2] Although a painter who could capture an individual likeness, Bunny here fails to present even a racially accurate face.

Australia's modern artists — Boyd, Tucker, Perceval, Nolan, Lanceley — sought their artistic fortunes in Europe in the 1950s and 1960s, much as Streeton, Phillips Fox, Preston and Proctor, among many others, had done before them. Donald Friend was among the few to choose Asia. He visited Sri Lanka (then Ceylon) in 1962, and had a long association with Bali, living there from 1967 to 1982, where he documented his stay in vignettes and sketch-portraits of the people he met, sending examples back to his Australian dealers.[3]

Margaret Preston's interest in Asia was stimulated, at least in the first instance, by her study of Japanese techniques during a stay in France and Germany from 1904 to 1907.[4] It is clear that from her reflection on Japanese art she derived a sense of outline, flattened space and strong contrast — as if forms were drawn in ink. These approaches lent themselves to the linearity of the woodcut through which she made her reputation. (While in the Japanese print it is the ink outline that shapes the form, in the woodcut the raised area that is not chiselled out creates the delineation.) Preston is known to have bought a book of Japanese prints,[5] and in 1934 visited Japan specifically to study woodcuts by Hiroshige, as well as to travel widely throughout Asia with her husband.[6] *Blue Mountains Theme* (Figure 32), an oil-on-canvas work painted in 1941, has a Chinese look that demonstrates an integrated adaptation discovered first-hand rather than through interpretations by European artists. Here, the grand vista is geometrically formalised and natural features are simplified, with limited modelling and brushstroke texture.

Humphrey McQueen relates how Preston dismissed her contemporary colleagues as 'a bunch of copyists'[7] who were only involved in imitations of styles developed in Europe. He argues that Preston wished to establish a popular Australian art based on the formal symmetry she felt existed in work by European masters.[8] She saw this balance as particularly evident in the paintings of J. M. W. Turner and John Constable and wished to emulate their compositional procedures which, she believed, could be effectively exploited to portray Australian subject matters. Reaching out to Chinoiserie and Japonisme was also part of her rationale. Just as Picasso set the vogue in appropriating African art, Preston looked to Aboriginal and Asian cultures, which, along with the superficiality of her interest, may indicate not only that she saw decorative possibilities in their work,[9] but also that Asian peoples enjoyed the status of primitive natives whose work was available for reinterpretation. However, the anti-Asian feeling stimulated by the Second World War appears not to have deterred her interest.

FIGURE 32
Margaret Preston, *Blue Mountains Theme*, c. 1941, oil on canvas, 50.7 x 51.3 cm. Collection: Shepparton Art Gallery, Victoria

McQueen quotes Preston as saying 'they [Chinese] paint the Spirit; we paint the Object'.[10] It is clear that for *Blue Mountains Theme* Preston's objective technique is indeed indebted to Chinese art, but in achieving this Chinese quality she appears to lose the 'spirit' of Australia. Although she was influenced by the art of China, she seems not to have been particularly interested in China itself. Although it is such a highly populated country, it is not the Chinese people who engage her, but their artistic techniques in representing the landscape.

It was not until the 1960s that Australians began to become acquainted with Asian people rather than just the Asian landscape in reproduction. The Vietnam (television) War introduced the world to individual Asians in extreme circumstances. It provided a new stereotype, improving on that of the 'Yellow Peril', the less than human enemy of the Second World War.

Regularly in the evening, the modern world, far removed from the battlefields, ate its TV dinners while watching terrified women and children finding some semblance of protection from guns and bombs by huddling together. We saw injured babies and their dead relations and realised that Vietnamese skin and flesh and fears hurt, too.

Among children fleeing a misplaced napalm strike targeted for North Vietnamese foxholes is a young girl who tears the burning skin from her body (Figure 33). We are presented with the ultimate vulnerability: a naked child who is accidentally wounded. We suffer the knowledge that she will bear her scars for ever. She comes to symbolise the inequality of the battle with its major-power capacities and defenceless human victims. She becomes known worldwide as Kim Phuc, the nine-year-old girl who helped to bring about an end to the Vietnam War.

Probably for the first time on television news, as opposed to fictional film, a man was shot in the head (Figure 34). In the television footage, he falls to the ground.

Associated Press reported that the victim, who has his hands tied behind his back, was a Vietcong guerilla captured near the Quang Pagoda in Saigon during the Tet Offensive of 1968. The executioner was Nguyen Ngoc Loan, a chief police officer who was reported to have calmly replaced his pistol in his holster after the shooting, John Wayne-style, declaring: 'They killed many Americans and many of my people.'[11] Here are two pure-evil stereotypes within the one racial group. Asians are becoming more complicated! The photograph, taken by Eddie Adams from Associated Press, won a Pulitzer Prize and was used by anti-Vietnam War demonstrators to exemplify the futility of the war.

Mahatma Gandhi had represented a mysterious Asian type when he made powerful political decisions that influenced international politics without the paraphernalia and ritual that usually accompany men of power. In 1906, working for the cause of the poor and aligning himself with the so-called 'untouchables', he instigated the *satyagraha* — a Sanskrit term which translates literally as soul force — through which he encouraged non-violent acts of civil disobedience. In working against British rule in India, Gandhi's impact was felt universally and he became a forerunner to the Indian guru who was taken up so enthusiastically by the West in the 1960s. The Maharishi Mahesh Yogi was one of a number of eastern mystics who based their philosophies either on Buddhism, Hinduism or versions of

FIGURE 33 (TOP)
Nick Ut, *Children Fleeing Napalm Strike Near Saigon, 10 June 1972*.
Photograph courtesy AP/AAP

FIGURE 34 (ABOVE)
Eddie Adams, *Shooting of Vietcong Guerilla Tet Offensive, 1 February 1968*.
Photograph courtesy AP/AAP

both that were homogenised for western consumption. The Maharishi became famous for receiving a personal visit by the Beatles, who observed his teachings for a time.

With a superficial introduction to meditation, and perhaps with the memory of Gandhi, the peace-loving Asian stereotype was retained. Although still unequal to a westerner, the non-uniformed, civilian Vietnamese demonstrated an endearing, peace-loving nature, but one that was perceived to be characterised by an inferior docility, like that of a gentle animal. Gandhi's *satyagraha* policy was emulated in the United States, first in Black civil-rights campaigns and then in anti-Vietnam War activities. Flower power arrived and the war ended.

In Australia, it took artists to recognise that there is much to be learned from Asia, the politicians following in earnest several decades later. Godfrey Miller (see chapter one) undertook a study of eastern philosophies in the 1950s, but better-known were Asianoid examples by Brett Whiteley. In 1968 Whiteley painted his controversial response to the Vietnam War, entitled *The American Dream*. Based on the American Pop artist James Rosenquist's format of message writ-large, it consists of eighteen panels, and parodies the American idea of peace via destruction. Whiteley's biographer, Sandra McGrath, relates that, on returning from England in 1964, Whiteley saw Australia as 'a political infant smothered by … apron strings stretching across two oceans, two continents and hundreds of islands', that connected it to Mother Britain.[12] McGrath says Whiteley felt that until Australia came to terms with Asia it was 'doomed to an inane existence'.[13]

With reference to the application of Asian philosophies in his art, Whiteley said: 'At this moment, the moment you get bored with the idea of predictability — then you reach for the furthest opposite: to be perpetually shifting and not holdable, to be mercurial and Zen!'[14] He captured this idea in a work titled *To Arrive at a Point of Cublessism*, 1961, in which there is the sense of the cube without recourse to the predictability of the cube shape. Whiteley used this Zen reference to describe his attempts to balance extremes so that ideas and art methods from the peripheries are not lost but incorporated simultaneously, much as is advocated by the Buddhist 'middle way'. According to Zen philosophies, enlightenment may be achieved suddenly, immediately and directly, as opposed to occurring after a long period of continuous dedication. Whiteley's attempts to capture the essential Zen appear to have suited his inclination towards the dramatic. Artistically, they appear as the pared-down form until it is a simple dominating line which journeys the female body, as well as along the road ahead, to become a recurring feature of his landscapes.

When in the 1960s and 1970s Australians saved to go 'overseas' they made only brief stops in Asian countries en route to Europe. Australian teenagers took a trip to England via Asia, like a final year of study with which to complete their education.

The Beatles split up, flower-power organisers cut their hair, gave up marijuana and melded into the middle class. Batik and other handicrafts of Asia went out of fashion. The nostalgia towards Asia that sounded the end of the Vietnam War continued for as long as it kept its place as a distant continent. But the world was becoming smaller with globalised media expansion in the 1970s and 1980s. Asia was seen to be more appealing, but as a relaxing holiday destination — the association was still superficial. 'I've been to Bali, too' the song went, and everyone brought back a souvenir, a kitsch piece of craft made specially for the tourist trade.

In the 1980s, with dramatic economic development in Asia, a new stereotype arose: that of a people with a dangerous capacity to work all day and half the night to improve their circumstances. But at least now the Asian person, although not yet recognised as having a thoroughly distinct regional culture, was seen to possess

PLATE 27
Vladimir Tretchikov, print, 61 x 55 cm.
Private collection. Photograph: John Brash

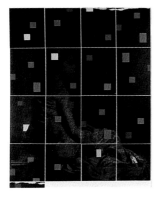

PLATE 28
Pat Hoffie, *Hotel Paradise,* **1989–90,**
laser copy on board, 145 x 336 cm.
Photograph: Elvira Gonzalez Lopez

a more complicated personality of interchangeable and even contradictory stereo-types: dangerous Communist hordes when en masse, and submissive and peace-loving when encountered on an individual basis.

Pat Hoffie has commented on the superficiality of the Australian acquaintance with Asian people, in *Hotel Paradise,* 1989–90 (Plate 28). Influential in her formulation of this work was her recollection of the Tretchikov portraits that were readily available at such department stores as Coles in the 1950s and 1960s, and commonly used for interior decoration (Plate 27).[15] But rather than any stylistic impression, Hoffie was left with a sense of the deficiency and distortion in their characterisation. These women were generalised Eurasian beauties of an indeterminate age from somewhere exotic. The mystique associated with their foreignness was heightened by their skin colour being given a greenish tinge. Tretchikov, a Russian-born resident of South Africa, gave his dark beauties Asiatic eyes but modified European faces, with superficial signs of their purported origins, such as a Chinese collar on their shirts.

Hoffie redesigned these images with an injection of realism. There is the inference that the woman who sits on the bed may be part of a new exploitation of Asia by the dominant white élite. The young woman, perhaps from Thailand, could be awaiting a client, as she may be the next stop on the sex tour. To the world outside her immediate family she is identified only by her ability to bring sexual pleasure to non-Asian men. She is not a personality but an object for acquisition, much like the souvenir. The grid produced by the computer-generated image places her as if behind bars, and although more lifelike than the Tretchikov woman she is now part of a new technologised commercial system. Push the button at the travel agent and up comes whatever-her-name-is for your enjoyment.

Only since the late 1970s has the notion of syncretism — the generalisation of the peoples of Asia into one homogenous whole — been questioned, and more recently still in any wholesale way. Similarly, the realisation has emerged that it was not Asia who named itself so but those external to it. Awareness is dawning on the West that the Asian continent consists not of one country with regional differences but many distinct cultures with inconsistent, even discordant, geneses to their heritage.

The people of these countries are now living as Australians, and as our colleagues, neighbours and friends. But, of course, they always have! There were 24,000 Chinese people in Victoria alone in the late 1860s,[16] many of whom, as is well known, were drawn to the State to mine in the goldfields. Some 200 Chinese people were furniture-makers in the 1890s but it was required that their products be stamped 'Chinese made'.[17] As Alison Carroll has mentioned, there are few references to these original Chinese in art. She writes: 'The low arts acknowledge[d] Asia while the "high" arts made a point of not doing so.'[18]

One of the earliest artistic references to Chinese people occurs in 1880 in a sketch by Aboriginal artist Tommy McRae (Figure 35). As well as being one of the few depictions of Chinese in Australia, it documents the animosity felt by Aborigines towards the Chinese who were mining their land. This is an early example of a cross-cultural exchange in which both partners are to some extent foreign to the dominant, white, middle class.

An Aboriginal-Chinese connection of an impersonal, abstract kind occurs in the work of Ian Fairweather, who was himself something of an outsider to Australian culture. Fairweather travelled to a number of Asian countries, including China, India, Korea and Hong Kong, in 1933, when the already complicated surface of his work was beginning to grow its contradictory, textured layers. These seasoned in the late 1920s and 1930s into the more sophisticated responses to China. By the 1960s, Fairweather had developed an imagery in which gestures are fused to become hybrid characters from a Chinese-Aboriginal language and yet these markings are still recognisable as illustrations of the mangrove swamps at Bribie Island, off the Queensland coast, where he is reputed to have lived the hermit's life. In *Mangrove*, 1961–62 (Figure 36), hieroglyphics like Chinese characters form the complexity that emerges from the swampy brown. Further intricate layers produce a twisted, abstract pattern that also resonates inhabitation among the mangrove.

While most people's first encounter with Asian art occurs with the purchase of a mass-produced object through the tourist trade, Asian art of a more sophisticated kind has been collected by Australian museums for more than a hundred years. In 1879 a sizeable quantity of Japanese art, in Sydney on exhibition, was donated by the Japanese government to the Art Gallery of New South Wales, beginning its Asian collection.[19] Consequently, Japanese art has been of continued interest to the gallery, followed by Chinese and Southeast Asian art. The National Gallery of Victoria has acquisitions from China, although this has not been an area of major interest to it.[20] Since 1993 the Queensland Art Gallery has led the way in the collection of contemporary art from the Asian region.

As curator and author Michael Brand has pointed out, a positive result of Australia's syncretic attitude towards Asia has been the assemblage of works from across the continent in a number of Australian galleries and museums, whereas in Asia, where this bias does not exist, collectors have concentrated on one or two countries.[21] As a result, the National Gallery of Australia in Canberra, for example, boasts one of the world's most comprehensive collections of decorative textiles from Southeast Asia.[22]

Works from these collections have been put on display from time to time, but one of the first exhibitions to explore Australia's reaction to Asian art was held in Melbourne in 1990 at the Heide Museum of Modern Art. Significantly, it was an anthropologist, rather than an art historian, who was asked to write the introductory essay for the exhibition, titled 'Out of Asia'. The writer argued that 'shameless economistic logics currently exhort Australia to embrace a relationship with Asia', clearly

FIGURE 35
Tommy McRae, *Aborigine Chasing Chinese Man*, 1880, pen and ink, 17.5 x 10 cm. Collection: National Library of Australia, Canberra

Ian Fairweather, *Mangrove*, 1961–62,
synthetic polymer paint and gouache on
cardboard on hardboard, 82 x 122 cm

asserting that it would be better if the relationship were based on higher motives, but also suggesting that doing trade with Asia has different and sinister implications that do not exist in trade with, say, Britain or New Zealand.[23] In the same essay, the 1990 organisers of the Sydney Biennale were criticised for considering eastern and western traditions so dissimilar as to preclude the incorporation of artists from what were referred to as third-world countries.[24]

With the first Asia-Pacific Triennial exhibition at the Queensland Art Gallery in 1993, the response from the press, as well as from some quarters of academia, was somewhat cynical. Although the art was appreciated, the question was asked as to why large amounts of government funding were being expended on the encouragement of interaction when this was all motivated by government policy to improve trade relations. Much of the coverage by ABC Radio's main arts program, 'Arts Today', was similarly dedicated to the question of whether or not this was money well spent, given that the exhibition had a political, economically driven basis. But given Australia's apparent ethnocentric concealment of Asian art, either held or produced in Australia, this position may be interpreted as no more sensitive than the 1860s stamp on Chinese-made furniture to identify and emphasise that the wood was handled by someone other than a European Australian.

The first Asia-Pacific Triennial exhibition convinced the more than 60,000 people who viewed it that Asia has many flourishing centres of contemporary art, as well as those directed to the crafts of the tourist trade. Three years later the second Asia-Pacific Triennial reinforced this message to the approximately 120,000 people who attended. The Third Asia-Pacific Triennial in 1999 attracted 150,000 visitors. Media in all events included sculpture, painting, photography, video and installation, but the first exhibition, focusing on the theme of tradition and change, demonstrated a special interest in performance, through which many of the countries participating have a still extant, direct link to traditional ritual and dance. This is the case even though Asian contemporary art performances now often involve politically driven metaphor and symbolism. For the first Asia-Pacific Triennial, Dadang Christanto covered himself with clay to signify a nostalgia for a pre-industrial land, creating a memorial to those violated, whether by military means, through media reports or in artistic representation.[25] In *For Those Who Have Been Killed*, 1993 (Figures 37A and 37B), Christanto directed his audience's attention to a universal denial of the prevalence of violence, and stressed that this is particularly the case with the policies of censorship that apply in his country of Indonesia.[26] Christanto here circumvented established news channels to put a perspective that would otherwise be unseen, in a lamentation of past deaths and, as is clear years later, one that prefigured violence to come.

FIGURE 37A AND 37B
Dadang Christanto, *For Those Who Have Been Killed*, 1993, performance at Queensland Art Gallery, Brisbane

FIGURE 38

Brenda Fajardo, *Ako ay Babae, Ako ay Pilipina*
(I Am Woman, I Am Filipino), **1993**, from the
'Cards of Life – Women's Series', pen and ink with
goldleaf on handmade paper, 52.5 x 72 cm.
Collection: Queensland Art Gallery, Brisbane,
The Kenneth and Yasuko Myer Collection of
Contemporary Asian Art, purchased 1993 with
funds from the Myer Foundation, Michael Myer
and Anne Gamble Myer through the Queensland
Art Gallery Foundation

Brenda Fajardo, from the Philippines, showed her 'Cards of Life' series of paintings on handmade paper (Figure 38). The series features a modernised and humanised tarot spread that predicts the future, not just for one woman but for most Filipinas whose prospects are as limited as the tarot reading suggests, and similarly beyond their control. As the cards fall, so lies their destiny. Their possibilities are limited to inauspicious options, such as employment as a house cleaner, or the dubious pleasures of life as a mail-order bride.[27] Fajardo here poses a question with important social ramifications, if not one of human rights, that rarely arises in the Australian context.

At the turn of the century, Australia is playing a leading role in the contemporary arts of the region, providing curatorial advice, as in the case of the curators' training workshop held in Kuala Lumpur in 1995 (to cite just one example) at which five Australian museum professionals acted as advisers. An ongoing dialogue is maintained through Asialink, a body established to foster Australian–Asian artistic relations, including programs of exchange and exhibition. The number of independent projects with Asia continues to increase as commercial galleries showcase their artists. These activities highlight the new transcultural nature of artmaking, in which the issue of nationality is less straightforward now that easier international travel and a greater awareness of other cultures are advancing the dissolution of fixed attitudes towards geographical and racial difference.

At the second Asia-Pacific Triennial in 1996, the Japanese artist Yukinori Yanagi produced an international emblem made of thirty-six flags from countries that

FIGURE 39
Xu Bing, A Case Study of Transference, 1994,
performance at Han Mo Art Centre, Beijing.
Photograph: Xu Zhi Wai

influence the region. His composite flag installation, called *Asia-Pacific Ant Farm*,
1996 (Plate 29), was made of coloured sand housed in perspex boxes. Attached to the
boxes were perspex tubes in which ants had been placed. These tubes were connected
to one another so that as the ants moved among the perfectly described flags, one
country's nationality became confused with another.

A further concern that has arisen through Australia's attempts to affirm its
geographical place in Asia, as well as to improve its relationships with Asia-Pacific
countries, is that these activities may be interpreted as motivated by a desire to
impose a form of post-colonial cultural imperative. At the same time, it must be
acknowledged that information and expertise on the arts are being freely donated by
Australia and that its need to retain a cultural place in the massive Asian market may
become all the more intense as the enormity of Asian economic, population and
cultural growth joins with international globalisation to ultimately impact on
Australian art by threatening to overwhelm it.

In a Chinese performance held in China, the original and recent meanings of the word 'chauvinism' are reinforced by two live pigs who are watched as their animal behaviour symbolises human cultural relationships. The boar, with Latinate characters printed on his back, chases the sow that wears Chinese-styled characters, and ultimately copulates with her. In human terms, he may be regarded as raping and violating her. In the realms of international relations, this would constitute an invasion. Culturally, there is the suggestion of western domination over the East. The artist could have been confident the pigs would either roll in the books that appear to play the part of western imperialist academicism, defecate, urinate or copulate on them, any one of which presents a declaratory rejection of it. But has the artist recognised that the very medium used — modern art performance in its contemporary form — derives from the United States? Orchestrated by Xu Bing, this performance, called A *Case Study of Transference*, 1994 (Figure 39), was held at the Han Mo Art Centre in Beijing.[28] It was reported in the Australian-produced *ART AsiaPacific* journal, first published in 1994, which is sold internationally and, apart from the Asia-Pacific Triennial exhibitions, marks the most significant Australian artistic foray into the region. The question as to how much Asian contemporary art — whose media, born of Europe and the United States — differs from its parental form is as yet in the distilling. (There are attempts in China to develop a new form of distinct conceptual art.)

While much art at the end of the twentieth century is political, it has tended towards the universal: gay rights, for example, involves similar issues in the United States as in Australia. But among Asian artists there is a differentiation of issues that is specific to the countries from which they derive and which in western terms concerns major infringements of human rights. This is not to suggest that all Asian contemporary art is political; some is deeply personal with no wider social ramifications. But when it does involve a political dimension there is, arguably, a basis generally unexperienced by non-Aboriginal Australian artists.

The issue arises as to whether or not Australian artists will retain their European-Australian vision or develop a new Australian-Asian hybrid art. The examples given indicate that, with rare exceptions, the degree to which Asian art has influenced Australian artists to date is slight.

Tony Clark, who has been included in two important Australian exhibitions considering Asian-influenced work by artists resident in Australia, paints what he calls Chinoiserie landscapes, in which two-dimensional images of maquettes in a Chinese architectural style are set against walls decorated with shapes derived from Islamic script (see Figure 40).[29] As art historian Roger Benjamin has argued, Clark's pagodas are themselves architecturally hybrid,[30] originating from small Italian temples or tomb structures that, with upturned cantilevers, develop a Chinese dialect. Clark has mentioned his interest in the sixteenth-century Italian fresco painter Mantegna, whose figures have a sculptural, three-dimensional quality, as if they were made of brass or stone. Clark emphasises that it is the very corruption of the image, and its removal from its source, that engages him for the ironic possibilities that arise.[31] But, however theoretically interesting and visually enigmatic, these are not expositions on Chinese culture. While it is the artist's prerogative to work in this manner, the decision to select him to represent transcultural Asian-inspired work appears to indicate that there was at the time little thoroughgoing consideration of Asian art among contemporary artists in Australia, and perhaps points to the absence of any other work that might be more 'Asian'. In this event, the argument is brought back to Rupert Bunny and the dim sim.

Despite her incorporation of disparate elements of exotic decoration, Margaret Preston's emphasis in 1942, that it was not just for the purposes of diversion but

PLATE 29
Yukinori Yanagi, *Asia-Pacific Ant Farm,* 1996,
installation, ants, coloured sand, plastic box,
plastic tube, plastic pipe and video documentation
on LCD monitor, dimensions variable,
Queensland Art Gallery, Brisbane

FIGURE 40
Tony Clark, *Chinoiserie Landscape*,
1986–87, acrylic on canvasboard,
three panels, 30.5 x 68.4 cm overall.
Courtesy Roslyn Oxley9 Gallery, Sydney

a matter of necessity that new Australian–Asian art be created, was extraordinarily prescient, and more apposite than many commentators are in the 1990s. She wrote:

> The change in the world situation of Australia, made by the War, will compel her artists to readjust their relationship to the Art of the European continent and Great Britain. They will have to realise that any help they wish culturally lies nearer to their own shores. Australia will find herself at the corner of a triangle; the East, as represented by China, India, Japan, will be at one point, and the other will have the United States of America representing the West. It will be in the choice of one of these corners that the future of Australian Art will lie.[32]

A long-standing resistance to Asian influence in Australia has been reflected in political policy. The White Australia policy has existed in various forms since activities on the Victorian and New South Wales goldfields, when violence flared towards industrious Chinese and restrictions were placed on their immigration. The policy was significantly reformed in the 1970s. As late as 1919, when immigrants were required to undertake a dictation test in English, a language with which they were not necessarily familiar, the policy was hailed as 'the greatest thing we have achieved' by Prime Minister William Morris Hughes. By the 1940s, this attitude was still current and reiterated by John Curtin, who proclaimed, 'this country shall remain for ever the home of the descendants of those people who came here in peace in order to establish in the South Seas an outpost of the British race'.[33]

From 1966, non-European immigration gradually increased, but race was not removed as an entry criterion until the Whitlam government took steps to alter the legislation in 1973, with further wide-ranging reforms undertaken in 1978 to significantly increase numbers. At the turn of the century, most immigrants are derived from New Zealand, the United Kingdom, China, Hong Kong, India and Vietnam.[34]

While it remains to be seen whether the perspective put by Pauline Hanson and her One Nation Party is an aberration or a lasting feature of Australian politics to be revived by another such identity or organisation, there are other more frivolous indications that an attitude of inequality prevails. Even without leaving the sitting room there is the example of the cat stuck in a suburban tree that takes precedence in commercial television news bulletins over the loss of thousands of people in a disaster in an Asian country, such as Bangladesh.

5

Picturing Life Together:
The Community and
the Visual Arts

In Aboriginal traditions, the ritual of body painting — in which the artwork is produced cooperatively by a number of artists — is an early example of what now has a label and definition. A more recent example occurs among Country Women's Associations, through which Australian women produce various needlework artefacts and decorations for festivals and church ceremonies. These activities constitute an institutionalised form of community art. ➤

PLATE 30
Bob Jankowski and Carol-Anne Harris (Artistic
Coordinators), *Berrivale Community Mural,*
1985, Berrivale Orchards, Sturt Highway, Berri,
6 x 75 m. Photograph: Italo Vardaro

The community art that is produced by non-professionals for exhibition in public spaces has origins that predate the modern city, but in a new, bureaucratised form it has become very much a part of contemporary urban life. The location of modern community artwork outside the gallery is fundamental to its purpose. It is of the community, unlike the sometimes remote, authoritative art system. It is intended for general information or entertainment and may also perform a proselytising function. It can be viewed by anyone at any time, as opposed to being on show in accordance with a particular exhibition schedule for a select audience who attend an opening by invitation only. To accommodate these requirements, the most suitable medium and location is the oil-painted mural on a public wall.

The 75-metre-long Berrivale Community Mural in South Australia's Riverland district (Plate 30) describes and celebrates the agricultural industry of this desert region that has been greened by irrigation from the Murray River. Painted in 1985 by school-children under the guidance of their art teachers, Bob Jankowski and Carol-Anne Harris, the mural traces the relationship between the people of the area and the land, and at the same time identifies the many elements that constitute local character.

The mural begins with a portrayal of Aboriginal methods of harvesting indigenous plant life. It moves on to the exploitation of early agricultural machinery by white settlers, through to the present technological production that makes this area of eastern South Australia a major producer and exporter of grapes, citrus, stone fruit and almonds. Painted on the Berrivale orchard fence that borders the Sturt Highway at Berri, the mural is a reminder that ultimately it is individual human labour that drives this industry, no matter how large-scale its markets and capacities, and that most people of the area are touched in some way by a commitment to fruit production. The multicultural mix from which the community has evolved, and which has created its personal and economic character, is alluded to in the national flags included in the mural. Reference is made to the first settlers, who were Canadian, and to those from Germany, as well as more recent arrivals from India and Turkey, many of whom brought know-how from homelands with long histories of commercial fruit and nut production.

This mural indicates, in keeping with its many counterparts around Australia, that for such artistic efforts to be effective it is necessary to employ a vocabulary common to all concerned so that complexity and ambiguity are avoided, and alternative misreadings do not occur. In banding together to produce art, community groups are motivated by the desire to communicate as strong and clear a message as possible in order to reach as wide an audience as practicable. Since their art production is inde-pendent of the private and institutional gallery system they are often obliged to exercise economies of means, both in the visual style adopted and the resources employed. There is a concern that audiences read the artists' intentions accurately so that rather than functioning solely as an item of decoration the artwork will inform or inspire a change of attitude towards its makers and the group it represents. At the very least, the artwork must be distinctly identifiable as belonging to a particular community.

PAGE 112
Carole Wilson, *Strike while the iron's hot,* 1987
(detail), screenprinted poster, 76 x 51 cm

The *From Bonboniere to Barbed Wire* mural (Figure 41), painted over several months from 1985 to 1986, portrays a wide cross-section of women and compares the various roles they perform. It is painted on the Gas and Fuel building situated at the corner of Smith Street and Queens Parade in the inner Melbourne suburb of North Fitzroy. The mural presents the argument that it is a diversity of character from which the 'general woman' of the feminist movement is comprised. Painted by Megan Evans and Eve Glenn at a time when the main thrust of the movement was for female equality, it was all too possible to lose sight of the fact that the needs of this vast group were more disparate and complex than was apparent in the hold-all phrases adopted. As the mural illustrates, the elderly woman has requirements that are very different from those of the middle-aged and the black woman. Their needs and aspirations are different again from those of the wife who works in the family greengrocer's, and can be at odds with those that will advance the cause of the young white woman pursuing a business career. In relation to all of these, the imprisoned woman, who is referred to as living behind barbed wire in the mural title, has quite specific desires and obligations. All these types are visible in the crowded, multicultural Fitzroy streets surrounding the mural. The message that appears on the screen at the top of the painting: 'Sisters are doing it for themselves' — taken from the Annie Lennox hit song that was popular in the mid-1980s[1] — optimistically asserts that women are not only ignoring male oppression, they are refusing to wait for the necessary change to be brought about in the predominantly male institutions that would normally control their advancement.

FIGURE 41

Megan Evans and Eve Glenn, *From Bonboniere to Barbed Wire*, 1985–86, Gas and Fuel building, Smith Street, North Fitzroy, Melbourne. Photograph: John Brash

Besides such political aims, community artists are concerned to create more than a simple slogan, and therefore aspire to a level of sophistication appropriate to the work being designated as art. While recognising this objective, the art style chosen is almost always figurative. Art historian Sandy Kirby has argued that a contributing factor in this representative approach lies in attitudes formed in the 1930s and 1940s, when social realism — the realist style with a political inclination — was chosen as the vocabulary through which the process of change via art was most effectively articulated.[2] Realism is also the most apt medium for the self-descriptive element that is a significant feature of community art, and which parallels the interest that arose in the 1980s in written local social histories. Both historical and artistic views were symptoms of the egalitarian position that art was not the exclusive domain of the élite. Another important influence was the splintering of every aspect of the art system, as postmodernism and its complicating mission took effect. In recognition of the fact that art can be made by anyone, anywhere, through multifarious thought patterns, the new postmodern system became less strictly hierarchical, and new career channels emerged. Australian society as a whole became more

FIGURE 42

Barry Drinan, Copy of Rembrandt's *The Two Philosophers* **(1628), 1997,** on footpath near the forecourt of the National Gallery of Victoria, Melbourne. The original hangs inside

heterogeneous and less amenable to simple classification. As interest in art participation grew, there was a need for artistic languages that would facilitate the communication of many diverse personalities, while the quest for a definition with which to describe the new artist group mirrored the need to cross other categories, such as public and urban art, political art and that of minority cultures.

Falling outside the divide of so-called consumerist and conceptual art, community art is not usually designed to be marketable, neither does it incorporate the metaphorical idea-base or the installation form with which conceptual and postmodern art are associated. In certain circumstances, such as that of the footpath-artist, community art involves small-scale commercialism. In approximating a depiction of the Old Master work, without the expense required for a specially prepared surface or quality oil paints and preservatives, the chalk artist needs his or her audience to perceive at a glance that it is, say, Leonardo's *Mona Lisa (La Gioconda)* they are viewing, so that a response is made within the time it takes to walk past the image. These enterprises belong to that category of artist whose work is ephemeral: it is walked over and washed away by the rain, erased almost as soon as completed.

In certain city districts there are strict guidelines as to where, from what materials, and even how footpath art should be painted. In Melbourne's central business district the footpath artist is required to submit work for assessment by a government employee (presumably with no training in art connoisseurship) before he or she can begin work.

The French philosopher Jean Baudrillard's ideas on the new simulated art are here interestingly exemplified. The simulacra — the footpath version of Rembrandt's important masterpiece which has been sketched with great perfection in a morning — arouses greater interest than the original that hangs inside the accredited, established art institution.

The banner provides another public art surface and again may be classified as community art since its exhibition occurs outside the gallery system and a number of artists are usually engaged in its production. It enables portability of the message and gives an added personal emphasis by being held by its makers or their followers. Promoting causes from industrial to nationalistic, the banner signals the importance of the trade union movement in the genesis of community art and exemplifies the element of transgression that has prevailed as an aspect of community art's history. Despite the level of expertise and attention to detail involved in the production of early Australian banners, such as that of the Australian Plumbers and Gasfitters Employees Union, c. 1920 (Plate 31), it would not, at the time, have been an acceptable

PLATE 31
Artist unknown, *Banner of the Australian Plumbers and Gasfitters Employees Union*, c. 1920, oil on canvas, 270 x 315 cm. Photograph: Greg Weight

form of art for inclusion in a public collection. Its medium was enough to eliminate it, but its association with the working class may well have been another criterion brought to bear in the assessment process.

Typically, banners were professionally painted (and sometimes embroidered), with clients often attributing great significance to the work and calling for high standards of design and workmanship that involved a painstaking approach to detail.[3] Besides promoting the cause of the union from which the commission was received, the banner lent the suggestion of an affiliation between art and worker to both the worker and the viewer. But the Plumbers and Gasfitters banner, with its highly sophisticated level of artistry and design, rather than advancing the cause of its union with a zealous or militant energy, presents a romanticised vision of its workers' duties. The artful design directs the eye to the patterned bathroom floor tiles, the playful curves of the pipes and the contrasting red rose, all of which create a distance between the plumber and the grime, stench and sweat of the labour devoted to the management of human waste. The benign spirit of this particular banner aside, the trade union movement and its progenitor, Marxism, espoused collective effort to achieve ends unattainable by the individual working in isolation. In this regard, the inclusive role of the banner in the nineteenth century went side by side with important changes in attitudes towards working-class involvement in art, laying foundations for the modern community art movement. Sandy Kirby has written of the Communist Party's early contribution towards the promotion of working-class participation in the arts that coincided with the widespread popularity of the party in the 1930s and 1940s.[4] The redefinition of artists as artworkers followed, and the slogan 'Art is a Weapon' promoted art's politicisation.[5]

The 1960s boost to union membership, said to have occurred with the heightened sense of political awareness that was a consequence of second-wave feminism and opposition to the Vietnam War, is believed to have expanded the artistic community and created a greater awareness of its activities. Also significant in the widespread community art interest of the 1970s were general political developments. The sense of national identity that emerged in the Whitlam years of 1972–75, when the national anthem was changed from the British 'God Save the Queen' to the expression of home-grown attitudes inspired by 'Advance Australia Fair', coincided with a desire for new and more broadly representative voices. The counter-culture movement was now ten years old and had seeded its own cottage industries and craft styles.[6] Important also was the establishment of the Australia Council and its provision of assistance to artists, which produced a new local vitality.

In 1971 a Trades Union Council for the Arts was established and arts officers were appointed to trades and labour councils, with various initiatives resulting.[7] Professional artists were employed to coordinate amateurs,[8] and funds were raised for the preservation and restoration of photos, murals and banners,[9] so registering the stamp of historic and artistic value on such materials. The Art and Working Life policy adopted in 1982 by the Australia Council demonstrated government support towards Labor movement culture, an association that was to continue and grow.[10] In 1990 four major building industry unions adopted policies stipulating that one per cent of the total cost of a building, if it amounted to more than $1 million, be devoted to Australian artwork for inclusion in the completed building.[11] Again, this bred a cross-fertilisation, with the agreement seeing union members becoming better acquainted with the arts and the artistic community inheriting new acolytes and receiving additional funding.

Oliver Strewe played with the work-and-art theme in a photograph he took while engaged as a professional photographer for the Australian Workers Union. Although

PLATE 32
Carole Wilson, *Strike while the iron's hot*,
1987, screenprinted poster, 76 x 51 cm

the subject matter for trade union artists is usually men at work, it is the rest-break that concerns Strewe in his amusing irony on Tom Roberts's *Shearing the Rams,* 1890. *On the Boards, Kentucky Station, NSW,* 1985 (Figure 43), offers many interpretations. The workers' exhaustion after their labour may be the defiant subject of the photograph, but since they take the sheep's place in the well-known painting there is a reference to exploitation; that it is human labour on whose back the economy rides, as it once did on the sheep. At the same time, the workers' status is raised in their being considered a subject worthy of portrayal as high art.

Community arts writer Gay Hawkins has argued that the whole notion of contemporary community art is an 'official' invention, given the extent to which government support is involved.[12] With a chequered history of assistance followed by cutbacks, government policies over the past twenty-five years have remained generally supportive of community art.[13] The first Community Arts and Development Committee was established in 1973 by the Whitlam Government to function under the auspices of the Australian Council for the Arts. In 1977, with the Fraser Government calling for cuts, local councils were considered the most appropriate source for funding community art projects and, according to the *Towards a National Agenda for the Arts* report, were still considered so in the 1990s, given the closure of the Community Arts Board that operated from 1978 to 1987.[14] This same report recommended further diversification of government support, suggesting that local municipalities with populations of more than 30,000 employ at least one community arts officer and that there be the provision of more community cultural centres.

The women's group called The Jillposters operated from 1983 to 1987 without government support; it was also unusual among art movements in having been formed to address issues beyond the art sphere. Primarily, the group formed to lobby for social justice issues, such as disarmament and the abandonment of uranium mining, as well as to pursue what were then known as women's issues, such as the extension and improvement of child-care facilities. The health implications of irradiating food were considered, as was the unacknowledged incidence of rape in the domestic and war domains, and the vexed question of who is responsible for domestic chores. In one postcard, a many-handed woman, like an all-powerful Hindu goddess, performs manipulative feats in order to fulfil a multitude of household tasks — but still she has too few hands. The Jillposters's artwork, consisting of striking postcards and witty posters, was mass-produced, although by non-mechanical means.

Jillposters members included Carole Wilson, Deej Fabyc, Julia Church, Julie Higginbotham, Lesley Baxter and Zana Dare, some of whom adopted pseudonyms for personal, and others for political, reasons. Carole Wilson, a key artist in the group, recalls: 'We didn't bother to apply for grants; we knew we were too far on the fringe to be successful and we weren't that formal. We wanted to do whatever we liked whenever we liked.'[15] The lack of money was also overcome by the use of makeshift equipment. The laundry became a darkroom; between seventy and a hundred copies were printed in the garage. Postcards were hung up on the clothesline to dry. Non-artist members provided such facilities as access to workshops and transport. A rock band called the Jillettes was formed to play at functions for a small door charge. When it was dark the women would turn to law-breaking by pasting up their work around inner-city streets.[16]

As members gradually left the group it lost its impetus and was disbanded in 1987, by which time its posters and postcards had been distributed through bookshops and galleries around the country, and acquired by the State Library of Victoria and the National Gallery of Australia.

The communal face of the women's movement was important in influencing the expansion of community art, providing evidence of the effectiveness of coordinated joint efforts. The collapse of the exclusivity that had been an art system feature also encouraged changes to the individual artist profile. Gender and race were becoming less relevant as factors dictating the progress of an art career. The system was looking beyond the promotion of work by middle-aged white men and began to include that of Aborigines, women, the young and those for whom English is a second language. With the diffusion of the artistic mould, the notion of the creator as rare genius was questioned. When more people were recognised as possessing artistic ability, accolades once granted to the very few were more liberally dispensed, and it became apparent that it was not necessary for an artist to possess exceptional talents to produce acceptable artwork. It became palpably clear also that interesting art could be created without the artist living the eccentric life, or demonstrating character traits usually associated with those of the so-called insane. An artist was someone who could live next door, as well as several centuries ago on the other side of the world. Indeed, it became clear that an artist of some sort might lurk inside everyone.

FIGURE 44

Deej Fabyc, *Wipe Out War Not Women*, c. 1983, screenprinted poster, 76 x 51 cm

FIGURE 45
Graffiti, inner Melbourne

But, as if to secure their position, the entrenched élite mounted a rearguard action. The conceptual art that was promoted by the art intelligentsia of the 1960s led to the development of narrow enclaves that again served to exclude those without the contacts, the means, the desire, or, it must be said, the intellectual capacity to follow this artistic stream, which was once again the province of the white, middle class, educated — if no longer middle-aged — male. The artist Vivienne Binns has argued that this new form of élitism inadvertently advanced the genesis of new languages and modes that posed alternatives to those of the established system.[17] These could be taken up by that part of the general population finding itself so rigorously excluded. Those whose access to the 'fine' art system was barred, or who felt disenchanted by it, turned instead, Binns has suggested, to revive interest in the crafts, and in doing so also contributed to the expansion of community arts.[18] Another impulse in the development of an alternative 'system' was a reaction against the promotion by some commercial galleries of art as interior decoration. It was a development considered inappropriate among those who believed art to be not only creatively constrained by market concerns but ethically devalued by them.

While not everyone interested in participation in the arts wished to pursue a professional artistic career on a full-time basis, many wanted an involvement in an activity through which they could express their political views. At the same time, much work produced in the 1980s and 1990s included distinctly apolitical examples, with scarcely any other intention than to serve as amusement for the community while still paying homage to the democratic principles of cooperation. It was now felt that through joint effort, the individual possessed an influential voice, and that art was a legitimate and effective means through which to express desired change. The new artist sometimes teamed up with the new art sponsor who first became a visible phenomenon in the 1980s.

By the late 1990s, however, community art fell subject to the processes that gave rise to the category itself. The rigid boundaries differentiating community and institutional art blurred, so that tattooing, for example, while an established community folk-art, in that it has its own cultural language of aesthetics, symbolism, conventions and patronage, was given the prestige of being included in a touring exhibition of public galleries (see chapter six). As an artform, tattooing relates to some of the earliest community arts, such as ritual body painting among tribal peoples, but in a more recent form has possessed the connotation of rebellion, until becoming a widely worn fashion accessory in the late 1990s.

Graffiti, the stage set to hip-hop music from the black ghettos of New York in the early 1980s, had lost some of its power as a transgressive device only ten years later. Once the ultimate in rebellious art, the act of placing a political statement on someone else's property without their permission became domesticated. Passersby get a glimpse inside 'Robo's' mind from the graffito he painted to decorate the house he lives in himself.

The more community art becomes officially and publicly sanctioned, so the need for such involvement declines. Some critics decry community artists as a ragbag of disadvantaged, passive people who are using art as therapy, but they are a dying breed in that the whole notion of artistic outsider-art is becoming a less meaningful category. While a very small percentage will have their work exhibited in a major public gallery, many can now find the acknowledgment they seek. The prisoner who paints on his cell wall may become an artist, even from inside gaol. Similarly, the migrants, the women, the elderly, the underprivileged Black are taken seriously as proponents of their artforms.

Racial and Sexual Versions: The Art of Minority Cultures

6

In his essays on history and sexuality, the British academic and writer Jeffrey Weeks queried the efficacy of adopting the routine methodology of employing the past to explain the present. How can we be sure, he argued, that we can ever really know the past when we were not there?[1] Equally, how can we really know others when we are not them? ➤

Art by urban Aboriginal people has a singular history in that its style and subject matter is often only partially linked with the past, given the abrupt and radical propulsion of Aboriginal people from their millennial cultures. They may still retain links with their land, but choose not to represent this attachment in their art. Similarly, their work may not illustrate their story in the traditional sense, but may still be identifiably Aboriginal. Despite the interest that has developed since the late 1960s in indigenous art, that dealing with Aboriginal political causes has tended to fall outside all existing art historical categories.

Having its own particular genesis, coding and messages, traditional Aboriginal art was, in effect, put on trial in the 1970s by the established white art system which analysed and deliberated on it to determine its validity as art as opposed to anthropological ethnography. Associated with the attitude that gave rise to this reconsideration and reclassification is the historical fact that Aborigines were not counted in the census, and therefore not regarded as Australian citizens until 1967, when a referendum was passed amending discriminatory sections of the Constitution. As Chicka Dixon, acting president of the Foundation of Aboriginal Affairs, said at the time: 'For most Aborigines the referendum is basically and most importantly a matter of seeing white Australians finally, after 179 years, affirming at last that they believe we are human beings.'[2]

A consequence of citizenship was the right to vote in an election. However, the qualification applied to the legislation granting Aboriginal suffrage served to reduce its impact in expunging Australia's racist history in that it did not require Aboriginal people to vote or enrol on a compulsory basis, as was the case for citizens from other racial groups, a situation not amended until 1983.[3] A remaining problem, given official, verbal recognition in 1999, is that their indigenous status is not mentioned in the constitution, a fact which has led to the suggestion that it still reads as if Australia were *terra nullius* (vacant land) when white settlers arrived.[4]

A recognition on the part of the wider community — as a result of action by Land Rights groups and the popularity of Aboriginal art — that there was a need for redress, gave rise to important legislation. The 1992 High Court Mabo decision rejected the notion that Australia, prior to white settlement, was owned by no one. The Court recognised that indigenous people had rights to land before white settlement, and that, in some areas, these rights — called Native Title — continued to the present day.

In 1996 the High Court Wik decision ruled that Native Title may co-exist alongside the interests of pastoral leaseholders. The Court also stated that where there is a conflict between the rights of a leaseholder and Native Title rights, those of the leaseholder would come first. In 1998 the Howard Government amended the previous Labor government's Native Title Act 1993, requiring that Native Title claimants pass a test to access the right to negotiate in relation to mining and certain other developments.

The purchase of traditional Aboriginal art was begun in the 1970s by a small number of collectors, the best known of whom was Margaret Carnegie. Interest grew, both locally and overseas, and the art boom of the 1980s further encouraged speculation in indigenous art, with merchandising increasing spectacularly. Works made in the Outback found their way onto the walls of New York and other cities around the world. It has been estimated that there were more than fifty commercial exhibitions of Aboriginal art throughout Australia from 1987 to 1989.[5] By the 1990s major exhibitions had been held in public galleries, and a number of specialist indigenous art galleries had opened. Aboriginal art's imitators, who made a mélange of cross-cultural designs for sale as souvenirs, were also profiting from its expansion, until growth could be described as explosive. Images were being exploited as decoration for

PAGE 124

Lin Onus, *Fruit Bats,* 1991 (detail), foam, fibreglass, resin, acrylic enamel paint, Hills Hoist, 250 x 250 x 250 cm. Collection: Art Gallery of New South Wales, Sydney. Reproduced with permission of VI$COPY Ltd, Sydney

PLATE 33
Trevor Nickolls, *Deaths in Custody*, **1990,**
synthetic polymer paint on canvas, 150 x 150 cm.
Collection: National Gallery of Australia,
Canberra

PLATE 34
Lin Onus, *Fruit Bats,* **1991,**
foam, fibreglass, resin, acrylic enamel paint,
Hills Hoist, 250 x 250 x 250 cm. Collection:
Art Gallery of New South Wales, Sydney.
Reproduced with permission of
VI$COPY Ltd, Sydney

everything from T-shirts to tea-towels, and the issue of intellectual copyright protection was raised. Legal action followed with important precedents being set in 1989, when the Aboriginal artists concerned were acknowledged as creators of an original image.[6] A largely ignorant western audience had supposed these designs to be generalised Aboriginal symbolism. The notion of the traditional Dreaming totem, which is owned by a particular clan and passed on through generations, became clarified in ensuing discussions. Confusing the issue was the realisation that imaginative input was not relevant to traditional Aboriginal art, as their procedure was to repaint images designed by their ancestors, with details as to how these should be executed described by family or clan members.

In the 1970s and 1980s, the classification of 'outsider' art was extended by a growing interest in community art projects and the attendant feeling that it is artists themselves who are best equipped to tell their own stories. Accordingly, the government-sponsored company Aboriginal Arts and Crafts Pty Ltd was established in 1971 to manage the sale of Aboriginal work, including that produced in outback community art centres. The company reported a $2.5 million result from arts and crafts made in 1979–80 alone.[7]

As these developments were occuring the distinction emerged between authentic Aboriginal art made with reference to traditional methods, and urban art which deployed a contemporary style and metaphorical depictions. Souvenir craft produced for the tourist trade was another product again and was usually relatively cheap and mass-made. That known as traditional involved modifications to original methods — such as using canvas instead of bark, or simply making marks in the sand — while retaining styles, images and techniques. Urban art was produced by city dwellers who predominantly used twentieth-century western methods to depict aspects of the Aboriginal political cause.

Trevor Nickolls describes the routines of a white life as they are experienced with a Black soul. Often his depictions are clearly divided into mechanised and spiritual sections, as if there are two clearly separate and even opposing ways of interpreting the world. This phenomenon is best described in words coined by Nickolls himself and used to title a 1984 work, *Machine Time and Dream Time*. One of the first to develop a hybrid white–Aboriginal iconography, Nickolls was using non-traditional methods as early as the 1970s.[8]

The sociologist Vivien Johnson has noted that significant to the development of urban Aboriginal art was the introduction of its artists to each other. She cites the exhibition 'Koori Art '84' at Artspace in Sydney as pivotal in demonstrating that a number of artists, working independently, were unwittingly adopting similar methods.[9] Important to Trevor Nickolls, stylistically, was his exposure in the late 1970s to the Central Desert Papunya painters.[10] Following this experience, he incorporated the dotted brushstroke into his scenes of Australian city life in the 1980s and 1990s. In *Deaths in Custody*, 1990 (Plate 33), Nickolls depicted one of the ongoing great tragedies for Aboriginal people whose essential nomadism means they are impossibly constrained by incarceration.

The desire to refer to contemporary society while retaining links with an ancestral past resulted in the ironically amusing and yet poignant *Fruit Bats*, 1991 (Plate 34), by Lin Onus, a work used to publicise the opening of the Yiribana gallery of Aboriginal and Torres Strait Islander art at the Art Gallery of New South Wales in November 1994. With its reference to mundane suburbia, the rotary clothes-hoist possesses a powerful symbolism in illustrating a white Australian method of marking territory. The natural habitat is taken over, a house is built, the family moves in and the rotary clothes-hoist is erected like a modern sculpture and given pride of place in

FIGURE 46

Fiona Foley, *Badtjala Woman: Native Blood Series*, 1994, black-and-white photograph, synthetic polymer paint, 72 x 61 cm

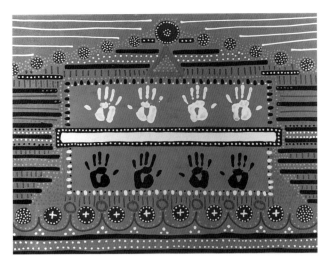

the back garden. Suggesting that Aboriginal culture has a greater respect and appreciation for the natural environment, Onus decorated the fruit bats with the traditional cross-hatching or rarrk strokes that typify painting from Western Arnhem Land.[11] Onus insinuates that the trees from which the fruit bats would normally hang are replaced by urban equipment which supports the needs of humans first. At the floor of the sculpture, illusionistic animal droppings represent the fruit bat's payback — a natural odour capable of overpowering that of the chemical whiter-than-white washed clothes.

While it is generally a key minority group aim to increase awareness of its members' situation in order to gain equal rights and lose the 'Other' tag, there is a feeling among some Aborigines that the differences between the many clans that comprise what are generally known as one Aboriginal culture are not yet fully understood. The concern is that acknowledgment be paid to the distinctions between each particular Aboriginal group:[12] the discrete symbolism derived from the specific topography, flora and fauna of a region, the rituals practised, and the language spoken only by them.

In her paintings and installations, Fiona Foley has emphasised the cultural and visual traits of her indigenous group, the Badtjala people of Hervey Bay and Fraser Island, and has spoken of her commitment to winning recognition for them. In her photographic self-portrait series she has a foot in both camps. The main thrust of the work is the revisitation of unnamed ancestors and the location of their portraits in a current context. This displacement highlights the fundamentally intrusive nature of anthropological activities, and of photography itself.

In *Badtjala Woman: Native Blood Series*, 1994 (Figure 46) Foley presents herself as the Aboriginal native in a grass skirt, whose every action and, most importantly, every physical characteristic, is documented. But she adopts a clichéd pose of twentieth-century white male photography that is characteristically used with a young woman as the subject, and is designed to portray her as sexually coquettish by concealing her nudity behind the back of a chair. In adopting the footwear of today and painting it in the red, black and yellow of the Aboriginal Land Rights Flag, Foley indicates she has literally stepped out of her past. She acknowledges with pride that her background remains physiologically visible to her audience and that it is felt by her both spiritually and psychologically.

Anthropological methodologies, which are so much a focus of Aboriginal indignation, have been refined and redirected in the latter part of the twentieth century in order to render approaches less judgmental and therefore more sympathetic to other cultures. The art historian is similarly subject to reproach for failing to appreciate that there are profound obstacles to a thorough understanding when there are cultural disparities. This is especially pertinent in the Aboriginal case since there are very few indigenous Australian art historians. The French theorist Gilles Deleuze and, more particularly, Michel Foucault have been influential in creating this new awareness in defining what they describe as the 'indignity of speaking for others' — a situation, it is argued, in which the speaker will inevitably assume the stance of the system that holds the reins of power.[13]

But another exigency arises, in that to omit the Aboriginal vision is to warp history and re-institute the neglect that has dominated Australian white–black relations. In order to refer effectively to elements of Aboriginal identity, images have often been separated from the mainstream discourse and analysed as an art apart.

Although it would seem time to include these images in the broader history of the art landscape, the concentration on politics in urban Aboriginal art continues to direct attention towards these distinctions, emphasising its difference from the art of other Australians.

Problematic also is the matter of whether or not the portrayal of Aboriginal circumstances should be the sole domain of indigenous people. Is it always inappropriate for non-Aboriginal artists to broach the issue, even when their position is sympathetic? *Hands off*, 1982 (Figure 47), by Stephen McCarthy, who first came to prominence as a member of the Melbourne Roar group of artists, is clearly influenced by the traditional dot painting, commonly employed by Aboriginal artists of the Central Desert region. Although capable of signifying many and profound things to the people whose ancestors devised their use as a descriptive technique, for McCarthy these dots are merely a patterning device that alludes to Aborigines and their art.[14] The handprints of the work suggest the marks of ancient rock artists, but they also comment on land ownership. The grasping white hands vie with those of the black to dramatically alter the pattern of the painting and the course of history.

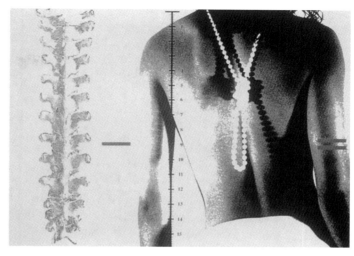

FIGURE 48

Rea, *If One Green Bottle Should Accidentally Fall ...*, 1995 (detail), triptych, edition of fifty, digital cibachrome, 59.5 x 76.5 cm

The process of redefinition that has accompanied Aboriginal activism and the attempts to rewrite Australian history from the Aboriginal point of view have resulted in a number of changes in common parlance, so that whites are characterised as invaders rather than settlers, for example. Artist Destiny Deacon has suggested the re-spelling of the word 'black' as 'blak' to enable a fresh consideration, and a re-emphasis of the original colonial language.[15] Of Koori descent, Rea took a one-word name as an adult artist after studying her ancestry. Born near Coonabarabran in New South Wales, she was originally called Regina Morris, having been denied an Aboriginal name because she was born on an Anglican mission where the practice of traditional ceremonies was banned and the contravention of this regulation punished.[16] The convention of naming Aboriginal people after the white manager of the mission, a practice through which she was given the name Morris, bore no relation, she felt, to her

FIGURE 49

Rea, *Lemons IV*, 1994, from the 'Lemons I–IV' series, edition of four, digital C-type photograph, 45 x 90 cm

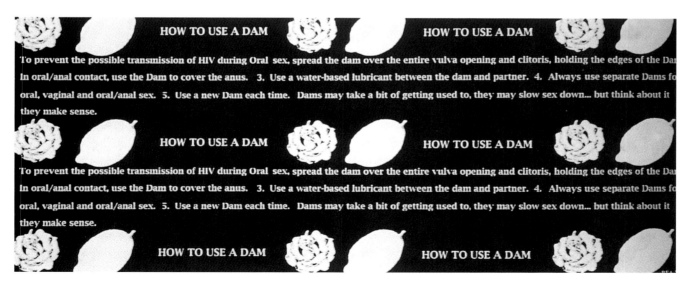

HOW

can we possibly be worse role models for our children than a mainstream society which condones the rape of everything from babies to the planet.

The **Lovely Mothers** series is part of **Word of Mouth III** lesbian visibility project.
Photos by Marion Moore. Concept co-ordination Elsa Holt & Catherine Fargher.
Thanks to lovely mothers and offspring for their input.

FIGURE 50

Marion Moore, _How,_ 1994, from the 'Lovely Mothers' series, photograph, print, poster, billboard, 42 x 60 cm

cultural identity.[17] While at first a simple nickname, 'Rea' (pronounced 'ree') became a more significant choice as she saw its relevance to her work. The preposition 're' in the sense of referring to, and 're' as a prefix, occur often in the titles of her work, such as in the words 'reconstruct' or 'refer'.[18]

By using the most modern of technologies that expressly signify whiteness, as well as masculinity, Rea subverts the 'scientific' method once used to describe Aboriginal difference, as well as extant racist views that question Aboriginal competency. Through computer imaging, she stresses that these studies were concentrated on the body, the most obvious site of racial difference, and suggests that the legacy of this approach is still current. Taking another perspective on the deaths in custody issue considered by Trevor Nickolls, Rea has suggested that death while employed as a servant is as unjust and humiliating, and was once as commonplace an experience among Aboriginal people as dying in a gaol is today.[19]

The gradual recognition of the human right to an 'identity' that has proven empowering for Aboriginal people also has negative ramifications. While the concept of a racial subgroup, allowing governments to engage in such activities as the forced removal of mixed-race children from their Aboriginal families is no longer acceptable, there is still a perception that a uniformity exists among Aboriginal people, overshadowing the many aspects from which individuality is comprised. The result is to lose sight of the fact that Aboriginal people play a multitude of roles in society, as public servants, academics, factory workers, lawyers, fathers, sportspeople, and so on.

Rea counters this emphasis on a uniform identity by her stance as a lesbian Aboriginal artist. In _Lemons IV,_ 1994 (Figure 49), she puts forward frank instruction on safe sex in a computer-generated image that plays on the contrary sweet and sour connotations of rose and lemon, and the possible pleasant or dire consequences of sampling the sexual sensation. Her no-nonsense instruction is provided to make the point that the same words can be used in a discriminatory or non-discriminatory way, but Rea's primary concern in this work is to 'give the lesbian and lesbian presence, a gallery presence' also.[20]

Although the lesbian 'herstory' of misinterpretation and discrimination has been documented, it has arguably not been studied as thoroughly as has the persecution of gay men, who are now generally known to have a continuing history of exposure to torture and indiscriminate acts of violence, as well as social and legal injustice. The lesbian or, as she is often defined, 'the woman-identified woman', has been thought of as unnatural, confused, at least psychologically defective and at worst a fully fledged witch, with Freudian analysis assisting in the discriminatory cause.[21] According to art historian Elizabeth Ashburn, the attitude towards lesbians in Nazi Germany involved the public display of her 'disgrace' in the form of a black triangle that was to be worn wherever and whenever she went.[22] Academic Annamarie Jagose has traced the history of lesbianism and has shown that sexual affection between women was not pathologised until the twentieth century, changing with reactions to first-wave feminism.[23]

An ironic statement regarding attitudes towards lesbians is provided by the Sydney artist Marion Moore, whose poster entitled _How,_ 1994 (Figure 50), shows a mother and daughter in a casually affectionate pose. Alongside is the inscription: 'How can we possibly be worse role models for our children than a mainstream society which condones the rape of everything from babies to the planet.' The poster was from the 'Lovely Mothers' series of photographs that were made into billboards and displayed on many Sydney buildings.

Although Australia is by no means the least tolerant of nations (as is evident from attendance at the annual Sydney Gay and Lesbian Mardi Gras), attitudes towards female homosexuality have been so misunderstood that it has failed to rate the dubious qualification of crime in Tasmania. This legislation, ruling that homosexual acts between men are a criminal offence, has only recently been repealed, although it is recognised that no-one in Tasmania has been prosecuted for an act of male homosexuality for nearly half a century. Similarly, the apparent lack of awareness of female-to-female sexual engagement that has resulted in its omission from the statute books is no longer as widespread.

In her important study of lesbian art in Australia, Elizabeth Ashburn argued that lesbian artists have an invisible history.[24] Without legitimate artistic personae, without supportive constructs, and with no accurately representative voice, lesbians exist outside the art discourse and are last in line among marginal groups. Ashburn has explained that certain women were reluctant to be included in her book in the event they would be branded 'lesbian marginal artist' when they had greater opportunity, and some had already realised success as a female or feminist artist.[25]

The search for the cause of lesbianism has been largely motivated by the desire to correct it or to find a cure for what has been seen as a problem. Historically, theories have argued for it being inherited or resulting variously from a defective central nervous system, faulty genes, female seduction, rejection in heterosexual love and masturbation.[26] But the actual, causal factor appears to refuse rigorous philosophical and scientific enquiry. As is the case with gay men, scientific studies have shown that hormone levels in lesbians lie within the same range as those of the heterosexual population.[27]

The feminist essentialism debate is given a different perspective when placed in the lesbian context. If a woman says she feels she was born lesbian she espouses the argument that sexual differences are biologically determined. In so doing, she sides with biological dominance in the old nature–nurture argument, now re-addressed in the gender context as the essentialist–constructionist debate, in which essentialists hold that sexual orientation is inherent, and social constructionists believe it to be culture-dependent. The former is problematic in that it negates the widely held belief that social circumstances are influential in the shaping of attitudes and behaviour. But it is now demonstrably true that it is social factors rather than lack of capability that have precluded women in general from adopting high-level leadership occupations, for example, and similarly clear that it is the lack of training that fails to encourage nurturing and child-caring capacities in men.

A further clarifying issue in this debate is the distinction between sex and gender. If the word 'sex' is used to define the physiological characteristics of men and women, 'gender' explains cultural differences and expressions. In this paradigm, 'social roles do not follow inevitably from biological facts' but involve elements from both domains.[28] Jagose explains how similar elements in the argument have been used to support opposing positions. She cites essentialist claims (that homosexuals are born with an innate preference for same-sex partners) being used to secure civil-rights-based recognition for homosexuals, while the constructionist position (that homosexuality is acquired) has been taken to argue that such an inclination may be corrected.[29]

Resolution of the essentialist–constructionist argument lies in a rejection of the precise, binary nature of the essentialist–constructionist and heterosexual–homosexual models. Ashburn's emphasis that there is no group lesbian identity, but that the term 'lesbian' should be taken to indicate numerous sexualities,[30] accords with the belief

David McDiarmid, *It's My Party and I'll Die If I Want To Sugar*, 1995, computer-generated Canon laser print and mixed-media, 26 x 21 cm. Photograph courtesy Tolarno Galleries, Melbourne

that context and time are important influences in the application of such categories.

The homophobic power of those who have perpetrated anti-homosexual views and actions has been diminished by the new visibility of homosexual people and the growing confidence in publicly identifying themselves as gay. The open and often confrontational approach among politicised homosexual people since the 1980s has seen them taking up the slights and taunts levelled against them and incorporating them into a new, 'proud' persona. Accordingly, now that words such as 'queer' and 'dyke' are used within the gay community, they are stripped of their power for those who would apply them to disparage. What was couched as 'coming out of the closet' in the 1970s might now be rephrased as 'doing the street' or 'going gay shopping'. Because the issue of homosexuality is less stigmatised and markets have discovered the value of the 'gay dollar',[31] public expressions of affection by gay people have become a new, specific focus of political action.[32]

As in the Aboriginal context, changing political directions have been accompanied by a developing language. The term 'queer', originally coined to differentiate ideologically fashionable homosexual people from homosexuals of the old school, and to categorise those who are more radical in style than that sanctioned by the norm, has come to be used to refer to any non-heterosexual person.[33] Its quirky adaptability to the requirements of media and advertising headlines has also lent the term a vague chic that belies its inventors' intentions, and perhaps even their dreams. The 'Queerography' exhibition which originated at Sydney's Roslyn Oxley9 Gallery in 1994 — a landmark year for homosexuality in Australian art — and went on to tour regional galleries, demonstrates this point, as well as encompassing more substantial ramifications. The exhibition was widely reviewed and significant in suggesting that the hitherto fringe interest of gay art was not a purely political matter but a legitimate art subject, and as worthy of art commerce as any other. It demonstrated the distinctive features of queer as opposed to gay art, in which the former is the more radically sexually orientated and less likely to involve standard art approaches and materials. Theoretically, the point is made that art with an explicit sexual component offends the conventional sense of what constitutes 'fine' art, and is subject to being dismissed on the grounds that it is mere propaganda. Exemplifying this point in the

'Queerography' exhibition was Andy Davey's 'X (actual photo)', 1994, a series of twenty-eight photographs of erect penises. Lachlan Warner's *The Sight of Being*, 1994 (Figure 51), perhaps more erotic in its moderation, involved covers of *GQ: Gentleman's Quarterly for the Modern Man* magazine, in which the pin-ups are whited out, and fragmented descriptions of desire are written over them in black felt-tipped pen.

Curated by Ted Gott in 1994, 'Don't Leave Me This Way: Art in the Age of AIDS' at the National Gallery of Australia, was, as its title suggests, an important first exhibition of art on the subject of AIDS that also presented a survey of homosexual art in Australia and located it in an international context. Included in the exhibition was a series of provocative, tragic and amusing slogans by David McDiarmid that characterised gay life in the 1990s. His related 1995 series was equally bitter, while at the same time both were intensely heartfelt and jocular. *It's My Party And I'll Die If I Want To Sugar*, 1995 (Plate 35), epitomises the defiance expressed by gay men at such events as the Sydney Gay and Lesbian Mardi Gras, with its spectacle of colour and sparkle. Gott has noted that these images are important in representing the way death and grief 'have been brought blazingly to the foreground' in western culture since the impact of the AIDS epidemic.[34] Other titles include: *Lifetimes Are Not What They Used To Be; The Family Tree Stops Here Darling*; and *Honey, Have You Got It?*. The 1995 slogans are superimposed over suffused stripes of orange, grading to purple. The earlier series is 'written' over the colours of the rainbow, after the Gay Rainbow Flag, which, as Ted Gott has mentioned, was designed by American, Gilbert Baker, for the 1978 Gay Freedom Day Parade in San Francisco.[35] These works are particularly poignant in the context of McDiarmid's death from an AIDS-related illness shortly after making the second series.

Among the earliest explicit considerations of sexuality in Australian art were those painted by Juan Davila in 1981. Davila has explained that his interest was not to illustrate his own sexual attitudes, disgorging so-called unconscious images from his own psyche, but to find a way to bring sexual iconography, or imagery, into art history. Sexual images, including references to male homosexuality, are slotted in at random, among his many quotations from other artists and well-known identities. These are interrupted by 'irrational irrelevancies', such as a sign, for example, that points to Marilyn Monroe but indicates the age of Sigmund Freud, a technique which functions to block any tendency to narrative flow.[36] Crucial to Davila's approach is his rejection of the Freudian visual unconscious and the notion that it can be tapped to produce material for either analysis or artmaking.[37] Davila has argued that his use of pornographic images in the context of high art, such as a Marilyn Monroe figure masturbating, functions to change their meaning, as well as to collapse high and low art into a new medium.[38]

More directly political in attempting to acquaint its viewers with gayness, and in particular with the notion that there is no typical lesbian person, is *A Gay Morning Tea!*, 1994 (Plate 36), by Tina Fiveash. Her photographic reconstruction includes 1950s domestic trappings that make the sight of two stereotypically beautiful housewives abandoned to their sexual passion a hilariously ridiculous shattering of the middle class, purer-than-white mores of that time.

Again involving a self-deprecating humour, Philippa Playford satirises the gay and lesbian fascination with country dance and music. Her plaque, *Cowdyke*, 1995 (Figure 52), is crowned with cow horns and decorated with American sheriff stars. Naturally, it has tassels hanging from its base.

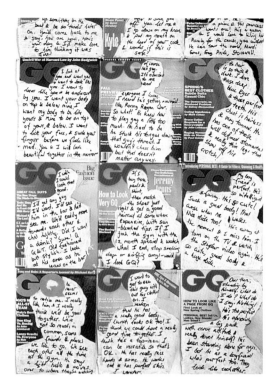

FIGURE 51
Lachlan Warner, *The Sight of Being*, 1994, printed pages with ink and acrylic paint, fifteen panels, 137 x 62 cm overall

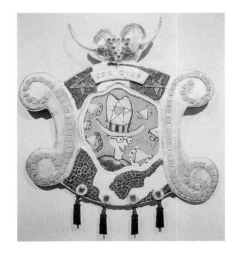

FIGURE 52
Philippa Playford, *Cowdyke*, 1995, mixed media, 110 x 70 cm

PLATE 36
Tina Fiveash, *A Gay Morning Tea!*,
1994, from the 'Stories for Girls' series,
C-type photograph, 48 x 42.5 cm

In *Spectre #1*, 1996–97 (Figure 53), eX de Medici, who styles herself via an art-historical nom de plume, uses the medium of the tattoo to make the lesbian woman not only more visible but permanently so. The commitment to the tattoo may be fleeting but it cannot be removed; it is registered at the cellular level but is always visible. In more tolerant times, she advocates the same procedure as adopted in Hitler's Germany, but to exalted rather than demeaning ends, by advocating the wearing of the badge indicating sexual category at a skin-deep level. According to the artist: 'Tattooing is inscribing blood — it's a pact … The fact that a queer symbol is inscribed and engraved in blood is also a sign of a much deeper kind of commitment to those kinds of ideals. We could probably have a Rainbow sticker on our car, but that is removable; if things get hot, then you can take that one off.'[39]

A fundamental appeal that may also accrue to the tattoo wearer is its power as a sign of the transgressive — the tattoo functioning to locate its wearer outside the average and predictable and within a culture of machismo values and violence.

FIGURE 53
eX de Medici, *Spectre #1*, 1996–97, coloured pencil, 228 x 240 cm

eX de Medici arrived at the tattoo as her means of expression through the predicaments she experienced as an underpaid artist.[40] Through tattooing she found a way to combine the practice of her craft and receive an income. She has explained, however, that on fraternising with the tattoo subculture she felt an uneasiness with many of its values. She found herself in the situation of producing what she has described as 'beautiful signs for ugly people'.[41] In the provision of her ornamentation, eX de Medici works to a clientele she does not fully respect and one which uses her art to make statements with which she often does not agree. To render some of the designs requested more acceptable to the artist, they are re-codified according to a symbology from different or earlier societies. In the case of the swastika, for example — a design in great demand — she prefers to dwell on the positive aspects that she believes are emphasised in its earlier interpretation in Nordic culture, rather than its 'thwart(ing) by Nazism'.[42] To redirect the meaning of the swastika, it is placed on a square rather than a diamond, thus, she argues, sending its referent back to antiquity.[43] Unwittingly, the artist here instinctively relates to the Hindu interpretation of the swastika's design origins, in which it is cast as a positive, supportive symbol. (The source for the swastika was the farmer's gate that consisted of two pieces of wood locked together.)[44] eX de Medici places the swastika on a bed of worms to suggest a speedy passage towards decay, with the renewal phase of the cycle shortly to follow. At the same time, as she has explained, 'I was wanting a feeling of pestilence to prevail'.[45]

As is clear from the vulnerability of young women, who are the most photographed, and the models to which many women aspire, prominence need not equate with power. With the politicisation of lesbianism, Elizabeth Ashburn suggests a new concern arises, which is that through its fashionability it may become subsumed into the mainstream and find its political edge weakened. Ashburn points out that homophobia can play a positive role in providing a shared sense of identity, so that the lesbian becomes 'a subject, rather than the object of oppression'.[46] But as is the case with Aboriginal people, a perhaps better scenario still would be one in which gay, lesbian, queer — and whatever new words are coined to identify sexually different people — are celebrated for their difference, and at the same time granted equality.

7

Portraits in Prayer: Eastern Philosophies in Australian Art

Asian art has been influential to Australian artists in two main ways: some have been attracted to traditional Asian motifs, and others to its ancient philosophies, with the latter group incorporating aspects of Buddhism, Hinduism, Taoism, Islam or Shinto into their work. ➤

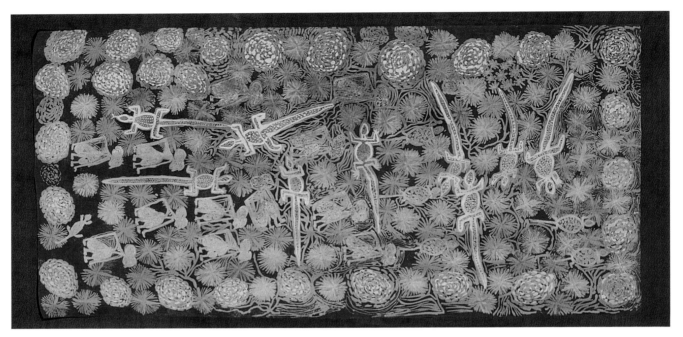

A relationship between art and meditation was unexpectedly discovered during a cross-cultural experiment in 1994 when Aboriginal and Indonesian artists worked together to decorate cloth using traditional batik methods. Besides producing interesting visual results, connections were made between the two cultures that have ramifications for the practice of art itself.

At Utopia in north-eastern Central Australia, the Anmatyerr and Alyawarr people first made batik in the late 1970s, as the 'hippy' interest in handicrafts had extended to outback Aboriginal communities.[1] Batik processes were then adopted as a decorative method which was combined with the growing folk-art movement to create a new hybrid decoration. Aboriginal designs were derived from ritual, ochre body painting that depicted the personal totem, as there was no textile production in their tradition.[2] These were applied in wax with a hand-held tool called a canting, and with brushes. When the cloth was dyed, the waxed areas resisted colour and, once removed, left a contrasting pattern.

In 1994, when the women of Utopia travelled to the Brahma Tirta Sari Batik Studio in Yogyakarta, Central Java, they worked alongside Javanese artists and experimented with ancient Indonesian Kejawen symbols, incorporating them into their own motifs. In an example by Lena Apwerl (Plate 37), a design based on wattle blossom and goannas, traditionally used in Aboriginal decoration, is placed alongside an Indonesian Wayang shadow-puppet character. In an example by James Bennett (Plate 38), who curated an exhibition for the Museum and Art Gallery of the Northern Territory from designs produced at these workshops, Tantric teachings — otherwise known as Hindu and Buddhist mystical scriptures — are used for their ability to represent a generalised idea and personal symbolism. Bennett's application of bone images in Tantric teachings, suggesting the dissolution of the ego that is an important aim of Buddhists, here also refers to the death of a friend from HIV/AIDS.[3]

In his analysis of the work produced, Bennett stressed the need for caution in any desire to discover similarities of approach or common areas of interest between Australian and Asian cultures, owing to the fundamental difference in our notions of the function of art.[4] He went on to warn that even sensitive and sophisticated

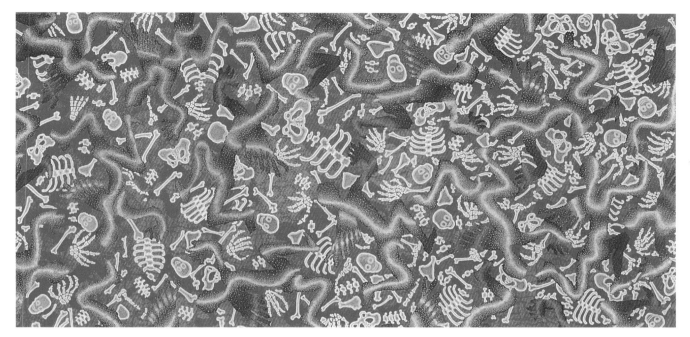

interpretations of Asian culture may still be flawed. Esoteric images, Bennett argued, such as those of Aborigines which are categorised as 'secret', and equally Indonesian imagery deriving from a culture and language that is foreign to Australians, may never be fully accessible to outsiders. Unlike the western tradition, in which art acts as a medium for individual free expression, in Indonesia, Bennett noted, the concern is to produce work that suggests 'sincerity, balance and order … providing the nurturing, creation and development of art and culture in society'.[5]

Nevertheless, while Asian iconography is often untranslatable, methods of practice may provide clues to comprehension. While observing the Anmatyerr women working at their batik decoration, Bennett saw that the soft, rhythmical chanting of their *awely* songs appeared to influence the way they applied the hot wax, so affecting the final design. It appeared that they transferred their musical mood through their hands to the cloth with which they were working. Bennett compared their singing with the more direct prayer orientation of mantra-chanting in Buddhist–Hindu traditions and suggested that there could also be a spiritual dimension to artmaking by Aboriginal people.[6] Indeed, artistic creation is often considered to be a form of meditation in Hindu and Buddhist cultures. Finding another ancient connection between the two cultures, Bennett mentioned that in one language of Central Australia the word *walbiri*, meaning song, also refers to a visible mark.[7]

The generalised eastern philosophies espoused throughout the western world in the 1960s and 1970s were given focus in Australian art by Brett Whiteley. The Buddhist concept of reincarnation was incorporated into a portrait of Patrick White called *Patrick White as a Headland*, c. 1981 (Figure 54), in which White's facial features can be read either as a portrait with the head turned onto its side, or as details of the landscape. According to Whiteley's inscription, the work was painted 'after a discussion about reincarnation'.

A less literal interpretation of the process of reincarnation occurs in Whiteley's transposition of the abstract line as it takes a cyclical journey towards 'endlessnes-sism'.[8] In a self-portrait titled *Remembering Lao Tse (Shaving off a Second)*, 1967, Whiteley referred to the originator of Taoism — the Chinese religion and philosophy

PLATE 38
James Bennett, *Bones and Angels*, 1994, batik cap/tulis on silk, 115.3 x 235.2 cm. Collection: Museum and Art Gallery of the Northern Territory, Darwin

FIGURE 54
Brett Whiteley, *Patrick White as a Headland*, c. 1981, oil on canvas, 39.4 x 49.7 cm. Private collection, Sydney

Matthys Gerber, *Let it Be Me,* **1987,**
oil and acrylic on canvas, 73 x 157 cm.
Courtesy Sarah Cottier Gallery, Sydney

of the sixth century — who advocated simplicity. Although there is nothing particularly simple in this self-portrait, there was often a spareness in Whiteley's calligraphy, such as that of his well-known female nudes who are often described with the fewest of lines. Given Whiteley's high profile, it is likely that this interest in eastern philosophies would have had an influential effect, encouraging a curiosity among other artists as well as his audience.

The vast Asian following of Islam is 'represented' in Australia by Matthys Gerber, who refers to the Islamic tradition of script as art in a work titled *Let it Be Me*, 1987 (Plate 39). In Islam, words from the Koran acquire a mysticism simply because they are a depiction of a 'truth'. Gerber's European maxim is highly decorated, and given as script rather than as a description of an idea, event or object. The ornamented script is presented as sufficient to signify its derivation from Islamic culture.

The Melbourne artist Domenico de Clario's performance titled *Seven-ness Sub-Lunar* (Figure 55) is based on yogic principles. Following the Hindu tradition, in which ceremonies and celebrations often occur on dates of the full moon, the performance was held at the date and time of the full moon on each of seven months from April to October 1995, in the gardens of the Heide Museum of Modern Art.

The significance in the work of the number seven derives from de Clario's perception of its frequency in universal systems, such as the seven-day week, the musical octave (in which the first and last notes are repeated) and the seven yogic chakras or energy sites which form the performance focus.[9] The association between colour and music recalls the same connection made by Roy de Maistre, although there is no direct relationship to de Clario's performance.

De Clario's main prop, an old Holden car, was brought into the mood of the moonlit night by the attachment of domestic lamps and other light fittings to each wheel (these were connected to the electricity supply) so that they emanated the colour associated with the energy or chakra site in the body. The wheel, the literal translation of the word 'chakra', here becomes the subject of puns. The word *chakravartin*, meaning 'the turning of the wheel', refers to the wheel of the gods' chariot.[10] Thus, the ephemeral but repetitive quality of life when it is shackled to karmic rejoinders is rendered visually as a cyclical pattern. In Hindu and Buddhist understanding, the pointless, repetitive life is transformed by yogic techniques, including meditation on the chakras, to become one lived rather as a spiral, in which modifications in behaviour move the soul forward.[11] Interestingly, the word yoga, meaning 'union', occurs in Hinduism, Buddhism, Jainism, Islamic Sufism and contemplative Christianity.[12]

De Clario's car also embodies the metaphor of his family, whose identity and character change alongside the acquisition and updating of the vehicle model. Skins are shed; major and minor periods in life pass by and begin again as new incarnations.[13]

Integral to the performance was de Clario's role as the unseeing innocent while he sat blindfolded at the piano making improvised but tuneful sounds. For each performance, a different key was used to announce the change of chakra and its associated colour. As the individual seeking spiritual enlightenment must — according to yogic theory — balance the body's hot or sun energy, and cold or lunar energy, so de Clario invited his audience to experience the subtle cooling of the moon in contrast to the blazing crassness of the midday sun. Perhaps there was the suggestion that Kundalini, the body's counterpart to cosmic consciousness, would be awakened. Should perfect balance be attained, she would travel through the chakras as each is meditated upon, to facilitate the harmonious benefits of perfect sight and pure consciousness.

For each performance, one of the colours associated with the passage of Kundalini was featured. Some major aspect of it reflected either red, orange, yellow, green, blue,

FIGURE 55
Domenico de Clario, *Seven-ness Sub-Lunar*, 1995, performance in the gardens of the Museum of Modern Art at Heide, Melbourne, fourth performance in a series of seven, 12 July 1995

PLATE 40
Claire Day, *Adya Sakti,* **1994,**
oil on canvas, 91.5 x 83.5 cm.
Photograph: John Brash

Geoffrey Goldie, *Guilt, Possession, Death*,
1994, synthetic polymer paint, collage on board,
80 x 61 cm. Private collection. Photograph:
John Brash

Geoffrey Goldie, *Dasa Mahavidya: Ten Great*
Paths to Wisdom, **1994,** synthetic polymer paint
on canvas, 112 x 213 cm. Photograph: John Brash

violet or indigo, as Kundalini was to travel, at least theoretically, from the base of the spine, through the areas of the genitals, the navel, the heart, the throat and the middle of the brow to the crown of the skull. Just as Kundalini's journey follows the body's mainstay — the spine — so the world, according to the theory, rests on a similar axis. This micro–macro model also applies to the universal elements of fire, earth, air, water and the ether, all of which are similarly said to be found in the body's physiology. Once again, a balancing of these is sought. De Clario's performance counterparts include a fountain which erupts alongside an orange tent that houses him and his piano for the genital chakra. A circle of electric fans is used to cool the globe as he sits surrounded by a green holly bush for the heart chakra. To suggest the powers of the base chakra, red lights were thrown upon a massive oak tree. Requiring water, air, the warmth of the sun to grow, the cooling influence of the moon to rest and rejuvenate, this red aura suggested all the influences that were to come in later performances.

The piano was played for the precise duration of the full-moon period, which occurred at any time from evening to dawn, and lasted a number of hours. In his dedication to his task, regardless of the time of night or weather conditions, de Clario reflected the yogic teaching that it is through the relentless and persistent practice of its principles that the divine is incorporated into life. But in keeping with postmodern approaches, rather than proselytising de Clario invited his audience to bring their experiences to the event and take away whatever they would.[14]

Claire Day has produced a series of works which attempt to define the ineffable state of meditation. A pale blue light merely exists. The meditator is deeply relaxed but still awake; present and yet uninvolved, present in body but not in mind. These moments are the beginning, the state of peace which gives rise to conception and gestation. Preparation is made to rejoin active life.

Claire Day's painting is titled *Adya Sakti*, 1994 (Plate 40), which is the name given to the Hindu goddess Kali when she is worshipped. 'Adya Sakti' translates as 'the beginning of all'. This is Kali just before her creative phase, when the powerful energy of Sakti is called upon. She is the feminine force whose genitalia signify a crucial aspect of her identity.

Geoffrey Goldie is a Melbourne artist who has incorporated considerable study of traditional Hindu and Buddhist representations into his work. After studying under George Bell, he travelled widely in Asia from the 1950s to the 1970s. His meeting and long friendship with the Indian classical dancer Chandrabhanu led to the production of his stage-set designs for the Melbourne Bharatam Dance Company.[15] Goldie successfully paints a melded interest in Jungian theory and Hindu philosophy, while retaining a concern for a textural surface that aligns him with such 1950s Melbourne landscapists as Boyd, Williams, Tucker, Perceval and Pugh who are his chronological peers in age.

In a series of ten paintings called 'Dasa Mahavidya: Ten Great Paths to Wisdom', 1994 (Plates 41 and 42), Goldie takes the viewer on a meditative journey through the 'spiritual' colours to enlightenment.[16] The act of painting itself is considered by him to be a meditative, transforming one, much as it is for the Anmatyerr artists from Utopia.

The notion of archetypes, as coined by Carl Jung, relates theoretically and representationally to Kali whose manifestations Goldie features with an awareness of her archetypal nature. Kali occurs throughout the ancient world, in the differing cultures of Calcutta as the anglicised Kalikata, and as the Irish prehistoric Kelles, the origin of the name Kelly, as well as in the Greek Kalli.[17]

Along with her main ten manifestations, the 'Dasa Mahavidya' or ten paths of wisdom, she is said to have roles as creator, preserver and destroyer and can occur in a partial way in every woman. The symbolic representation, or the yantra of Kali, includes references to her character. The pattern through which she is characterised

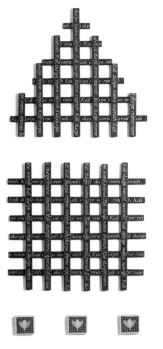

FIGURE 56A
Carole Wilson, *Kali House II*, 1994,
oil on wood with brass wire, 100 x 120 cm.
Private collection. Photograph: John Brash

FIGURE 56B
Carole Wilson, *Kali House II*, 1994 (detail),
oil on wood with brass wire. Private collection.
Photograph: John Brash

is codified and intended to be read as levels of consciousness. If contemplation upon aspects of this design can aid the quality and depth of meditation, painting the yantra may well, as Goldie suggests, be a meditative experience in itself. The yantra relates to Jung's interest in the mandala — the circular pattern of Hinduism and Buddhism referring to the universe or consciousness that is also sometimes used in psychoanalysis. Jungian psychologists also have an esoteric symbology assigned to the mandala which, Jung argued, following his notion of archetypes, is a basic form or shape found throughout nature. Jung also contended, in a western reinterpretation, that the mandala occurs in dreams and that it may be read as a symbol of human wholeness.[18]

In taking up the idea of Kali as the archetypal woman, Goldie goes on to relate her to Medea from the Greek play by Euripides.[19] Medea acts as an interesting symbolic companion to Kali as they cross cultures and become interchangeable. According to the mythology, Medea is filled with vengeance for the infidelity of her lover, Jason, whose desire to marry a Corinthian princess he justifies as ensuring the security of Medea and her children. But in an act which has been seen as a peculiarly female jealousy, Medea poisons the princess. And in another archetypal act which arouses the same fascination that inspired the Lindy–Azaria Chamberlain preoccupation, she goes on to murder their children. The mother is always good but here she creates the ultimate ethical and logical dilemma in acting against her own basic nature.

Traditionally, Kali possesses a purely female ability to calm demonic forces. She is said to have arisen from the brow of Durga to assist in the suppression of the most difficult evils, and Durga, according to the mythology, in answer to the prayers of the gods for assistance to combat the powers of evil, was herself welcomed as a goddess to join them.[20] Kali has been adopted by the women's movement as a symbol of their purpose in that she possesses all that is positively female and yet is still powerful.[21] She can be shown in a number of colours, including black, white and red. The triangular shape that is representative of the stylised female genitals is Sakti, who is the embodiment of female energy, and who emphasises the creative, sexual aspects of womanhood.[22]

This accent on the female gender exemplifies the fact that these goddesses occur in a matriarchal culture in which men aspire to the feminine, providing the context in which the female genitals are revered.[23] Cutting across this mythological interest is the caste system in which, according to her family status, a woman may be killed at birth or accept an automatic leadership role. Nevertheless, theoretically, it is considered that the creativity of the individual female reflects the creation of the larger cosmos, as well as cosmic consciousness.[24]

When, at the age of seventy, Goldie considered a female mythology in his work, he could not have ventured further from the sources of subjects considered by his contemporaries in Australian art.

Carole Wilson, who is best known as a member of the Jillposters group, brought a western feminist consciousness to her observations of traditional art observed on a journey through India in 1988. In mood and meaning, her wooden shrine titled *Kali House II*, 1994 (Figures 56A and 56B), relates to this tradition. But while the lotus bud that decorates the work refers to the important role of this flower in Buddhism as signifier of beauty, symmetry and purity, she was aware that the shape of the lotus flower in bud, and exposed

PLATE 43A
Anne Marie Power, *Shrine,* **1991**, Japanese
Shinto shrine, prints, plastic buttons, hair pins,
75 x 45 x 38 cm

PLATE 43B
Anne Marie Power, *Shrine,* **1991** (detail),
Japanese Shinto shrine, prints, plastic
buttons, hair pins

in full bloom, is representative of female genitalia. To her fleshy description, she added a cross-cultural recuperation of pink from its pre-feminist position as an unacceptable, female colour considered inappropriate for high art.[25] Wilson has said she also had the pink buildings of India in mind when making her adaptation.[26] The lotus is shown against the words 'Kali', 'namo' and 'durge' (both durge and durga spellings occur in the literature), which are repeated in the form of a mantra. 'Namo' is used here to mean salutation.[27]

Wilson's *Kali House I* and *Kali House II* are collectively titled 'Prayers and Mantras' and serve as souvenir shrines recalling those that often appear in India, as if accompanying the traveller along the way. As it does for a surprising number of Australian artists, the shrine is central to the work of Anne Marie Power, whose altarscape installation titled *Shrine*, 1991 (Plates 43A and 43B), crosses cultural boundaries in that it involves objects usually present in a Japanese context, such as fans and saki cups, and others that appear representative of the West. A coloured crayon and a plastic car-shaped button, for example, therefore appear oddly placed. Having worked as an exchange artist in Yokohama in 1991, Power saw Shinto family shrines that reminded her of those from the Roman Catholic tradition of her Australian childhood that were used, along with the rosary beads, in the name of 'Our Lady'. Objects for this Australian–Japanese shrine are chosen to represent a cross-cultural, and particularly female, statement. Everyday items that fill a woman's life in the home are worshipped here: the Japanese print decorates a coaster; hatpins mimic Japanese combs.[28]

Ironically, despite the conscientious methodology involved in interpretations of eastern practices and traditions, they are not particularly representative of everyday life in Asia today. This may mean that our understanding of Asian culture remains limited and misconceived, much as it has always been. In a book introducing the science of yoga, B. K. S. Iyengar writes:

> How is it that in India, where we have six hundred million people, very few are attracted by meditation? And how is it that by contrast so many Westerners are? My colleagues in yoga work with you in a certain way because you cannot control your nerves. You are always under stress. To work is a stress. To sleep is a stress. To go to the toilet is a stress for people in the West! You are almost always under stress, so you are given what may be called passive meditation, and when you are made to remain silent for a while, you think you have reached yoga, or that your kundalini has awakened! Easterners are more relaxed, so to tell them to do this kind of meditation has no meaning. On the contrary, they have to be taught to be more active, and that becomes an active meditation for the East.[29]

Perhaps a more apposite portrayal of the function religious philosophy performs in an Asian country today is provided by the Thai artist Montien Boonma, whose sculptural installation titled *Lotus Sound* (Figure 57), was purchased by the Queensland Art Gallery following its exhibition at the first Asia-Pacific Triennial in 1993. As an integral part of the Buddhist ceremonial tradition, the ceramic bell is here stilled and silent as a wall that conceals and protects the mysteries of the lotus flower. But Boonma goes beyond simply holding the bell in reverence, as an Australian artist might in an attempt to pay appropriate respect to a foreign religious culture. He has observed poverty first-hand and considers the role of religion in a materialistic world, making a pun on the bell, which is lined up in readiness for sale through the tourist trade.

As more Asians are becoming Asian–Australians, they are providing an authentic sense of their identity and may do so as powerfully as Hanh Ngo describes how she lost and regained hers, fleeing South Vietnam via a seventeen-metre boat across the Gulf of Siam to Malaysia, and on by air to Australia.[30]

Ngo's weaving skill, learnt in an Australian art school, continues and develops the tradition still practised in her country of origin. Her work displays, in stark black and white contrasts, her bleak circumstances and the total disruption to her life and identity that was involved in relocation. Her self-portrait, *Identity*, 1995 (Figure 58), takes the place of a destroyed photograph and a lost life. Although Vietnamese are not black-skinned, they are non-white and as such remain outsiders. Ngo has said that in Australia she has always been aware that her hair is blacker than black.[31] The numbers on her lower tapestry plaque have a private significance but at the same time evoke memories of other situations of war and incarceration, in which individuals are stripped of their culture, name and possessions. Here, Ngo lists the significant dates that constitute her identity: her birthday, the refugee boat number, the date she left Vietnam, the day she arrived in Malaysia.[32]

This poignant account of personal distress is made by an Asian–Australian who attended an Australian art college. It deals with the individual. But, according to Hindu and Buddhist philosophies, individualism is misguided, since life occurs without barrier from the greater whole, from the earthly universe and its living beings, and from cosmic consciousness. The cosmic being, including humanity, exists organically in relationship with everything else. In expressing her individual response to adversity, Ngo was asserting her Australian-ness. While more Asian artists are adopting the contemporary art practices developed by the West, when Australian artists concern themselves with broader philosophical issues, there are times when they articulate as Asians once did.

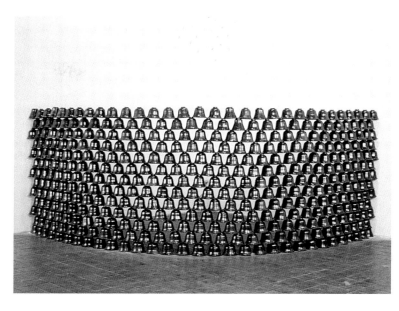

FIGURE 57
Montien Boonma, *Lotus Sound*, 1993, installation, terracotta bells, gilded wood, 300 x 350 x 300 cm. Collection: Queensland Art Gallery, Brisbane

FIGURE 58
Hanh Ngo, *Identity*, 1995, tapestry, weaving, cotton, wool, 30 x 30 cm. Private collection

conclusion

Everything Old is Cool Again:
The Contemporary Context

With the turn of the century, attempts to anticipate and define the art that will be produced in a new age take on a greater urgency. The question of identity, always something of a preoccupation in Australia, is required to orientate itself towards answers. The failure of the republic referendum reveals that the 'cultural cringe' continues to exert its influence. The 'virtual republic',[1] when it is made fact, may settle some matters of equivocation and insecurity. Could it be, however, that the moment ripe for the expression of a 'true' and unitary artistic voice is long lost in the rush to participate in matters of international fashion? Now, a single Australian identity is replaced by many, and old ideas of country are giving way to influences that extend beyond national boundaries. ➤

PLATE 44
Rosalie Gascoigne, *Firebird,* **1991,**
retro-reflective road-signs on plywood,
135 x 103 cm. Photograph courtesy
Roslyn Oxley9 Gallery, Sydney

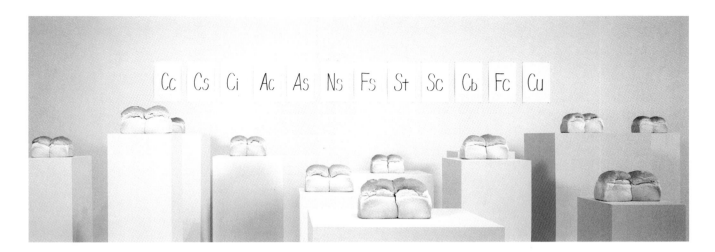

FIGURE 59
Robert MacPherson, *Sundog: 12 Frog Poems (Green Wizzer) for J.B.*, 1988–89,
twelve loaves of white bread on plinths,
twelve fibre-tipped pen drawings on paper,
courtesy Yuill Crowley, Sydney

Against many predictions, painting has survived the competitive onslaught from its old rival, photography, through to the electronic and digital media that have threatened to supplant it. Similarly, representation endures, albeit of a metaphorical kind, along with abstraction and conceptual art, or as aspects of either. The art object, not always gaining definition in the theoretical context, is being returned to its old place at the forefront of consideration.

Rosalie Gascoigne's *Firebird*, 1991 (Plate 44), constructed from the material used for reflective road signs,[2] has a spareness that recalls cool 1960s minimalism while conveying properties that it did not. It is sculptural installation, abstract design or representation, depending on the viewer's perspective. Once the road signs are attached to plywood, taking on the dimensions of a work of art, they possess a seductive radiance. The material, unexpectedly displaced from road to gallery, becomes charged with a sensual energy; there is the desire to reach out and touch its smooth, glowing surface. And once given a metaphorical title, it acquires and conveys an animate quality that replaces and reinterprets notions of landscape representation.

In the most discreet of ways, the landscape appears in the conceptual installation work *Sundog: 12 Frog Poems (Green Wizzer) for J.B.*, 1988–89 (Figure 59), by Robert MacPherson. Here, cloud formations appear as an idea via esoteric meteorological references: 'Cc' is the abbreviation for cirrocumulus; 'Cu' stands for cumulus.[3]

Referring to his broader opus, MacPherson has described himself as a 'satirical formalist',[4] thus directing the viewer back to ideas espoused by Clement Greenberg, and many who preceded him, for whom the purpose of art was to display the purely visual effects of the work's construction. But while MacPherson's cute pairs of loaves sit for all the world like high-art still-lifes, even more than Duchamp's urinal they are of the ordinary and everyday. We laugh at them, and the loaves laugh back at our search for the concept which is only an artistic conceit on the idea that art can be too pretentious and clever by half.

Rather than replacing traditional forms, new media have adapted or incorporated them. Tracey Moffatt's photographs, for example, have been influenced by film. Since she works with props, sets and extras,[5] like a director on a film set, Moffatt gives the impression that her photographs are, as curator Gael Newton has suggested, remnants of some lost movie.[6] The shack, for example — the central 'prop' in her photoseries *Something More*, 1989 (Plate 45) — has a two-dimensional appearance, and the demeanour of the woman in the petticoat is overly dramatic for a realistic documentary tableau. With a postmodern 'disorganisation', panels may be read from left to

PAGE 152
Edite Vidins, *Internet Supersonic Blah Blah*, 1995 (detail), phaser III wax prints,
56 x 135 cm

Tracey Moffatt, *Something More No. 1*, 1989,
one in the series of nine direct positive colour
photographs and gelatin silver photographs,
each 90 x 150 cm. Collection of the artist
and Roslyn Oxley9 Gallery, Sydney

right or from top to bottom, and there is sufficient ambiguity for the viewer to discover his or her own interpretation of events. Along with the fictional element of the series that takes it beyond documentary or photojournalism, the omission of information and the combined techniques of selected close-up shots and frozen-motion also serve to dramatise and distort.

As post-structuralism heralded the development of a personal questioning, so post-colonialism encouraged the expression of a national or group identity. It would take an extreme regime or a major economic catastrophe to change the democratic character of Australian art, which, like the nation itself, incorporates the voices of many minorities. Without such overwhelming eventualities, it is possible to propose that the need for the art of those who currently class themselves as minorities will decline, much as multicultural art and literature have become subsumed into the general national consciousness. From the audience point of view, Australians are less ready to accept the clichéd or simplistic now that their national character has become more complex. The fluidity of a complicated, organic art culture refuses containment and constantly demands the refinement of its analytical devices — which are by definition a step behind the art they describe.

Although art by those who in the 1980s and 1990s characterised themselves as gay, lesbian, queer or Black often involves an expression of this aspect of their identity, there are times when they have become categorised into minority groups by the media, curators or art historians, according to criteria they have not wished to emphasise or have felt are not accurately descriptive of them. Accordingly, Moffatt will not participate in exhibitions of Aboriginal art, in order to blur her Aboriginal identity and reduce the apparent significance of her experience as a foster child of white parents.[7]

In *Something More*, Moffatt casts herself as a vulnerable Eurasian who sets out on a fateful adventure which takes place in an Americanised Australian outback, 300 kilometres from Brisbane. The date of Moffatt's disturbing drama is also fugitive, given that women do not generally dress in silk underwear in an outback shack, and the Chinese character with a pigtail and straw hat has probably not been seen anywhere, except in film, for at least a hundred years. In this Cinderella gone-wrong tale the flawless, naive beauty of the heroine is complicated by her worn, torn dress that implies a worldliness not evident in her face.

Moffatt confuses usually fixed details, such as place, time and the precise beginning and end of her narrative, as well as the conventions that circumscribe the way her medium is presented. But as innovative as her approach appears to be it is another permutation of an artistic method with a long tradition. Newspaper cartoons were reproduced in oil by Roy Lichtenstein in the 1920s in the United States, and notable, photo-realist style portraits were painted by the Americans Alfred Leslie in the 1920s and Chuck Close in the 1940s. Examples from this book are David Wadelton's and Tony Clark's paintings of sculpture, eX de Medici's drawing of a tattoo, Yukinori Yanagi's sculpture of a flag, Judy Normand's embroidery of a cartoon, Hanh Ngo's textile self-portrait and Brett Whiteley's portrait that is also a landscape.

The mimicry and absorption of electronic effects now appear in alternative media. Pixilation, regularly used on television news bulletins to conceal a subject's identity, and the rectangular insert of the CD-ROM, are generalised to many other visual forms. Notions regarding spatial dimensions and their relationships within an image are also changed. Associated with the new video, digital and laser arts, are different ways of viewing images.

However, subjects for art are not so radically divergent. Even when travel extends beyond the planet through space, distorting time, the pictures that are relayed back to earth are of the newly discovered landscape. Even when travel occurs virtually,

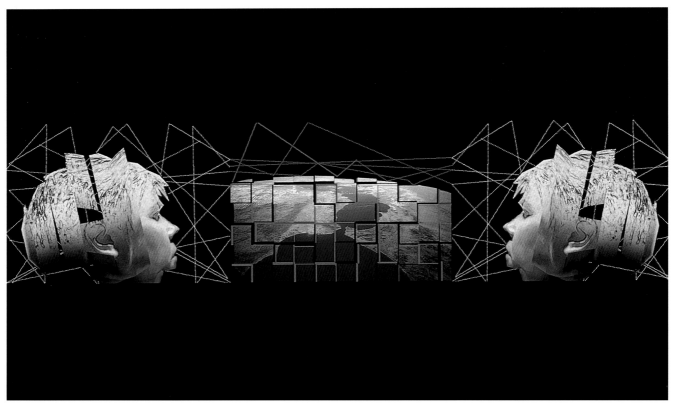

distorting concepts of space, the subjects of concern are not dramatically different. Those that haunt life at the millennium — concerns for personal and national security and the place of the individual in the technological age — were considered in an exhibition titled 'Technothelyogia' at the Monash University Gallery in Melbourne in 1997, and received treatment that reflects their time. The cliché of the violent male and the force that drives him is given fresh humour with the illustrative potential of a Type-C photograph and air-brushing techniques. Michele Barker and Anna Munster illustrate the thought process as it unfolds on news of the latest shooting, in *Easy Access to Power,* 1995 (Figure 60).

Although only a minority of men are uncontrollably aggressive, most violent crimes are committed by them rather than by women. However, updating and reinterpreting the one-dimensional essentialist jibe, this gun does not derive from a phallus but a dildo. As such, violence asserts a learned rather than a biological basis and may influence a persona assumed by either gender in a society which condones its use. Anxiety over individual survival and that of the planet must always have existed, however, even if the means to achieve ultimate destruction have not.

What are perceived to be the diminishing effects of experiencing the world via the Internet are captured in a photograph by Edite Vidins, *Internet Supersonic Blah Blah,* 1995 (Plate 46), in which the landscape is viewed via a grid on a computer screen. The obvious impoverishment of the natural world is matched by the computer operators who, plugged into their machinery, are metamorphosed into a uniform appearance.

But while technologies have the capacity to undermine the democratic character of art to some degree (given the expenditure involved in their operation), on the broader scale the fear that humanity will be overwhelmed by technological expansion would have, no doubt, been as real with the introduction of the telephone, the car and the aeroplane. Art, at least, has seen it all before.

Since most art relates in some fleeting or profound way to the human experience, however that is characterised, it is bound to cyclical reconsiderations, such as the latest in language fashion that has 'cool' and 'groovy' travel from fashionable to hackneyed and de rigueur once more. It is remarkable, however, how ably art may be adapted to exploit anything in its path for the creation of a new and different expression. It can, for example, as exemplified in the work reproduced in this book, reinterpret folktales, aspects of music, politics, nature, mathematics, geography, literature, philosophy, anthropology and science, enable the experience of new spatial dimensions, or refer to art's own history. Indeed, as the French philosopher Jean Baudrillard has argued, art is less an imitator of life than vice versa.[8] Tune in to the latest currents in art to see what will happen next!

FIGURE 60
Michele Barker and Anna Munster,
Easy Access to Power, **1995,**
type-C photographs, each 66.5 x 79 cm

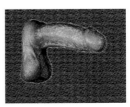

endnotes

Introduction

1. From an interview with Clement Greenberg by Paul Taylor, in *Art and Australia*, vol. 18, no. 2, 1980, p. 143.
2. Paul Foss, 'Theatrum mondum cognitorum', in *The Foreign Bodies Papers*, eds C. Burns and P. Botsman, Local Consumption, Sydney, 1981, p. 17.
3. A. A. Phillips, 'The cultural cringe', *Meanjin*, vol. 9, no. 4, summer 1950, pp. 209–302.
4. Alan McCulloch and Susan McCulloch, *The Encyclopedia of Australian Art*, Allen and Unwin, Sydney, 1994, p. 789: 'it represented a major assault on popular and academic taste'. In *Australia: National Journal*, no. 3, December – February 1937–40, pp. 52–70, and discussed in Richard Haese, *Rebels and Precursors: The Revolutionary Years of Australian Art*, Allen Lane, Ringwood, Victoria, 1981, pp. 61, 297, writing about the 1941 Contemporary Art Society (CAS) exhibition: 'this show was a massive assault on all assumptions about art in Australia … The exhibition … was a landmark in Australian art and in its own way as important as the *Herald* Exhibition.'
5. L. F. Crisp, *Australian National Government*, Longman, Melbourne, 1970, p. 363.
6. From an article by Basil Burdett entitled 'Modern art in Melbourne', *Art in Australia*, no. 15, November 1938, and referred to by Jan Minchin in her article 'Basil Burdett', *Art and Australia*, vol. 17, no. 4, 1980, pp. 369–73.
7. McCulloch and McCulloch, op. cit., p. 789.
8. Robert Hughes, *The Art of Australia*, Penguin, Ringwood, Victoria, 1970, pp. 236, 250.
9. ibid.
10. Charles Green, 'Robert Rooney', in *From the Homefront: Robert Rooney Works 1953–1988*, Monash University Gallery, Clayton, Victoria, 1990, p. 6.
11. John Whiteoak, 'Robert Rooney and the McKimm/Rooney/Clayton music collaboration: Melbourne 1960s', in Green, ibid., p. 19.
12. *Kind-Hearted Kitchen-Garden IV*, 1967.
13. 'The Field Now', Heide Park and Art Gallery, Bulleen, Victoria, 4 September – 21 October 1984.
14. Critic Alan McCulloch considered the exhibition a 'wholesale imitation of another country's abstract art', reprinted in Catharine Lumby's *The Art of Flux: An Australian Perspective, Antipodean Currents, Ten Contemporary Artists from Australia*, exhibition catalogue, Guggenheim Museum, New York, 21 June – 6 August 1995, p. 17. Regarding 'The Field' exhibition, Bernard Smith wrote: 'The local painters were at the disadvantage of being carriers rather than originators of the style. It is not surprising therefore, that … in the matter of quality, [it] did not meet the expectations either of the participating artists themselves or the public', in Bernard Smith and Terry Smith, *Australian Painting 1788–1990*, Oxford University Press, Melbourne, 1992, pp. 443–44. In Bernard Smith's *The Death of the Artist as Hero: Essays in History and Culture*, Oxford University Press, Melbourne, 1988, p. 213, the exhibition is referred to as 'unfortunate'. Terry Smith wrote of 'The Field' being a strong local movement 'following Noland, Olitski, Stella and others', in his essay 'The provincialism problem', reprinted in *Anything Goes: Art in Australia 1970–1980*, ed. Paul Taylor, Art + Text, Melbourne, 1984, p. 49.
15. Telephone interview with the artist by Traudi Allen, 24 June 1997.
16. Pamela Hansford, *Peter Tyndall: Dagger Definitions*, Greenhouse Publications, Richmond, Victoria, 1987, p. 28.
17. ibid., p. 22.
18. ibid., p. 48.
19. Smith and Smith, op. cit., p. 453.
20. Andrew Milner, *Contemporary Cultural Theory: An Introduction*, Allen and Unwin, Sydney, 1991, p. 78.
21. Roland Barthes, *Barthes: Selected Writings*, ed. Susan Sontag, Fontana, London, 1983.
22. Sandy Kirby, *Sight Lines: Women's Art and Feminist Perspectives in Australia*, Craftsman House, Sydney, 1992, p. 102.
23. See Milner, op. cit., p. 68.
24. The distinctions between Derrida, Foucault and Lacan are outlined in Milner, op. cit., pp. 72–7.
25. Edward S. Casey and J. Melvin Woody, 'Hegel, Heidegger, Lacan', in *Interpreting Lacan: Psychiatry and the Humanities*, eds Joseph H. Smith and William Kerrigan, Yale University Press, London, vol. 6, 1983, p. 80.
26. Wilfried Ver Eecke, 'Hegel as Lacan's source for necessity in psychoanalytic theory', in Smith and Kerrigan, op. cit., p. 114.
27. Telephone interview with David Wadelton by Traudi Allen, 16 June 1997.
28. Milner, op. cit., p. 73, identifies this as occurring first in Barthes's study of Balzac's short story 'Sarrasine', in *S/Z*, translated by R. Miller, Hill and Wang, New York, 1974.
29. Jacques Lacan, *The Four Fundamental Concepts of Psychoanalysis*, translated by Alain Sheridan, State University of New York Press, Albany, 1995.
30. Richard Haese, 'Waiting for postmodernism', *Art Monthly*, no. 78, April 1995, p. 7.
31. Telephone interview with Dennis Passalick by Traudi Allen, 6 July 1997.
32. ibid.
33. Margaret A. Rose in *The Post-modern and the Post-industrial: A Critical Analysis*, Cambridge University Press, Oakleigh, Victoria, 1991, pp. 6–7, shows that one of the earliest uses of the term was by Joseph Hudnut in 1945 in an article titled 'Post-modern house'. Rose does point out, however, that there were earlier usages, p. 43.

34. Conrad Hamann, with Michael Anderson and Winsome Callister, *Cities of Hope: Australian Architecture and Design by Edmond and Corrigan 1962–1992*, Oxford University Press, Melbourne, 1993, p. 119.

35. ibid.

36. *The Abolition of the 'White Australia' Policy*, Department of Immigration and Multicultural Affairs, Canberra, 1997.

37. Nevill Drury, *Images 2: Contemporary Australian Painting*, Craftsman House, Sydney, 1994, p. 255.

38. 'The life-motif', interview with Imants Tillers by Jennifer Slatyer, *Art Monthly*, no. 9, April 1988.

39. Imants Tillers mentioned his reading of Terry Smith's article in an interview with Louise Adler on 'Arts Today', ABC Radio, 12 August 1997.

40. Terry Smith, 'The provincialism problem', *Artforum*, September 1974; reprinted in *Anything Goes*, op. cit.

41. For example, in 1995 five Australian museum professionals ran a curators' training workshop in Kuala Lumpur. In the same year a series of exhibitions was sent to the region through Asialink, a body established to foster Australia's artistic relationship with Asia. There are now numerous other such examples.

42. Elizabeth Ashburn in *Lesbian Art: An Encounter With Power*, Craftsman House, Sydney, 1996, p. 21, writes that since sexuality is experienced differently there cannot be a homogeneous lesbian point of view; see also p. 35.

Chapter One

1. The urban landscape is the main concern in Chris McAuliffe's *Art and Suburbia*, Craftsman House, Sydney, 1997. Also, in 1997 the Queensland Art Gallery mounted an exhibition entitled 'The Urban Edge: Historical and Contemporary Works from the QAG Collection'.

2. Works by Graham Sutherland, Henry Moore and Paul Nash all exemplify this trait.

3. Leigh Astbury argues a link to Jean François Millet in 'What should Australian artists paint?', in *City Bushmen*, Oxford University Press, Melbourne, 1985, pp. 8–9.

4. Astbury details the role of literature in the maintenance of the bush myth, ibid., p. 81.

5. ibid., p. 4 and throughout.

6. *Montagne Sante-Victoire*, 1885–87, Courtauld Institute, London. Examples of work in which this compositional structure is involved include: *Young Gums*, 1888, by Arthur Streeton; *Picnic at Box Hill*, 1886, and *The Artists' Camp*, 1886, by Tom Roberts; *While the Billy Boils*, 1886, by Frederick McCubbin; and *Spring*, c. 1895, by Sydney Long. Roberts was in England in 1903 and Italy in 1911 (Bernard Smith and Terry Smith, *Australian Painting 1788–1990*, Oxford University Press, Melbourne, 1992, pp. 152, 154) and in Paris in 1885 (Helen Topliss, *The Artists' Camps: Plein air Painting in Australia*, Hedley Australia, Alphington, Victoria, 1992, p. 172).

7. See example in Topliss, op. cit., p. 68.

8. Smith and Smith, op. cit., p. 161.

9. Colin Thiele, *Heysen of Hahndorf*, Rigby, Adelaide, 1976, pp. 53–5.

10. Letter to Lionel Lindsay dated June 1923, ibid., p. 53.

11. McAuliffe, op. cit., p. 73.

12. Brian Adams, *Sidney Nolan: Such is Life*, Hutchinson, Hawthorn, Victoria, 1987, p. 59.

13. In *Rebels and Precursors: The Revolutionary Years of Australian Art*, Allen Lane, Ringwood, Victoria, 1981, p. 195, Richard Haese argues that Matisse was the guiding influence. Brian Adams claims it was Cézanne whom Nolan was influenced by, in Adams op. cit., p. 58.

14. Haese, 1981, op. cit., p. 280, used this as a paraphrase of an extract from an article by John Reed. Reed wrote: 'and for many of us who have experienced perhaps for the first time, a complete realisation of themselves as Australians, as part of a unique country which gives them qualities recognisably different from others and of special value', *Art and Australia*, vol. 5, no. 2, 1967, p. 443.

15. The apparent reference to Cézanne is confirmed by Deborah Edwards, 'Subsiding to the heart of things: Godfrey Miller, the works', in *Godfrey Miller 1893–1964*, exhibition catalogue, Art Gallery of New South Wales, Sydney, 1996, pp. 12, 20, 29, 32, 38.

16. See Ann Wookey, 'Godfrey Miller and mathematics', in *Godfrey Miller 1893–1964*, op. cit., pp. 110–15.

17. Letter from Miller to C. V. Allen, London, 28 September 1938, ibid., pp. 112, 114.

18. Edwards, op. cit., p. 16.

19. ibid., p. 61.

20. Miller writes: 'Steiner uses the word web-like. Lattice is the word of my own', ibid., p. 64.

21. ibid., pp. 13, 22 and throughout.

22. ibid.

23. The evident influence of Turner is confirmed by Renee Free in *Lloyd Rees: The Last Twenty Years*, Craftsman House, Sydney, 1990, p. 13. She mentions Constable as an equally significant source.

24. ibid., p. 167, Rees speaking to Renee Free.

25. ibid., p. 15.

26. ibid.

27. ibid.

28. Sandra McGrath, *Brett Whiteley*, Bay Books, Sydney, 1979, p. 10: 'Undoubtedly his feelings for harbours, waves and open seas, associated with these family days of long walks, fishing and exploring the rocks, made Whiteley return often to these themes … Every year his mother and father … and Brett spent their holidays at Boat Harbour, a tiny fishing village cowering at the feet of tremendous escarpments north of Sydney.'

29. Frannie Hopkirk, *Brett: A Portrait of Brett Whiteley by his Sister*, Alfred A. Knopf, Sydney, 1996, p. 38.

30. Patrick McCaughey, *Fred Williams*, Bay Books, Sydney, 1980; James Mollison, *A Singular Vision: The Art of Fred Williams*, Australian National Gallery, Canberra, 1989.

31. McCaughey, ibid., p. 11.

32. ibid., p. 107.

33. Referring to the Whitechapel exhibition, Bernard Smith writes: 'we were packaged as exotica and became, like Omai the Tahitian, high fashion for a season and then discarded', in Smith, *The Death of the Artist as Hero: Essays in History and Culture*, Oxford University Press, Melbourne, 1988, p. 212. This idea was refuted by Patrick McCaughey in an interview for the ABC television 'Express' program, 24 March 1997. Clifton Pugh's *Self Portrait*, 1960, showing the artist standing in a desert landscape, was chosen to illustrate the review written by the art critics, the *Times*, 3 June 1961 and the *Sunday Telegraph*, 11 June 1961.

34. Haese, op. cit., p. 294.

35. 'Fred Williams: A major exhibition', an interview by Annabel Davie with Lyn Williams and James Mollison, *Art Monthly*, no. 5, October 1987, p. 6.

36. ibid., p. 7.

37. Ian Burn, 'What can Nolan mean today?', *Art Monthly*, no. 3, August 1987, pp. 1–4.

38. ibid., p. 2.

39. Ted Snell, *Howard Taylor: Forest Figure*, Fremantle Arts Centre Press, Fremantle, Western Australia, 1995, pp. 46–7.

40. In 1987 Jan Senbergs visited the Davis Base at Antarctica, which was established in the 1950s.

41. Interview with Jan Senbergs by Traudi Allen at the artist's studio, North Melbourne, 14 August 1997.

42. Interview with Michelle Harris, Done Gallery Administrator, 16 April 1997, who said that this figure derives from sales at the Done Gallery in The Rocks in Sydney, from the Surfers Paradise gallery and other outlets.

43. Ken Done, writing on his painting *Nice Day at the Beach*, 1985, in *Ken Done: Paintings, Drawings, Posters and Prints*, Craftsman House, Sydney, 1986, p. 109.

44. Interview with Mandy Martin by Traudi Allen for video, *Women's Art and Feminism*, distribution Video Education Australasia, Bendigo, Victoria, 1994.

45. Terry Smith mentions the mining of red ochre pigment by Aborigines in Smith and Smith, op. cit., p. 546.

46. Interview with Mandy Martin, op. cit.; Susan Sontag, *The Volcano Lover: A Romance*, HarperCollins, Canada, 1992.

Chapter Two

1. Bernard Smith, *The Death of Artist as Hero: Essays in History and Culture*, Oxford University Press, Melbourne, 1988, p. 200. The article was published in *Education*, February 1943, and was one of Smith's first reviews.

2. Bernard Smith and Terry Smith, *Australian Painting 1788–1990*, Oxford University Press, Melbourne, 1992, pp. 276–87.

3. Geoffrey Serle, *From Deserts the Prophets Come: The Creative Spirit in Australia 1788–1972*, Heinemann, Melbourne, 1974, p. 169.

4. Richard Haese, *Rebels and Precursors: The Revolutionary Years of Australian Art*, Allen Lane, Ringwood, Victoria, 1981, p. 26.

5. Janine Burke, *Joy Hester*, Greenhouse Publications, Richmond, Victoria, 1983.

6. Max Harris, catalogue essay, *Angry Penguins and Realist Painting in Melbourne in the 1940s*, exhibition catalogue, Hayward Gallery, London, 1988.

7. The foreword was written by Richard Frances and Sandy Nairne, ibid., p. 10.

8. Bernard Smith, 'Realist art in wartime Australia', in Harris, op. cit., p. 58.

9. Haese, op. cit., p. 233, writes that Tucker was given two pounds per week from 1942 and that this was increased to six pounds in 1946.

10. Yvonne Boyd, telephone communication, 6 November 1997.

11. Traudi Allen, *John Perceval*, Melbourne University Press, Melbourne, 1992, p. 117.

12. Haese, op. cit.; Haese acknowledges the reluctance of Boyd and Perceval to commit themselves to the Reeds and their aspirations: 'Perceval and Boyd stood to one side of the central group since both were held by strong communal bonds of family and friendship to the Boyd encampment in Murrumbeena, with its attraction for young University intellectuals', p. 124.

13. See Peter Herbst, *Modernism, Murrumbeena and Angry Penguins: The Boxer Collection*, Australian Government Publishing Service, Canberra, 1981, pp. 4–9.

14. ibid., p. 6.

15. Haese, op. cit., p. 121.

16. Interview with Arthur Boyd by Haese, 2 December 1974, typescript at Bundanon, reprinted in Barry Pearce, *Arthur Boyd Retrospective*, exhibition catalogue, Art Gallery of New South Wales, Sydney, 1993, p. 13.

17. Recollection by Yvonne Boyd communicated via Bundanon curator Nicki Mortimor.

18. I have seen one of the very few extant paintings by Mary Boyd, an oil entitled *The Chinese Restaurant*, which was painted on the reverse of a work by John Perceval. This one example supports the argument that Mary Boyd is an interesting artist.

19. The gift of a house is mentioned in the film *The Good Looker*, directed by Claire Jager.

20. Jeanette Hoorn argues for Hester having been considered 'at best a marginal figure', in *Strange Women: Essays in Art and Gender*, Melbourne University Press, Melbourne, 1994, p. 27.

21. Heather Johnson, *Roy de Maistre: The Australian Years 1894–1930*, Craftsman House, Sydney, 1988, p. 31.

22. ibid., p. 38.

23. Humphrey McQueen, *The Black Swan of Trespass: The Emergence of Modernist Painting in Australia to 1944*, Alternative Publishing Cooperative, Sydney, 1979, p. 141: 'It was indicative of the superficiality of *Angry Penguins* Modernism that John Reed dismissed her work with the same condescending praise, [as] "decorative".' Hoorn, op. cit., p. 27: 'Unsurprisingly, once Modernism was recognised as a dominant discourse it became the province of men. The Angry Penguin artists and the social realists, with the exception of Joy Hester … were all men.'

24. Helen Topliss, *Modernism and Feminism: Australian Women Artists 1900–1940*, Craftsman House, Sydney, 1996, p. 18.

25. Reprinted in Michael Heyward's *The Ern Malley Affair*, University of Queensland Press, St Lucia, Queensland, 1993, p. 21.

26. See Joanna Murray-Smith, 'The Angry Penguins as cultural gesture', in *Ern Malley*, Allen and Unwin, Sydney, 1988, pp. 43–5.

27. Harris, op. cit., p. 25.

28. Albert Tucker interview with James Mollison and Nicholas Bonham in *Albert Tucker*, Macmillan, South Melbourne, 1982, p. 32.

29. Haese, op. cit., p. 238.

30. ibid., p. 242.

31. For a full analysis of this work see Traudi Allen, op. cit., p. 50.

32. Smith, op. cit., p. 198–9, writes of Barbara Blackman's account of the group's formation as being informed by her role as an 'apprehensive wife … who was not privy to the group's formal meetings'.

33. The manifesto is reproduced in Smith, ibid., p. 194.

34. Smith has written that he prepared the manifesto from 'a number of discussions and written statements prepared by some of the artists', ibid., p. 198.

35. ibid., pp. 201–3.

36. ibid., p. 199.

37. ibid., p. 200.

38. ibid., p. 202.

39. Margaret Plant, *John Perceval*, ed. John Henshaw, Landsdowne, Melbourne, 1978, p. 80.
40. Smith, op. cit., p. 213.
41. ibid., pp. 198–213.
42. ibid., p. 206.
43. Responding to my essay entitled 'The Antipodeans: Another chapter', Lauraine Diggins Gallery, Malakoff Fine Arts Press, Melbourne, for an exhibition of the same title from 17 October – 4 November 1988, Bernard Smith (letter dated 13 October 1988) dismissed my reference to the 'humanisation of nature' as implying the desire to involve the human figure as 'quite absurd', since 'landscape painting itself as a genre is a humanisation of nature'.
44. Ursula Hoff, *The Art of Arthur Boyd*, Andre Deutsch, London, 1986, p. 49.
45. Pugh mentioned to me that he had attempted to reproduce Aboriginal techniques in his paintings. The conversation took place after the publication of his biography in 1981.
46. According to Bernard Smith, the response was 'coolly neutral to dismissive; sales did not much more than cover expenses', in Smith, op. cit., p. 207.
47. In Smith, ibid., p. 204, David Boyd wrote that: 'The Vic Arts had never seen such a crowd. The galleries, balconies, and stairs were packed with an unusually animated assembly. The response was tumultuous.'
48. Terry Smith, 'The provincialism problem', reprinted in *Anything Goes: Art in Australia 1970–1980*, ed. Paul Taylor, Art + Text, Melbourne, 1984, pp. 46–53; referred to in greater detail in the introduction to this book.
49. Clement Greenberg, 'I meet a man who did not want to meet me', the *Australian*, 30 May 1968.
50. Smith, op. cit., p. 210.
51. ibid., p. 210.
52. ibid.
53. Traudi Allen, 'The Antipodeans: Another chapter', catalogue essay, Lauraine Diggins Fine Art, Nolan Gallery, S.H. Ervin Gallery, Malakoff Fine Arts Press, Melbourne, 1988–89.
54. Mike Brown, 'Kite II, Part 2: The heart of things', *Art Monthly*, no. 75, November 1994, p. 17.
55. Interview with Mike Brown by Traudi Allen for *The Annandale Imitation Realists*, video, Video Education Australasia, Bendigo, Victoria, 1994.
56. Mike Brown, 'Kite II, Part 1: What on earth are you saying, Colin?', *Art Monthly*, no. 73, September 1994, p. 4.
57. Brown, 'Kite II, Part 2', op. cit., p. 16.
58. ibid., p. 14.
59. ibid., p. 17.
60. Brown, 'Kite II, Part 1', op. cit., p. 5; and interview with Colin Lanceley by Traudi Allen for *The Annandale Imitation Realists*, op. cit.
61. Interview with Mike Brown by Traudi Allen, op. cit.
62. Richard Haese, *Power to the People: The Art of Mike Brown*, National Gallery of Victoria, Melbourne, 1995, p. 38.
63. Richard Haese, 'Waiting for postmodernism', *Art Monthly*, no. 78, April 1995, pp. 5–8.
64. Haese, *Power to the People*, op. cit., p. 38.
65. Colin Lanceley, 'Craven A: Surrealism and the Annandale Imitation Realists', *Art and Australia*, vol. 31, no. 4, 1994, pp. 482–9.
66. Brown, 'Kite II, Part 1' and 'Kite II, Part 2', op. cit.
67. Interview with Mike Brown by Traudi Allen, op. cit.
68. Van Gogh lived in the Yellow House at 2 Place Lamartine, Arles, from mid-September 1888. Gauguin spent nine weeks in the Yellow House, arriving on 23 October and leaving (it is thought) on 26 December 1888, although he told his wife that he would stay for six months. See Ronald Pickvance, *Van Gogh in Arles*, Metropolitan Museum of Art, New York, and Harry N. Abrams, New York, 1984, pp. 175, 201, 202, and Van Gogh letters to Theo (7, 9, 16 September 1888) reproduced in Pickvance, p. 23.
69. ibid., pp. 11–12.
70. In the case of Arthur Boyd, in its most pronounced form, this was limited to repetitive strokes from a heavily loaded brush in the early landscape works of Rosebud and the surrounding region, painted when Boyd stayed there with his grandfather in the 1930s. For Perceval the encounter was more profound. His *Van Gogh Sunflowers*, 1936–37, remains extant, and his entire oeuvre reveals an enduring preference for impasto. His contact with Arnold Shore lent a second-generation van Gogh influence also.
71. Letter from Vincent to Theo, in Pickvance, op. cit., p. 268.
72. Sandra McGrath, *Brett Whiteley*, Bay Books, Sydney, 1979, p. 230.
73. Joanna Mendelssohn, *The Yellow House 1970–1972*, Art Gallery of New South Wales, Sydney, 1990, pp. 9–10.
74. ibid., p. 9.
75. Telephone interview with Greg Weight by Traudi Allen, 30 October 1997.
76. Mendelssohn, op. cit., refers to *Woman's Day*, 15 June 1970 and *Dolly*, October 1971, pp. 12, 46.
77. Videotaped interview with George Gittoes by Traudi Allen, Bundeena, New South Wales, 16 November 1995.
78. Mendelssohn, op. cit., p. 11.
79. Interview with George Gittoes by Traudi Allen, op. cit.
80. Mendelssohn, op. cit., p. 10.
81. Mendelssohn, op. cit., mentions Gittoes's meeting with Greenberg.
82. See Mendelssohn, op. cit., p. 40 and throughout; and interview with Greg Weight by Traudi Allen, op. cit.
83. Interview with George Gittoes by Traudi Allen, op. cit.
84. ibid.
85. Mendelssohn, op. cit., p. 12.
86. David Bromfield, *Identities: A Critical Study of the Work of Mike Parr 1970–1990*, University of Western Australia Press, Perth, 1991, p. 8.
87. Among many examples of this interest was an article written by Mike Parr for *Art and Australia* in February 1976 titled 'Abesex to Zymasex (homage to Sigmund Freud)', which consisted of an alphabetical list of every word from the Funk and Wagnall's standard dictionary that ended in 'se' with 'x' added, *Art and Australia*, vol. 13, no. 4, 1976.
88. An extract from the rewritten press release appears in Bromfield, op. cit., p. 8.
89. ibid.
90. ibid., p. 9.
91. From a letter from Mike Parr to the critic Donald Brook, December 1970, reproduced in Bromfield, op. cit., p. 9: 'the gallery can be used in a highly private way. We have got audience control, insofar that it becomes possible to develop deliberate group situations on a basis that is selective and directional.'

92. Mendelssohn, op. cit., p. 11.
93. An extract from the letter appears in Bromfield, op. cit., p. 8.
94. Lucy R. Lippard (ed.), *Six Years: The Dematerialization of the Art Object from 1966 to 1972*, Studio Vista, London, 1973. In the 1997 edition of this book Parr, Kennedy and Johnson are mentioned. Sue Cramer refers to the relationship between Lippard and Inhibodress in *Inhibodress 1970–92*, Institute of Modern Art, Brisbane, 1989, p. 12.
95. Cramer, op. cit., p. 15.
96. ibid., pp. 5, 8, 9.
97. Anne Marsh, *Body and Self: Performance Art in Australia 1969–92*, Oxford University Press, Melbourne, 1993, p. 51.
98. ibid., p. 41.
99. Bromfield, op. cit., p. 10.
100. Donald Brook, *Studio International*, February 1971, excerpt reproduced in Bromfield, op. cit., p. 12.
101. Terry Smith, 'Bin for blurred rubbish', *Sunday Australian*, 19 September 1971, p. 19.
102. Cramer, op. cit., pp. 9–10.
103. These are listed by Bromfield, op. cit., p. 8. Bromfield mentions that the Inhibodress account books record a foundation membership of fourteen as opposed to the eleven listed in the press release, rewritten by Peter Kennedy in 1974, pp. 300–1.
104. *Artlink*, vol. 14, no. 2, 1994.
105. See Therese Kenyon, *Under a Hot Tin Roof: Art, Passion and Politics at the Tin Sheds Art Workshop*, State Library of New South Wales Press in association with Power Publications, The Power Institute of Fine Arts, University of Sydney, Sydney, 1995, which lists many groups who have been associated with Tin Sheds.
106. Boomalli originally operated from 27 Abercrombie Street, Chippendale, Sydney, and is now based in Annandale.
107. For a more comprehensive list see Traudi Allen, *Roar! And Quieter Moments From a Group of Melbourne Artists 1980–1993*, Craftsman House, Sydney, 1995.
108. See John Nixon, 'Art Projects 1979–84', *Art + Text*, no. 28, 1988.
109. ibid., p. 20.
110. ibid.
111. ibid.
112. Terry Smith in Smith and Smith, op. cit., p. 472.
113. For more on John Nixon see Sue Cramer and Carolyn Barnes, *John Nixon*, Roslyn Oxley9 Gallery, Sydney, 1991; Grant Hannan, 'John Nixon and the Russian Connection', *Art Monthly*, no. 16, November 1988; and Catharine Lumby, 'John Nixon interview', *On The Beach* (Sydney), no. 13, April 1988.
114. See quote by Mark Howson in Allen, *Roar!*, op. cit., p. 42.
115. Paul Taylor, 'Angst in my pants', *Art + Text*, no. 7, 1982, pp. 48–60.
116. Patrick McCaughey is an exception, see *Australian Art 1960–1986: Field To Figuration, Works From the National Gallery of Victoria*, National Gallery of Victoria, Melbourne, 1987.

Chapter Three

1. Simone de Beauvoir, *The Second Sex*, translated by H. M. Parshley, Picador, London, 1988, p. 16. In referring to Otherness, de Beauvoir quotes E. Levinas who expresses it as 'otherness' or 'alterity'.
2. Ian North, *Margaret Preston: Model of an Era*, exhibition catalogue, Art Gallery Board of South Australia, Adelaide, 1980, p. 7.
3. ibid.
4. Humphrey McQueen, *The Black Swan of Trespass: The Emergence of Modernist Painting in Australia to 1944*, Alternative Publishing Cooperative, Sydney, 1979, p. 145, see also chapter 4.
5. Andrew Milner, *Contemporary Cultural Theory: An Introduction*, Allen and Unwin, Sydney, 1991, p. 83. See whole chapter for feminist theory.
6. Joan Kerr (ed.), *Heritage: The National Women's Art Book*, Craftsman House, Sydney, 1995, p. 432.
7. North, op. cit. pp. 12, 15.
8. According to Helen Topliss, *Modernism and Feminism: Australian Women Artists 1900–1940*, Craftsman House, Sydney, 1996, pp. 53, 181, this was mentioned in an interview with Grace Cossington Smith.
9. While using it as an example of a wider attitude, Topliss attributes this view specifically to Thea Proctor, ibid., p. 25.
10. De Beauvoir, op. cit., p. 21.
11. Topliss, op. cit., p. 120.
12. Margaret Preston, *From Eggs to Electrolux*, 1927; reprinted in North, op. cit., p. 8.
13. Milner, op. cit., p. 88.
14. North, op. cit., p. 7.
15. Kerr, op. cit., p. 432.
16. Bernard Smith and Terry Smith, *Australian Painting 1788–1990*, Oxford University Press, Melbourne, 1992, p. 128.
17. See Kerr, op. cit. and Topliss, op. cit., especially chapter 8, pp. 141–71.
18. Topliss mentions that women outnumbered men at the National Gallery of Victoria Art School in 1890, op. cit., p. 47.
19. The first use of the term 'second wave' occurred on 10 March 1968 in *New York Times Magazine*. See Hester Eisenstein, *Contemporary Feminist Thought*, Allen and Unwin, Sydney, 1984, p. 147.
20. J. C. Ollenburger and H. Moore, *A Sociology of Women: The Intersection of Patriarchy, Capitalism and Colonization*, Prentice Hall, New Jersey, 1992, p. 19. The authors point out that such an argument is followed by John Stuart Mill in 'The subjection of women', in *On Liberty*, Oxford University Press, London, 1912.
21. Eisenstein, op. cit., p. 35.
22. ibid., pp. 35–6.
23. This point is made in Milner, op. cit., p. 103, and throughout the chapter on feminism, but is a critical issue of post-colonial discourse and dealt with widely in the literature.
24. Among the many sources in which this can be found is an extract: 'Jacques Lacan from "The Mirror Stage" (1949)', in *A Critical and Cultural Theory Reader*, eds Antony Easthope and Kate McGowan, Open University Press, Buckingham, 1994, pp. 71–6.
25. This point is made by Janet Wolff in *The Social Production of Art*, Macmillan, London, 1984, pp. 135–6.
26. Lois McNay, *Foucault and Feminism: Power, Gender and the Self*, Polity Press, Cambridge, 1992, p. 173.
27. See Craig Owens, 'The discourse of others: Feminists and postmodernism', in *Postmodern Culture*, ed. Hal Foster, Pluto Press, Sydney, 1985, p. 63. For a full discussion see Zillah Eisenstein, 'Constructing a theory of capitalist patriarchy and socialist feminism', in *Women, Class, and the Feminist Imagination*, eds K. V. Hansen and I. J. Philipson, Temple University Press, Philadelphia 1990, pp. 114f.

28. Sandy Kirby, in Traudi Allen, *Women's Art and Feminism*, video, distribution Video Education Australasia, Bendigo, Victoria, 1994; see also Sandy Kirby, *Sight Lines: Women's Art and Feminist Perspectives in Australia*, Craftsman House, Sydney, 1992, pp. 30–1.

29. Kirby, ibid., p. 31.

30. Janine Burke, *Joy Hester*, Greenhouse Publications, Richmond, Victoria, 1983.

31. Kerr, op. cit.

32. Interview with Jan Martin, dealer to Yvonne Audette, Lyttleton Gallery, North Melbourne, 3 February 1991; see Deborah Durie Saines, 'The will to paint: Three Sydney women artists of the 1950s', Master of Arts, University of Sydney, 1992, p. 51.

33. Interview with Jan Martin, ibid.

34. Yvonne Audette papers, c/- Jan Martin, Lyttleton Gallery, North Melbourne.

35. Recollection by Vivienne Binns in Therese Kenyon, *Under a Hot Tin Roof: Art, Passion and Politics at the Tin Sheds Art Workshop*, State Library of New South Wales Press in association with Power Publications, The Power Institute of Fine Arts, University of Sydney, Sydney, 1995, p. 62.

36. See David Bromfield, *Identities: A Critical Study of the Work of Mike Parr 1970–1990*, University of Western Australia Press, Perth, 1991, p. 8.

37. Lucy R. Lippard, *From the Center: Feminist Essays on Women's Art*, E. P. Dutton, New York, 1976.

38. For more on essentialism see Hester Eisenstein, op. cit., pp. xi, 3. Eisenstein devotes her entire book to an examination of the history of feminist ideology.

39. ibid., p. xi, gives the argument in summary.

40. ibid., pp. 47, 48, 96, 122; see chapter 14 for suggestions on further adaptations of this view.

41. ibid., p. 47.

42. Anne Koedt, 'The myth of vaginal orgasm', in *Radical Feminism*, eds Anne Koedt, Ellen Levine and Anita Rapone, Quadrangle Books, New York, 1973, pp. 198–207.

43. Kirby, op. cit., p. 22.

44. Mentioned in Kirby, ibid., pp. 80, 139.

45. Anne Marsh, *Body and Self: Performance Art in Australia 1969–92*, Oxford University Press, Melbourne, 1993, p. 173.

46. ibid.

47. Interview with Merren Ricketson, Director, Women's Art Register, 2 December 1996.

48. Letters, *Art Monthly*, June 1995, p. 18.

49. Kenyon, op. cit., p. 70.

50. See Kirby, op. cit., chapter 4, for the return to embroidery.

51. Megan Evans makes this point in her catalogue essay to 'The Art of Nursing' exhibition held on International Nurses Day, 1994, comprising work by the Australian Nursing Federation (Victorian Branch).

52. Interview with Mona Ryder by Traudi Allen for *Women's Art and Feminism*, op. cit.

53. Interview with Mona Ryder, 29 January 1990. Ryder maintains that she was unaware of Kahlo's use of tubing and that her application of this motif derives from her reference to the garden hose. Both used tubing as a metaphor to represent medical procedures on reproductive organs. Kahlo referred to her miscarriage in the work *Henry Ford Hospital*, 1942, and included six objects connected by tubing that were symbolic of her feelings at the time. See Hayden Herrera, *Frida Kahlo: The Paintings*, Bloomsbury, London, 1992.

54. Michel Foucault, *Discipline and Punish: The Birth of the Prison*, translated by A. M. Sheridan, Penguin, Harmondsworth, 1984.

55. P. Rabinow (ed.), *The Foucault Reader*, Penguin, Harmondsworth, 1984; reprinted in McNay, op. cit.

56. From Annette Bezor interview in Anna Voigt, *New Visions, New Perspectives: Voices of Contemporary Australian Women Artists*, Craftsman House, Sydney, 1996, p. 45.

57. Mary Daly, *Gyn/Ecology: The Metaethics of Radical Feminism*, Beacon Press, Boston, 1978; reconsidered in Hester Eisenstein, op. cit., p. 109.

Chapter Four

1. Joseph Eisenberg, 'Olive Crane', in *Heritage: The National Women's Art Book*, ed. Joan Kerr, Craftsman House, Sydney, 1995, p. 283.

2. For more on Bunny, see David King, 'Rupert Bunny's paintings of Sada Yakko', *Art and Australia*, vol. 25, no. 3, 1988.

3. Alan McCulloch and Susan McCulloch, *The Encyclopedia of Australian Art*, Allen and Unwin, Sydney, 1994, p. 271.

4. Humphrey McQueen, *The Black Swan of Trespass: The Emergence of Modernist Painting in Australia to 1944*, Alternative Publishing Cooperative, Sydney, 1979, p. 141.

5. Helen Topliss, *Modernism and Feminism: Australian Women Artists 1900–1940*, Craftsman House, Sydney, 1996, p. 123.

6. McQueen, op. cit., p. 158; Topliss, op. cit., p. 126.

7. McQueen, op. cit., p. 155.

8. ibid., p. 145.

9. This point is made in Topliss, op. cit., p. 126.

10. McQueen, op. cit., p. 154.

11. AAP files.

12. Sandra McGrath, *Brett Whiteley*, Bay Books, Sydney, 1979, p. 71.

13. ibid.

14. ibid., p. 113.

15. Pat Hoffie interview with Alison Carroll in *Out of Asia*, catalogue essay, Heide Park and Art Gallery, Bulleen, Victoria, 1990, p. 18.

16. Carroll, ibid., p. 6.

17. ibid.

18. ibid., p. 8.

19. Edmund Capon, *Asian Gallery Opens*, press release, Art Gallery of New South Wales, Sydney, 13 July 1994.

20. ibid.

21. Interview with Michael Brand, curator of Asian art, National Gallery of Australia, Canberra, 6 December 1995.

22. ibid.

23. Annette Hamilton, 'Dreaming the lotus: Aesthetic dialogue with "Asia"', in Alison Carroll, *Out of Asia*, op. cit., p. 4.

24. ibid.

25. For this and other performances by Dadang Christanto, see Astri Wright, *ART AsiaPacific*, vol. 3, no. 1, 1996, p. 75.

26. ibid., p. 77.

27. Brenda Fajardo interview with Traudi Allen for ABC Radio, September 1993.

28. See *ART AsiaPacific*, vol. 3, no. 1, 1996, pp. 44–51.

29. See Carroll, op. cit., pp. 14–15. Also, Roger Benjamin, *Transcultural Painting*, Ian Potter Gallery, Melbourne; Asialink; and the University of Melbourne, Victoria, 1994, pp. 23–27.

30. Benjamin, ibid., p. 25.

31. Tony Clark, speaking with Alison Carroll, *Out of Asia*, op. cit., p. 14.
32. 'The orientation of art in the post-war Pacific', *Society of Artists Book*, Sydney, 1942, p. 7, reproduced in Topliss, op. cit., p. 126.
33. *The Abolition of the 'White Australia' Policy*, Department of Immigration and Multicultural Affairs, Canberra, 1997.
34. ibid.

Chapter Five

1. Letter from Megan Evans to Traudi Allen, 10 July 1997.
2. Sandy Kirby, 'An historical perspective on the community arts movement', in *Community and the Arts: Australian Perspectives*, ed. Vivienne Binns, Pluto Press, Sydney, 1991, especially p. 27.
3. Ann Stephen and Andrew Reeves, *Badges of Labour, Banners of Pride: Aspects of Working Class Celebration*, Museum of Applied Arts and Sciences, Sydney, in association with Allen and Unwin, Sydney, 1985, gives a detailed example, p. 38.
4. Kirby, op. cit., pp. 19–30, especially pp. 24–5.
5. ibid., p. 25.
6. David Watt asserts that community art has its origins in the counter-culture movement in, 'Interrogating "community": Social welfare versus cultural democracy', in Binns, op. cit., pp. 55–65.
7. Sandy Kirby, *Artists and Unions — A Critical Tradition: A Report on the Art and Working Life Program*, Australia Council, Sydney, 1992, p. 13.
8. See examples in Kathie Muir, *Creative Alliances — Unions and the Arts: Art and Working Life in the 1990s*, Union Media Services, Trades Hall, Sydney, 1992.
9. ibid., p. 3.
10. ibid; and Kirby, *Artists and Unions*, op. cit., also provides a detailed analysis of the involvement of the trade union movement in the arts.
11. Muir, op. cit., p. 4.
12. Gay Hawkins, 'Reading community arts policy: From Nimbin to the gay mardi gras', in Binns, op. cit., p. 45.
13. Watt takes up this debate in Binns, op. cit., p. 59.
14. *Towards a National Agenda for the Arts*, report compiled by Arts Action Australia, February 1990, p. 15.
15. Interview with Carole Wilson, 15 July 1997.
16. ibid.
17. Binns, op. cit., p. 12.
18. ibid.

Chapter Six

1. Jeffrey Weeks, *Against Nature: Essays on History, Sexuality and Identity*, Rivers Oram Press, London, 1991.
2. Chicka Dixon, 'I want to be a human being', *Sun–Herald*, 21 May 1967; extract reprinted in *The 1967 Referendum, Or When Aborigines Didn't Get The Vote*, Bain Attwood and Andrew Markus with Dale Edwards and Kath Schilling, Aboriginal Studies Press, Australian Institute of Aboriginal and Torres Strait Islander Studies, Canberra, 1997, p. 50.
3. Interview with officer from the Australian Electoral Commission, 13 February 1997.
4. This issue is discussed in Attwood and Markus, op. cit., p. 71. For the Mabo debate, see Bain Attwood, *In the Age of Mabo: History, Aborigines and Australia*, Allen & Unwin, Sydney, 1996.
5. Michael A. O'Ferrall, *On The Edge: Five Contemporary Aboriginal Artists*, exhibition catalogue, Art Gallery of Western Australia, Perth, 1989, p. 4.
6. Action was brought on behalf of Bulun Bulun; see Martin Hardie, 'The Aboriginal copyright cases', *Artlink*, vol. 10, nos 1 and 2, 1992, pp. 39–40.
7. ibid., p. 5.
8. Wally Caruana, *Aboriginal Art*, Thames and Hudson, London, 1993, p. 185.
9. Vivien Johnson, 'Into the urbane: Urban Aboriginal art in the Australian art context', *Art Monthly*, no. 30, May 1990, pp. 20–3.
10. Michael A. O'Ferrall, *Australian Aboriginal Art: Convergence and Divergence*, catalogue, Art Gallery of Western Australia, Perth, 1990, p. 31.
11. For more on desert painting see Caruana, op. cit., p. 214.
12. Fiona Foley made this point on the SBS program 'Stretton on Saturday', September 1996.
13. From a conversation between Gilles Deleuze and Michel Foucault in *Language, Counter-memory, Practice*, p. 209, mentioned in Craig Owens, 'The discourse of others: Feminists and postmodernism', in *Postmodern Culture*, ed. Hal Foster, Pluto Press, Sydney, 1985, pp. 69, 80.
14. Wally Caruana, op. cit., p. 110, mentions a variety of uses of the dot, from simple design features to references to the supernatural.
15. Antonia Carver, 'Mind, body and soul', *ART AsiaPacific*, vol. 3, no. 2, 1996, p. 70 and footnotes p. 71.
16. Traudi Allen telephone interview with Rea, 10 December 1997.
17. ibid.
18. ibid.
19. ibid.
20. Elizabeth Ashburn, *Lesbian Art: An Encounter With Power*, Craftsman House, Sydney, 1996, p. 114.
21. A reference to the Freudian notion of penis envy and an often quoted letter by Freud to the parent of a prospective client in which he refers to 'the blighted germs of homosexuality' and reports that analysis is successful in treating some cases, *American Journal of Psychiatry*, April 1951, p. 786; extract reproduced in 'Freud, male homosexuality, and the Americans', in *The Lesbian and Gay Studies Reader*, eds Henry Abelove, Michele Aina Barale and David M. Halperin, Routledge, New York, 1993, pp. 381–2.
22. Ashburn, op. cit., p. 18.
23. Annamarie Jagose, *Queer Theory*, Melbourne University Press, Melbourne, 1996, p. 14.
24. Ashburn, op. cit., pp. 13–21.
25. ibid., p. 15.
26. Christine Browning, 'Changing theories of lesbianism: Challenging the stereotypes', reproduced in *Women-Identified Women*, eds Trudy Darty and Sandee Potter, Mayfield Publishing, California, 1984, p. 13. This book is a highly readable review of lesbian history and experience.
27. ibid.
28. Denise Thompson provides a thorough review of this argument in *Reading Between the Lines: A Lesbian Feminist Critique of Feminist Accounts of Sexuality*, Lesbian Studies and Research Group and the Gorgon's Head Press, Sydney, 1991.

29. Jagose, op. cit., pp. 8–9.
30. Ashburn, op. cit., p. 35.
31. Ashburn discusses the implications of the 'gay dollar', op. cit.; see also Danae Clark, 'Commodity lesbianism', in Abelove, op. cit., pp. 186–201.
32. Jeffrey Weeks, op. cit., writes of public expressions of gay sexuality as disrupting the distinction between public and private which structures modern understandings of sexuality. Public expressions of gay sexuality cut across distinctions between home, family and work, and challenge conventional notions that such behaviour belongs to the private domain.
33. Jagose, op. cit., pp. 72–100.
34. Ted Gott, 'Grief', Artlink, vol. 14, no. 4, summer 1994, p. 18.
35. ibid.
36. This example is seen in Davila's Miss Sigmund, 1981, reproduced in Hysterical Tears, ed. Paul Taylor, Greenhouse, Richmond, Victoria, 1985, p. 61.
37. Paul Foss interview with Juan Davila, in Taylor, ibid., pp. 10–16.
38. References to Marilyn Monroe occur throughout Davila's 1980–81 paintings; this particular image is from Stupid as a Painter, 1981, reproduced in Taylor, ibid., p. 62; for Davila's commentary on pornography see Taylor, ibid., p. 15.
39. eX de Medici interview with Ted Gott, 30 November 1996, reprinted in Indelible, exhibition catalogue, Australian Centre for Contemporary Art, Melbourne, 1997.
40. eX de Medici interview with Traudi Allen, Australian Centre for Contemporary Art, Melbourne, 23 January 1997.
41. ibid.
42. ibid.
43. ibid.
44. Robert E. Fisher, Buddhist Art and Architecture, Thames and Hudson, London, 1993, p. 31.
45. Traudi Allen interview with eX de Medici, op. cit.
46. Ashburn, op. cit., p. 3. For an overview of gay/queer issues I am indebted to Robert Schubert's lecture, 'That's Miss Faggot to you honey! Queer/gay art in Oz', Monash University, Clayton, Victoria, 18 March 1996.

Chapter Seven

1. James Bennett, Hot Wax: An Exhibition of Australian Aboriginal Indonesian Batik, catalogue, Museum and Art Gallery of the Northern Territory, Darwin, April 1995.
2. ibid.
3. Traudi Allen telephone interview with James Bennett, 12 April 1996.
4. James Bennett, 'Dialogue with Indonesia', in Contemporary Craft Review, ed. Jenny Zimmer, Monash University, Clayton, Victoria, 1996, p. 80. Bennett provides the Indonesian original: 'Keseriasan, keseimbangan dan keteraturan … sebagai bekai, pemelihara, pembinaan dan pengembangan kesenian serta kebudayaan dalam masyarakat', a quote from a lecturer in Indonesian textiles, Dr Nanang Rizali Surakarta.
5. ibid., p. 82; Bennett cites these observations as having been made by Indonesian anthropologist Agung Harjuno.
6. ibid.
7. ibid.
8. 'Endlessnessism' is the name of a company established by Brett and Wendy Whiteley.

9. Interview with Domenico de Clario by Traudi Allen, ABC radio 'Asia Focus', 19 June 1995.
10. Michael Brand, The Vision of Kings: Art and Experience in India, National Gallery of Australia, Canberra, and Thames and Hudson, Melbourne, 1996, p. 15.
11. Godfrey Devereux, The Elements of Yoga, Shaftsbury, Dorset, p. 3.
12. ibid.
13. Interview with Domenico de Clario by Traudi Allen, op. cit.
14. ibid.
15. Geoffrey Goldie papers, courtesy Lyttleton Gallery, North Melbourne.
16. Interview with Geoffrey Goldie by Traudi Allen, ABC radio, 19 June 1995.
17. Ajit Mookerjee, Kali: The Feminine Force, Thames and Hudson, London, 1995, p. 78.
18. Aniela Jaffe (ed.), C. J. Jung: Word and Image, Bollingen Series XCVII: 2, Princeton University Press, Princeton, New Jersey, 1979, p. 77.
19. Dr Chandrabhanu has produced a ballet on the theme of Medea.
20. Mookerjee, op. cit., p. 8.
21. ibid., p. 9.
22. ibid., p. 11; Mookerjee writes that in the Kaimur region of Central India archaeologists have found concentric triangles 'where concretionary sandstone and, especially, triangular laminae are set up as shrines for the worship of Shakti'.
23. ibid., p. 25, and many other references throughout.
24. ibid., p. 34.
25. Sandy Kirby makes this point in a general context in Traudi Allen, Women's Art and Feminism, videotape, Video Education Australasia, Bendigo, Victoria, 1994.
26. Traudi Allen interview with Carole Wilson, 2 May 1996.
27. ibid.
28. Interview with Anne Marie Power by Traudi Allen, 12 May 1996.
29. B. K. S. Iyengar, The Tree of Yoga, Fine Line Books, Oxford, 1988, p. 141.
30. Interview with Hanh Ngo by Traudi Allen, 21 April 1996.
31. ibid.
32. ibid.

Conclusion

1. 'Virtual republic' was coined by McKenzie Wark and is the title of his book, The Virtual Republic: Australia's Cultural Wars of the 1990s, Allen and Unwin, Sydney, 1997.
2. Rosalie Gascoigne interview with Nevill Drury, Images 2: Contemporary Australian Painting, Craftsman House, Sydney, 1994, p. 216.
3. Daniel Thomas, 'Everybody sing: The art of Robert MacPherson', Art and Australia, vol. 33, no. 4, 1996, p. 487.
4. ibid., p. 486.
5. Gael Newton, Tracey Moffatt: Fever Pitch, Piper Press, Sydney, 1995, p. 15.
6. ibid.
7. ibid., pp. 18, 22, n. 11.
8. Jean Baudrillard discusses the relationship between reality and effect in 'The precession of simulacra', translated by Paul Foss and Paul Patton, Art + Text, no. 11, 1983, pp. 32–3. See also Jean Baudrillard, 'The China syndrome' in Simulacra and Simulation, translated by Sheila Faria Glaser, The University of Michigan Press, Michigan, pp. 53–7.

bibliography

Introduction
Art Comes Out: Tracing the Development of
Contemporary Art

Appignanesi, Richard and Garratt, Chris. *Postmodernism for Beginners*, Icon, Cambridge, 1995.

Barthes, Roland. *The Death of the Author: Image-Music-Text*, essays selected and translated by Stephen Heath, Fontana/Collins, Glasgow, 1977.

Barthes, Roland. *Barthes: Selected Writings*, ed. Susan Sontag, Fontana, London, 1983.

Barthes, Roland. *Mythologies*, translated by Annette Lavers, Paladin, London, 1989.

Berger, John. *Ways of Seeing*, Penguin, Ringwood, Victoria, 1983.

Crisp, L. F. *Australian National Government*, Longman, Melbourne, 1970.

Drury, Nevill. *Images 2: Contemporary Australian Painting*, Craftsman House, Sydney, 1994.

Easthope, Anthony and McGowan, Kate. *A Critical and Cultural Theory Reader*, Open University Press, Buckingham, 1994.

Haese, Richard. *Rebels and Precursors: The Revolutionary Years of Australian Art*, Allen Lane, Ringwood, Victoria, 1981.

Hansford, Pamela. *Peter Tyndall: Dagger Definitions*, Greenhouse Publications, Richmond, Victoria, 1987.

Hughes, Robert. *The Art of Australia*, Penguin, Ringwood, Victoria, 1970.

Kirby, Sandy. *Sight Lines: Women's Art and Feminist Perspectives in Australia*, Craftsman House, Sydney, 1992.

Lacan, Jacques. *The Four Fundamental Concepts of Psychoanalysis*, translated by Alain Sheridan, State University of New York Press, Albany, 1995.

McCulloch, Alan and McCulloch, Susan. *The Encyclopedia of Australian Art*, Allen and Unwin, Sydney, 1994.

McQueen, Humphrey. *The Black Swan of Trespass: The Emergence of Modernist Painting in Australia to 1944*, Alternative Publishing Cooperative, Sydney, 1979.

Milner, Andrew. *Contemporary Cultural Theory: An Introduction*, Allen and Unwin, Sydney, 1991.

Rose, Margaret A. *The Post-modern and the Post-industrial: A Critical Analysis*, Cambridge University Press, Oakleigh, Victoria, 1991.

Smith, Bernard and Smith, Terry. *Australian Painting 1788–1990*, Oxford University Press, Melbourne, 1992.

Articles and catalogues
The Art of Flux: An Australian Perspective, Antipodean Currents Ten Contemporary Artists from Australia, exhibition catalogue, Guggenheim Museum, SoHo, New York, 1995.

Burdett, Basil. 'Modern art in Melbourne', *Art in Australia*, no. 15, November 1938.

Baudrillard, Jean. 'The Precession of simulacra', translated by Paul Foss and Paul Patton, *Art + Text*, no. 11, 1983.

Casey, Edward S. and Melvin Woody, J. 'Hegel, Heidegger, Lacan', in *Interpreting Lacan: Psychiatry and the Humanities*, eds Joseph H. Smith and William Kerrigan, Yale University Press, New Haven and London, vol. 6, 1983.

The Field, exhibition catalogue, National Gallery of Victoria, Melbourne, 1968.

The Field Now, exhibition catalogue, Heide Park and Art Gallery, Heidelberg, Victoria, 1984.

Foss, Paul. 'Theatrum mondum cognitorum', in *The Foreign Bodies Papers*, eds C. Burns and P. Botsman, Local Consumption, Sydney, 1981.

Green, Charles. 'Robert Rooney', in *From the Homefront: Robert Rooney Works 1953–1988*, Monash University Gallery, Clayton, Victoria, 1990.

Jameson, Fredric. 'Postmodernism and consumer society', in *Postmodern Culture*, ed. Hal Foster, Pluto Press, Sydney, 1985.

Minchin, Jan. 'Basil Burdett', *Art and Australia*, vol. 17, no. 4, 1980.

Lindsay, Robert. *Vox Pop: An Iconography of Popular Beliefs*, exhibition catalogue, National Gallery of Victoria, Melbourne, 1983.

Smith, Terry. 'The provincialism problem', in *Anything Goes: Art in Australia 1970–1980*, ed. Paul Taylor, Art + Text, Melbourne, 1984.

Taylor, Paul. 'Interview with Clement Greenberg', *Art and Australia*, vol. 18, no. 2, 1980.

Chapter One
A Continuing Romance: The Biography of the Tree

Adams, Brian. *Sidney Nolan: Such is Life*, Hutchinson, Hawthorn, Victoria, 1987.

Astbury, Leigh. *City Bushmen*, Oxford University Press, Melbourne, 1985.

Done, Ken. *Ken Done: Paintings, Drawings, Posters and Prints*, Craftsman House, Sydney, 1986.

Free, Renee. *Lloyd Rees: The Last Twenty Years*, Craftsman House, Sydney, 1990.

Haese, Richard. *Rebels and Precursors: The Revolutionary Years of Australian Art*, Allen Lane, Ringwood, Victoria, 1981.

Haese, Richard. *Sidney Nolan: The City and the Plain*, exhibition catalogue, National Gallery of Victoria, Melbourne, 1983.

Hopkirk, Frannie. *Brett: A Portrait of Brett Whiteley by his Sister*, Alfred A. Knopf, Sydney, 1996.

McAuliffe, Chris. *Art and Suburbia*, Craftsman House, Sydney, 1997.

McCaughey, Patrick. *Fred Williams*, Bay Books, Sydney, 1980.

McGrath, Sandra. *Brett Whiteley*, Bay Books, Sydney, 1979.

Mollison, James. *A Singular Vision: The Art of Fred Williams*, Australian National Gallery, Canberra, 1989.

Smith, Bernard and Smith, Terry. *Australian Painting 1788–1990*, Oxford University Press, Melbourne, 1992.

Snell, Ted. *Howard Taylor: Forest Figure*, Fremantle Arts Centre Press, Fremantle, Western Australia, 1995.

Thiele, Colin. *Heysen's Early Hahndorf*, Rigby, Adelaide, 1976.

Thiele, Colin. *Heysen of Hahndorf*, Rigby, Adelaide, 1976.

Topliss, Helen. *The Artists' Camps: 'Plein air' Painting in Australia*, Hedley Australia, Alphington, Victoria, 1992.

Van de Ven, Marie. *Ken Done's Graphic Design*, Powerhouse Publishing, Sydney, 1994.

Articles and catalogues

Barbour, John. 'Mandy Martin's mural', *Art Monthly*, no. 8, March 1988.

Burn, Ian. 'What can Nolan mean today?', *Art Monthly*, no. 3, August 1987.

Edwards, Deborah. 'Subsiding to the heart of things: Godfrey Miller, the works', in *Godfrey Miller 1893–1964*, exhibition catalogue, Art Gallery of New South Wales, Sydney, 1996.

Green, Charles. 'Thoughtful art', *Art and Australia*, vol. 34, no. 4.

Martin, Jan. *Important Works from North East Arnhem Land*, exhibition catalogue, Lyttleton Gallery, Melbourne, 1989.

Mollison, James; Williams, Lyn; and Davie, Annabel. 'Fred Williams: A major exhibition', *Art Monthly*, no. 5, October 1987.

Plant, Margaret. 'A singular vision', *Art Monthly*, no. 24, September 1989.

Reed, John. 'Sidney Nolan', *Art and Australia*, vol. 5, no. 2, 1967.

Senbergs, Jan. *Voyage Six: Antarctica*, exhibition catalogue, Powell Street Gallery, Melbourne, 1988.

Chapter Two
Managing Modernism: Australian Artistic Movements since 1940

The Angry Penguins

Allen, Traudi. *John Perceval*, Melbourne University Press, Melbourne, 1992.

Angry Penguins and Realist Painting in Melbourne in the 1940s, Hayward Gallery, London, 1988. (Contributions by Max Harris, Barrett Reid, Bernard Smith, Janine Burke, Charles Merewether, Christopher Heathcote and Christine Dixon.)

Burke, Janine. *Joy Hester*, Greenhouse Publications, Richmond, Victoria, 1983.

Dixon, Christine and Smith, Terry. *Aspects of Australian Figurative Painting 1942–1962: Dreams, Fears and Desires*, exhibition catalogue, The Power Institute of Fine Arts, University of Sydney, Sydney, 1984.

Eagle, Mary and Jones, John. *A Story of Australian Painting*, Pan Macmillan, Sydney, 1994.

Haese, Richard. *Rebels and Precursors: The Revolutionary Years of Australian Art*, Allen Lane, Ringwood, Victoria, 1981.

Haese, Richard. 'Images of Loss', in *Josl Bergner: A Retrospective Exhibition*, National Gallery of Victoria, Melbourne, 1985.

Harris, Max and Murray-Smith, Joanna. *Ern Malley: The Poems With Commentaries*, Allen and Unwin, Sydney, 1988.

Herbst, Peter. *Modernism, Murrumbeena and Angry Penguins: The Boxer Collection*, Australian Government Publishing Service, Canberra, 1981.

Heyward, Michael. *The Ern Malley Affair*, University of Queensland Press, St Lucia, Queensland, 1993.

Hoff, Ursula. *The Art of Arthur Boyd*, Andre Deutsch, London, 1986.

Hoorn, Jeanette (ed.). *Strange Women: Essays in Art and Gender*, Melbourne University Press, Melbourne, 1994.

Johnson, Heather. *Roy de Maistre: The Australian Years 1894–1930*, Craftsman House, Sydney, 1988.

Lippard, Lucy. *Six Years: The Dematerialization of the the Art Object from 1966 to 1972*, Studio Vista, London, 1973.

McQueen, Humphrey. *The Black Swan of Trespass: The Emergence of Modernist Painting in Australia to 1944*, Alternative Publishing Cooperative, Sydney, 1979.

Mollison, James and Bonham, Nicholas. *Albert Tucker*, Macmillan, South Melbourne, 1982.

St John Moore, Felicity. *Vassilieff and His Art*, Oxford University Press, Melbourne, 1982.

Pearce, Barry. *Arthur Boyd Retrospective*, exhibition catalogue, Art Gallery of New South Wales, Sydney, 1993.

Philipp, Franz. *Arthur Boyd*, Thames and Hudson, London, 1967.

Serle, Geoffrey. *From Deserts the Prophets Come: The Creative Spirit in Australia 1788–1972*, Heinemann, Melbourne, 1974.

Smith, Bernard. *The Death of the Artist as Hero: Essays in History and Culture*, Oxford University Press, Melbourne, 1988.

Smith, Bernard and Smith, Terry. *Australian Painting 1788–1990*, Oxford University Press, Melbourne, 1992.

Topliss, Helen. *Modernism and Feminism: Australian Women Artists 1900–1940*, Craftsman House, Sydney, 1996.

The Antipodeans

The Antipodeans: Another Chapter. Lauraine Diggins Gallery, North Caulfield, Victoria, 1988.

Benko, Nancy. *The Art of David Boyd*, Lidums, Adelaide, 1973.

Dickerson, Jennifer. *Against the Tide*, Pandanus Press, Brisbane, 1994.

Eagle, Mary and Jones, John. *A Story of Australian Painting*, Pan MacMillan, Sydney, 1994.

Gunn, Grazia. *Arthur Boyd: Seven Persistent Images*, Australian National Gallery, Canberra, 1985.

Hoff, Ursula. *The Art of Arthur Boyd*, Andre Deutsch, London, 1986.

Lindsay, Robert. 'The figure in the carpet: Some literary and visual sources in the work of John Brack', in *John Brack: A Retrospective Exhibition*, exhibition catalogue, National Gallery of Victoria, Melbourne, 1987.

Mendham, Dawn. 'Directions in Australian painting and art criticism 1938–1962', Litt. B thesis, Australian National University, Canberra, 1981.

Pearce, Barry. Catalogue essay, *Arthur Boyd Retrospective*, exhibition catalogue, Art Gallery of New South Wales, Sydney, 1994.

Philipp, Franz. *Arthur Boyd*, Thames and Hudson, London, 1967.

Plant, Margaret. *John Perceval*, ed. John Henshaw, Landsdowne, Melbourne, rev. edn, 1978.

Shapcott, Tom. *The Art of Charles Blackman*, Andre Deutsch Ltd, London, 1989.

Smith, Bernard. *The Antipodean Manifesto: Essays in Art and History*, Oxford University Press, Melbourne, 1976.

Smith, Bernard. 'The truth about the Antipodeans', in *The Death of the Artist as Hero: Essays in History and Culture*, Oxford University Press, Melbourne, 1988.

Smith, Terry. 'The provincialism problem', in *Anything Goes: Art in Australia 1970–1980*, ed. Paul Taylor, Art + Text, Melbourne, 1984.

The Annandale Imitation Realists

Allen, Traudi. 'Interview with Mike Brown', *The Annandale Imitation Realists*, video, Video Education Australasia, Bendigo, Victoria, 1994.

Brown, Mike. 'Kite II, Part I: What on earth are you saying, Colin?', *Art Monthly*, no. 73, September 1994.

Brown, Mike. 'Kite II, Part II: The heart of things', *Art Monthly*, no. 75, November 1994.

Catalano, Gary. 'The aesthetics of the Imitation Realists', *Meanjin*, vol. 35, no. 2, June 1976.

Catalano, Gary. *Years of Hope: Australian Art and Criticism 1959–1968*, Oxford University Press, Melbourne, 1981.

Haese, Richard. *Power to the People: The Art of Mike Brown*, exhibition catalogue, National Gallery of Victoria, Melbourne, 1995.

Haese, Richard. 'Waiting for postmodernism', *Art Monthly*, no. 78, April 1995.

Lanceley, Colin. 'Craven A: Surrealism and the Annandale Imitation Realists', *Art and Australia*, vol. 31, no. 4, 1994.

Lynn, Elwyn. 'Pop goes the easel', *Art and Australia*, vol. 1, no. 3, 1963.

Plant, Margaret. *The Annandales: Irreverent Sculpture*, Monash University Gallery, Clayton, Victoria, 1985.

Wright, William and Lanceley, Colin. *Colin Lanceley*, Craftsman House, Sydney, 1987.

The Yellow House

McGrath, Sandra. *Brett Whiteley*, Bay Books, Sydney, 1979.

Mendelssohn, Joanna. *The Yellow House 1970–1972*, Art Gallery of New South Wales, Sydney, 1990.

Pickvance, Ronald. *Van Gogh in Arles*, Metropolitan Museum of Art, New York, and Harry N. Abrams, New York, 1984.

van Gogh, Vincent. *The Letters of Vincent Van Gogh*, ed. Mark Roskill, Fontana, London, 1983.

Walther, Ingo. *Vincent Van Gogh 1853–1890: Vision and Reality*, Benedikt Taschen, Cologne, 1990.

Inhibodress

'The Art of Survival', *Artlink*, vol. 14, no. 2, 1994.

Bromfield, David. *Identities: A Critical Study of the Work of Mike Parr 1970–1990*, University of Western Australia Press, Perth, 1991.

Cramer, Sue. *Inhibodress 1979–1972*, Institute of Modern Art, Brisbane, 1989.

Kenyon, Therese. *Under a Hot Tin Roof: Art, Passion and Politics at the Tin Sheds Art Workshop*, State Library of New South Wales Press in association with Power Publications, The Power Institute of Fine Arts, University of Sydney, Sydney, 1995.

Lippard, Lucy. 'The dematerialisation of art', in *Changing: Essays in Art Criticism*, Dutton, New York, 1971.

Marsh, Anne. *Body and Self: Performance Art in Australia 1969–92*, Oxford University Press, Melbourne, 1993.

Smith, Terry. 'Bin for blurred rubbish', *Sunday Australian*, 19 September 1971.

Roar

Allen, Traudi. *Roar! And Quieter Moments From a Group of Melbourne Artists 1980–1993*, Craftsman House, Sydney, 1995.

Green, Janina. 'Roar or whimper', *Art + Text*, no. 14, 1984.

Nixon, John. 'Art Projects 1979–84', *Art + Text*, no. 28, 1988.

Pascoe, Joseph and Fraser, Katrina. *Roar Studios Touring Exhibition*, Shepparton Art Gallery, Shepparton, 1992.

Taylor, Paul. 'Angst in my pants', *Art + Text*, no. 7, 1982.

Art Projects

Cramer, Sue and Barnes, Carolyn. *John Nixon*, Roslyn Oxley9 Gallery, Sydney, 1991.

Hannan, Grant. 'John Nixon and the Russian connection', *Art Monthly*, no. 16, November 1988.

Lumby, Catharine. 'John Nixon Interview', *On The Beach*, no. 13, April 1988.

Smith, Bernard and Smith, Terry. *Australian Painting 1788–1990*, Oxford University Press, Melbourne, 1992.

Chapter Three
A Female Space: Australian Women's Art

de Beauvoir, Simone. *The Second Sex*, translated by H. M. Parshley, Picador, London, 1988.

Burke, Janine. *Joy Hester*, Greenhouse Publications, Richmond, Victoria, 1983.

Drury, Nevill. *New Sculpture: Profiles in Contemporary Sculpture*, Craftsman House, Sydney, 1993.

Eisenstein, Hester. *Contemporary Feminist Thought*, Allen and Unwin, Sydney, 1984.

Foucault, Michel. *Discipline and Punish: The Birth of the Prison*, translated by A. M. Sheridan, Penguin, Harmondsworth, 1984.

Hansen, K. V. and Philipson, I. J. (eds). *Women, Class and the Feminist Imagination*, Temple University Press, Philadelphia, 1990.

Herrera, Hayden. *Frida Kahlo: The Paintings*, Bloomsbury, London, 1992.

Kenyon, Therese. *Under A Hot Tin Roof: Art, Passion and Politics at the Tin Sheds Art Workshop*, State Library of New South Wales Press in association with Power Publications, The Power Institute of Fine Arts, University of Sydney, Sydney, 1995.

Kerr, Joan (ed.). *Heritage: The National Women's Art Book*, Craftsman House, Sydney, 1995.

Kirby, Sandy. *Sight Lines: Women's Art and Feminist Perspectives in Australia*, Craftsman House, Sydney, 1992.

Lippard, Lucy. *From The Center: Feminist Essays on Women's Art*, E. P. Dutton, New York, 1976.

McNay, Lois. *Foucault and Feminism: Power, Gender and the Self*, Polity Press, Cambridge, 1994.

McQueen, Humphrey. *The Black Swan of Trespass: The Emergence of Modernist Painting in Australia to 1944*, Alternative Publishing Cooperative, Sydney, 1979.

Marsh, Anne. *Body and Self: Performance Art in Australia 1969–92*, Oxford University Press, Melbourne, 1993.

Milner, Andrew. *Contemporary Cultural Theory: An Introduction*, Allen and Unwin, Sydney, 1991.

Ollenburger, J. C. and Moore, H. *A Sociology of Women*, Prentice Hall, New Jersey, 1992.

Smith, Bernard and Smith, Terry. *Australian Painting 1788–1990*, Oxford University Press, Melbourne, 1992.

Topliss, Helen. *Modernism and Feminism: Australian Women Artists 1900–1940*, Craftsman House, Sydney, 1996.

Voigt, Anna. *New Visions, New Perspectives: Voices of Contemporary Australian Women Artists*, Craftsman House, Sydney, 1996.

Wolff, Janet. *The Social Production of Art*, Macmillan, London, 1984.

Articles and catalogues

Allen, Traudi. *Women's Art and Feminism 1970–1994*, video, Video Education Australasia, Bendigo, Victoria, 1994.

Allen, Traudi. *Mother, Other, Lover: The Sculpture of Mona Ryder*, exhibition catalogue, Queensland Art Gallery, Brisbane, 1995.

Australian Women Artists: One Hundred Years, 1840–1940, exhibition catalogue, Ewing and George Paton Galleries, Melbourne University Union, Melbourne, 1975.

Eisenstein, Zillah. 'Constructing a theory of capitalist patriarchy and socialist feminism', in *Women, Class and the Feminist Imagination*, eds K. V. Hansen and I. J. Philipson, Temple University Press, Philadelphia, 1990.

Evans, Megan. *The Art of Nursing*, exhibition catalogue, Australian Nursing Federation (Victorian Branch), Melbourne, 1994.

Follent, Sarah. 'A private world with a familiar landscape', *Australian*, 15 October 1984.

Follent, Sarah (for Mona Ryder). *Australian Perspecta*, exhibition catalogue, 1985.

Koedt, Anne. 'The myth of the vaginal orgasm', in *Radical Feminism*, eds Anne Koedt, Ellen Levine and Anita Rapone, Quadrangle Books, New York, 1973, pp. 198–207.

Lacan, Jacques. 'Jacques Lacan from "The Mirror Stage" (1949)', *A Critical and Cultural Theory Reader*, eds Antony Easthope and Kate McGowan, Open University Press, Buckingham, 1994.

North, Ian (ed.). *Margaret Preston: Model of an Era*, Art Gallery Board of South Australia, Adelaide, 1980.

Owens, Craig. 'The discourse of others: Feminists and postmodernism', in *Postmodern Culture*, ed. Hal Foster, Pluto Press, Sydney, 1985.

Ricketson, Merren. 'Women's Register reaches 20 years', *Gallery*, National Gallery Society of Victoria, March 1995.

Chapter Four
Take Away or Eat Here? Decisions on the Digestion of Asian Images

Bail, Murray. *Fairweather*, Craftsman House, Sydney, 1994.

Broinowski, Alison. *The Yellow Lady: Australian Impressions of Asia*, Oxford University Press, Melbourne, 1992.

Humphreys, Christmas. *The Buddhist Way of Life*, Allen and Unwin, London, 1990.

Jaffe, Aniela. *C. G. Jung: Word and Image*, translated by Krishna Winston, Princeton University Press, Princeton, New Jersey, 1979.

McGrath, Sandra. *Brett Whiteley*, Bay Books, Sydney, 1979.

McQueen, Humphrey. *The Black Swan of Trespass: The Emergence of Modernist Painting in Australia to 1944*, Alternative Publishing Cooperative, Sydney, 1979.

Pearce, Barry. *Brett Whiteley: Art and Life 1939–1992*, Thames and Hudson in association with the Art Gallery of New South Wales, Sydney, 1995.

Said, Edward W. *Orientalism: Western Conceptions of the Orient*, Penguin, Harmondsworth, 1995.

Sayers, Andrew. *Aboriginal Artists of the Nineteenth Century*, Oxford University Press, Melbourne, in association with the National Gallery of Australia, Canberra, 1994.

Shelburne, Walter A. *Mythos and Logos in the Thought of Carl Jung: The Theory of the Collective Unconscious in Scientific Perspective*, State University of New York Press, New York, 1988.

Turner, Caroline (ed.). *Tradition and Change: Contemporary Art of Asia and the Pacific*, University of Queensland Press, St Lucia, Queensland, 1993.

Articles and catalogues
The Abolition of the 'White Australia' Policy, Department of Immigration and Multicultural Affairs, Canberra, 1997.

Allen, Traudi. 'Early morning illuminations', *ART AsiaPacific*, vol. 3, no. 1, 1996.

Benjamin, Roger (ed.). *Transcultural Painting*, exhibition catalogue, Asialink and Ian Potter Gallery, University of Melbourne, Melbourne, 1985.

Capon, Edmund. *Asian Gallery Opens*, press release, Art Gallery of New South Wales, Sydney, 13 July 1994.

Carroll, Alison. *Out of Asia*, exhibition catalogue, Heide Park and Art Gallery, Bulleen, Victoria, 1990.

Eisenberg, Joseph. 'Olive Crane', in *Heritage: The National Women's Art Book*, ed. Joan Kerr, Craftsman House, Sydney, 1995.

Ewington, Julie. *Localities of Desire: Contemporary Art in an International World*, exhibition catalogue, Museum of Contemporary Art, Sydney, 1994.

Hamilton, Annette. 'Dreaming the lotus: Aesthetic dialogue with "Asia"', in *Out of Asia*, exhibition catalogue, Heide Park and Art Gallery, Bulleen, Victoria, 1990.

King, David. 'Rupert Bunny's paintings of Sada Yakko', *Art and Australia*, vol. 25, no. 3, 1988.

Ngoch Phac, Nguyen. *The Umbilical Cord of Vietnamese Artists: Midnight Sun National Exhibition by Australian–Vietnamese Artists*, exhibition catalogue, National Gallery of Victoria, Melbourne, 1996.

North, Ian (ed.). *Margaret Preston: Model of an Era*, Art Gallery Board of South Australia, Adelaide, 1980.

Zimmer, Jenny and Mackenzie, Margaret. Exhibition catalogue, Dianne Tanzer Gallery, 1996.

Chapter Five
Picturing Life Together: The Community and the Visual Arts

Artists and the "Creation of Australia": A Discussion Paper With Positive Proposals, Arts Action Australia, Melbourne, 16–19 February 1992.

Binns, Vivienne (ed.). *Community and the Arts: Australian Perspectives*, Pluto Press, Sydney, 1981.

Kirby, Sandy. *Artists and Unions — A Critical Tradition: A Report on the Art and Working Life Program*, Australia Council, Sydney, 1992.

Latreille, Anne (ed.). *People for Places: Urban Spaces in Victoria*, Victorian State Urban Arts Unit, Melbourne, 1986.

McAuliffe, Chris. *Art and Suburbia*, Craftsman House, Sydney, 1996.

Muir, Kathie, *Creative Alliances — Unions and the Arts: Art and Working Life in the 1990s*, Union Media Services, Trades Hall, Sydney, 1992.

Stephen, Ann and Reeves, Andrew. *Badges of Labour, Banners of Pride: Aspects of Working Class Celebration*, Museum of Applied Arts and Sciences, Sydney, in association with Allen and Unwin, Sydney, 1985.

Towards a National Agenda for the Arts, compiled by Arts Action Australia, Sydney, February 1990.

Chapter Six
Racial and Sexual Versions: The Art of Minority Cultures

Abelove, Henry; Aina Barale, Michele; and Halperin, David M. (eds). *The Lesbian and Gay Studies Reader*, Routledge, New York, and Kegan Paul, London, 1993.

Ashburn, Elizabeth. *Lesbian Art: An Encounter With Power*, Craftsman House, Sydney, 1996.

Attwood, Bain. *In the Age of Mabo: History, Aborigines and Australia*, Allen & Unwin, Sydney, 1996.

Attwood, Bain and Markus, Andrew with Edwards, Dale and Schilling, Kath. *The 1967 Referendum, Or When Aborigines Didn't Get the Vote*, Aboriginal Studies Press, Australian Institute of Aboriginal and Torres Strait Islander Studies, Canberra, 1997.

Beier, Ulli. *Dream Time – Machine Time: The Art of Trevor Nickolls*, Robert Brown and Associates in association with the Aboriginal Artists Agency, Bathurst, New South Wales, 1985.

Caruana, Wally. *Aboriginal Art*, Thames and Hudson, London, 1993.

Darty, Trudy and Potter, Sandee. *Women-Identified Women*, Mayfield Publishing, California, 1984.

Drury, Nevill. *Images 2: Contemporary Australian Painting*, Craftsman House, Sydney, 1994.

Griffiths, Max. *Aboriginal Affairs: A Short History 1788–1995*, Kangaroo Press, Sydney, 1995.

Isaacs, Jennifer. *Aboriginality: Contemporary Aboriginal Paintings and Prints*, University of Queensland Press, St Lucia, 1992.

Jagose, Annamarie. *Queer Theory*, Melbourne University Press, Melbourne, 1996.

Taylor, Paul (ed.). *Hysterical Tears*, Greenhouse, Richmond, Victoria, 1985.

Thompson, Denise. *Reading Between the Lines: A Lesbian Feminist Critique of Feminist Accounts of Sexuality*, Lesbian Studies and Research Group and The Gorgon's Head Press, Sydney, 1991.

Weeks, Jeffrey. *Against Nature: Essays on History, Sexuality and Identity*, Rivers Oram Press, London, 1991.

Articles and Catalogues
Carver, Antonia. 'Mind, body and soul', *ART AsiaPacific*, vol. 3, no. 2, 1996.

Clark, Deborah. 'Lost in queer street', *Art Monthly*, no. 69, May 1994.

Eisenstein, Hester. 'Lesbianism and the woman-identified woman', in *Contemporary Feminist Thought*, Allen and Unwin, Sydney, 1984.

Foley, Fiona. 'A blast from the past', in *Performing Hybridity*, eds May Joseph and Jennifer Natalya Fink, University of Minnesota Press, Minneapolis, 1999, pp. 46–58.

Gott, Ted. 'Interview with the Artists, 30/11/96', in *Indelible*, exhibition catalogue, Australian Centre for Contemporary Art, Melbourne, 1997.

Gott, Ted. 'Grief', *Artlink*, vol. 14, no. 4, summer 1994.

Hardie, Martin. 'The Aboriginal copyright cases', *Artlink*, vol. 10, nos 1 and 2, 1992.

Johnson, Vivien. 'Into the urbane: Urban Aboriginal art in the Australian art context', *Art Monthly*, no. 30, May 1990.

McFarlane, Jenny. 'No dumb surface', in *60 Heads eX de Medici*, Canberra Contemporary Art Space Touring Exhibition, Canberra, 1996, 1997.

O'Ferrall, Michael A. *On The Edge: Five Contemporary Aboriginal Artists*, exhibition catalogue, Art Gallery of Western Australia, Perth, 1989.

O'Ferrall, Michael A. *Australian Aboriginal Art: Convergence and Divergence*, exhibition catalogue, Art Gallery of Western Australia, Perth, 1990.

Owens, Craig. 'The discourse of others: Feminists and postmodernism', in *Postmodern Culture*, ed. Hal Foster, Pluto Press, Sydney, 1985.

Schubert, Robert. 'That's Miss Faggot to you, honey! Queer/gay art in Oz', lecture, Monash University, Clayton, Victoria, 18 March 1996.

Smith, Terry. 'Aboriginal painting', in Bernard Smith and Terry Smith, *Australian Painting 1788–1990*, Oxford University Press, Melbourne, 1992.

Chapter Seven
Portraits in Prayer: Eastern Philosophies in Australian Art

Bennett, James. *Hot Wax: An Exhibition of Australian Aboriginal Indonesian Batik*, Museum and Art Gallery of the Northern Territory, Darwin, 1995.

Bennett, James. 'Dialogue with Indonesia', in *Contemporary Crafts Review*, ed. Jenny Zimmer, Monash University, Clayton, Victoria, 1996.

Brand, Michael. *The Vision of Kings: Art and Experience in India*, National Gallery of Australia, Canberra, and Thames and Hudson, Melbourne, 1996.

Humphreys, Christmas. *The Buddhist Way of Life*, Mandala, London, 1990.

Iyengar, B. K. S. *The Tree of Yoga*, Fine Line Books, Oxford, 1988.

Jaffe, Aniela (ed.). *C. J. Jung: Word and Image*, Bollingen Series XCVII: 2, Princeton University Press, Princeton, New Jersey, 1979.

Kirby, Sandy. In Traudi Allen, *Women's Art and Feminism*, video, Video Education Australasia, Bendigo, Victoria, 1994.

Mookerjee, Ajit. *Kali: The Feminine Force*, Thames and Hudson, London, 1995.

Conclusion
Everything Old is Cool Again: The Contemporary Context

Drury, Nevill. *Images 2: Contemporary Australian Painting*, Craftsman House, Sydney, 1994.

Newton, Gael. *Tracey Moffatt: Fever Pitch*, Piper Press, Sydney, 1995.

Newton, Gael. 'See the woman with the red dress on … and on … and on …', *ART AsiaPacific*, vol. 1, no. 2, 1994.

Technothelyogia, exhibition catalogue, Monash University Gallery, Melbourne, 1997.

Thomas, Daniel. 'Everybody Sing: The art of Robert MacPherson', *Art and Australia*, vol. 33, no. 4, 1996.

Wark, McKenzie. *The Virtual Republic: Australia's Cultural Wars of the 1990s*, Allen and Unwin, Sydney, 1997.

plates

PLATE 1

John Perceval, *Sulphur Smoke*, 1959, oil and tempera on composition board, 90.8 x 121 cm. Private collection, Melbourne

PLATE 2

Robert Rooney, *Slippery Seal III*, 1967, synthetic polymer paint on canvas, 106.7 x 106.7 cm. Collection: Monash University, Melbourne. Photograph: John Brash

PLATE 3

Dennis Passalick, *Myself Portrait/Hostile Landscape*, 1991, oil on canvas, 170 x 274 cm

PLATE 4

Imants Tillers, *Izkliede*, 1994, synthetic polymer paint, oilstick and gouache on canvasboard, 292 panels, 304 x 914 cm overall. Private collection, Sydney

PLATE 5

Tom Roberts, *A Summer Morning Tiff*, 1886, oil on canvas on board, 76.5 x 51.2 cm. Collection: Ballarat Fine Art Gallery, Victoria, Martha K. Pinkerton Bequest Fund, 1943

PLATE 6

Sidney Nolan, *Wimmera River*, c. 1942, ripolin enamel on cotton gauze on cardboard, 51.3 x 63.7 cm. Collection: National Gallery of Victoria, Melbourne, presented by Sir Sidney and Lady Nolan, 1983

PLATE 7

Sidney Nolan, *Landscape*, 1944, ripolin enamel on cotton gauze on pulpboard, 51 x 63.4 cm. Collection: National Gallery of Victoria, Melbourne, presented by Sir Sidney and Lady Nolan, 1983

PLATE 8

Godfrey Miller, *Blue Unity*, 1954–55, oil, pen and ink on canvas, 69.8 x 88.2 cm. Collection: National Gallery of Australia, Canberra

PLATE 9

Brett Whiteley, *The Jacaranda Tree (on Sydney Harbour)*, 1977, oil on canvas, 208 x 456 cm. Private collection

PLATE 10

Fred Williams, *Black Creek*, 1958, oil on composition board, 75.5 x 100 cm. Private collection, Western Australia. Reproduced courtesy Lyn Williams

PLATE 11

Howard Taylor, *Tree Line with Green Paddock*, 1993, oil on marine ply panel, 61 x 122 cm. Private collection. Photograph: Victor France

PLATE 12

Dale Hickey, *Cottlesbridge Landscape*, 1980, oil on canvas, 244 x 198.6 cm. Collection: National Gallery of Victoria, Melbourne

PLATE 13

Elizabeth Kruger, *The Last of the Cool Skies*, 1988, gouache, acrylic on hardboard, 31 x 92.5 cm. Collection: Moët & Chandon, France. Photograph: Gary Somerfield

PLATE 14

Ken Done, *Postcard from the Cabin*, 1981, oil on canvas, 95 x 125 cm. Private collection, Sydney

PLATE 15

Mandy Martin, *Red Ochre Cove*, 1987, oil on canvas, 121 x 280 cm. Commissioned for the Main Committee Room, House of Representatives, Parliament House, Canberra. Photograph: Parliament House Art Collection, Canberra. Reproduced with permission of VI$COPY Ltd, Sydney

PLATE 16

Arthur Boyd, *Half-caste Child*, 1957, oil, tempera on canvas, 150 x 177.5 cm. Private collection, Melbourne. Reproduced with permission of Bundanon Trust

PLATE 17

Yvonne Boyd (née Lennie), *Children, Fitzroy*, 1944, oil on muslin on cardboard, 64 x 75.5 cm. Collection: Bundanon Trust. Reproduced with permission of Bundanon Trust

PLATE 18

Albert Tucker, *Tram Stop (Image of Modern Evil # 26)*, 1945–46, oil on hardboard, 80 x 120 cm. Collection: ICI Australia, Melbourne

PLATE 19

Clifton Pugh, *Cat in a Rabbit Trap*, 1957, oil on composition board, 91.4 x 137.1 cm

PLATE 20

Mike Brown and Ross Crothall, *Sailing to Byzantium*, 1961, pencil, oil crayon and enamel on composition board, 91.5 x 122.1 cm. Collection: National Gallery of Australia, Canberra

PLATE 21

The Yellow House, 1970–72, 59 Macleay Street, Potts Point, Sydney. Photograph: Greg Weight

PLATE 22

Yvonne Audette, *Chinese Poem*, 1963, oil on composition board, 122 x 91.5 cm

PLATE 23
Vivienne Binns, *Suggon*, 1966, enamel on composition board, electric motor, synthetic polymer mesh, steel wire, 122.2 x 92 cm. Collection: National Gallery of Australia, Canberra

PLATE 24
Judy Normand, '*Normally I'd get a nurse to thread the needle, but with their strike on ...*', 1986, tapestry wools, embroidery cottons, theatre suture silk on canvas, 30 x 40 cm. Photograph: John Brash

PLATE 25A
Mona Ryder, *Mother, Other Lover*, 1995, sculptural installation, mixed media, Queensland Art Gallery, Brisbane

PLATE 25B
Mona Ryder, *Mother, Other Lover*, 1995 (detail), steel, leather, drumhide, hair

PLATE 25C
Mona Ryder, *Mother, Other Lover*, 1995 (detail), steel, leather, drumhide, hair

PLATE 26
Olive Crane, *Design for the 'Gum Tree Pattern' Plate*, c. 1920, watercolour

PLATE 27
Vladimir Tretchikov, print, 61 x 55 cm. Private collection. Photograph: John Brash

PLATE 28
Pat Hoffie, *Hotel Paradise*, 1989–90, laser copy on board, 145 x 336 cm. Photograph: Elvira Gonzalez Lopez

PLATE 29
Yukinori Yanagi, *Asia-Pacific Ant Farm*, 1996, installation, ants, coloured sand, plastic box, plastic tube, plastic pipe and video documentation on LCD monitor, dimensions variable, Queensland Art Gallery, Brisbane

PLATE 30
Bob Jankowski and Carol-Anne Harris (Artistic Coordinators), *Berrivale Community Mural*, 1985, Berrivale Orchards, Sturt Highway, Berri, 6 x 75 m. Photograph: Italo Vardaro

PLATE 31
Artist unknown, *Banner of the Australian Plumbers and Gasfitters Employees Union*, c. 1920, oil on canvas, 270 x 315 cm. Photograph: Greg Weight

PLATE 32
Carole Wilson, *Strike while the iron's hot*, 1987, screenprinted poster, 76 x 51 cm

PLATE 33
Trevor Nickolls, *Deaths in Custody*, 1990, synthetic polymer paint on canvas, 150 x 150 cm. Collection: National Gallery of Australia, Canberra

PLATE 34
Lin Onus, *Fruit Bats*, 1991, foam, fibreglass, resin, acrylic enamel paint, Hills Hoist, 250 x 250 x 250 cm. Collection: Art Gallery of New South Wales, Sydney. Reproduced with permission of VI$COPY Ltd, Sydney

PLATE 35
David McDiarmid, *It's My Party and I'll Die If I Want To Sugar*, 1995, computer-generated Canon laser print and mixed-media, 26 x 21 cm. Photograph courtesy Tolarno Galleries, Melbourne

PLATE 36
Tina Fiveash, *A Gay Morning Tea!*, 1994, from the 'Stories for Girls' series, C-type photograph, 48 x 42.5 cm

PLATE 37
Lena Apwerl, *Goanna and Wayang Puppets*, 1994, batik cap/tulis on silk, 240 x 112.3 cm. Collection: Museum and Art Gallery of the Northern Territory, Darwin

PLATE 38
James Bennett, *Bones and Angels*, 1994, batik cap/tulis on silk, 115.3 x 235.2 cm. Collection: Museum and Art Gallery of the Northern Territory, Darwin

PLATE 39
Matthys *Gerber, Let it Be Me*, 1987, oil and acrylic on canvas, 73 x 157 cm. Courtesy Sarah Cottier Gallery, Sydney

PLATE 40
Claire Day, *Adya Sakti*, 1994, oil on canvas, 91.5 x 83.5 cm. Photograph: John Brash

PLATE 41
Geoffrey Goldie, *Guilt, Possession, Death*, 1994, synthetic polymer paint, collage on board, 80 x 61 cm. Private collection. Photograph: John Brash

PLATE 42
Geoffrey Goldie, *Dasa Mahavidya: Ten Great Paths to Wisdom*, 1994, synthetic polymer paint on canvas, 112 x 213 cm. Photograph: John Brash

PLATE 43A
Anne Marie Power, *Shrine*, 1991, Japanese Shinto shrine, prints, plastic buttons, hair pins, 75 x 45 x 38 cm

PLATE 43B
Anne Marie Power, *Shrine*, 1991 (detail), Japanese Shinto shrine, prints, plastic buttons, hair pins

PLATE 44
Rosalie Gascoigne, *Firebird*, 1991, retro-reflective road-signs on plywood, 135 x 103 cm. Photograph courtesy Roslyn Oxley9 Gallery, Sydney

PLATE 45
Tracey Moffatt, *Something More No. 1*, 1989, one in the series of nine direct positive colour photographs and gelatin silver photographs, each 90 x 150 cm. Collection of the artist and Roslyn Oxley9 Gallery, Sydney

PLATE 46
Edite Vidins, *Internet Supersonic Blah Blah*, 1995, phaser III wax prints, 56 x 135 cm

figures

FIGURE 22
Greg Weight, *Yellow House*, photocollage, top row (left to right): Brett Whiteley, *Rembrandt* (detail); poetry recital; 'Rembrandt to Magritte' room. Second row: Brett Whiteley, Karen, Sebastian Jorgensen; Tim Burns, Mary in the bathroom; Brett Whiteley and Peter Wright. Third row: Peter Kingston and the geodesic tent; George Gittoes's puppet theatre; Martin Sharp and Tim Burns with Chris and Bruce Goold in the distance. Fourth row: Greg Weight and Albie Thoms reflected in the crystal ball; Peter Kingston; Martin Sharp in 'Magritte's Remembered Journey'. Fifth row: Brett Whiteley and bottom half of *Rembrandt* seen in top panel; Jam in the 'Cloud Room'; Martin Sharp; Moth of the White Company (mime)

FIGURE 23
Peter Kennedy and Mike Parr, 'Idea Demonstrations', 1972, installation view, corner group (from left to right): Tess Parr, unknown, unknown, Barbara Hall. Photograph: Peter Kennedy

FIGURE 24
Roar Gallery sign and logo

FIGURE 25
Judi Singleton with Mark Howson (left) and Pasquali Giardino, working on a joint painting for the National Gallery of Australia cafe, 1986. Photograph: John Gollings

FIGURE 26
John Nixon, *Self Portrait (Non-Objective Composition) 79*, installation view, seventy-nine paintings, Art Projects, Melbourne, 1982

FIGURE 27
Margaret Preston, *Flying Over the Shoalhaven River*, 1942, oil on canvas, 50.6 x 50.6 cm. Collection: National Gallery of Australia, Canberra

FIGURE 28
Clarice Beckett, *Bay Road, Foggy Morning*, c. 1926, oil on hardboard, 29 x 37 cm. Private collection

FIGURE 29
Marie McMahon, *D'Oyley Disco*, c. 1978, screenprint. Reproduced courtesy Tin Sheds Gallery, Sydney

FIGURE 30
Annette Bezor, *NO*, 1991, acrylic and oil on galvanised iron, two pieces: 120 x 150 x 10 cm

FIGURE 31
Rupert Bunny, *Geisha Girl*, c. 1901, oil on canvas, 160 x 118.2 cm. On loan to Stuartholme-Behan collection, University Art Museum, University of Queensland, Brisbane

FIGURE 32
Margaret Preston, *Blue Mountains Theme*, c. 1941, oil on canvas, 50.7 x 51.3 cm. Collection: Shepparton Art Gallery, Victoria

FIGURE 33
Nick Ut, *Children Fleeing Napalm Strike Near Saigon, 10 June 1972*. Photograph courtesy AP/AAP

FIGURE 34
Eddie Adams, *Shooting of Vietcong Guerilla Tet Offensive, 1 February 1968*. Photograph courtesy AP/AAP

FIGURE 35
Tommy McRae, *Aborigine Chasing Chinese Man*, 1880, pen and ink, 17.5 x 10 cm. Collection: National Library of Australia, Canberra

FIGURE 36
Ian Fairweather, *Mangrove*, 1961–62, synthetic polymer paint and gouache on cardboard on hardboard, 82 x 122 cm

FIGURE 37A
Dadang Christanto, *For Those Who Have Been Killed*, 1993, performance at Queensland Art Gallery, Brisbane

FIGURE 37B
Dadang Christanto, *For Those Who Have Been Killed*, 1993, performance at Queensland Art Gallery, Brisbane

FIGURE 38
Brenda Fajardo, *Ako ay Babae, Ako ay Pilipina (I Am Woman, I Am Filipino)*, 1993, from the 'Cards of Life – Women's Series', pen and ink with goldleaf on handmade paper, 52.5 x 72 cm. Collection: Queensland Art Gallery, Brisbane, The Kenneth and Yasuko Myer Collection of Contemporary Asian Art, purchased 1993 with funds from The Myer Foundation, Michael Myer and Ann Gamble Myer through the Queensland Art Gallery Foundation

FIGURE 39
Xu Bing, *A Case Study of Transference*, 1994, performance at Han Mo Art Centre, Beijing. Photograph: Xu Zhi Wai

FIGURE 40
Tony Clark, *Chinoiserie Landscape*, 1986–87, acrylic on canvasboard, three panels, 30.5 x 68.4 cm overall. Courtesy Roslyn Oxley9 Gallery, Sydney

FIGURE 41
Megan Evans and Eve Glenn, *From Bonboniere to Barbed Wire*, 1985–86, Gas and Fuel building, Smith Street, North Fitzroy, Melbourne. Photograph: John Brash

FIGURE 42
Barry Drinan, Copy of Rembrandt's *The Two Philosophers (1628)*, 1997, on footpath near the forecourt of the National Gallery of Victoria, Melbourne. The original hangs inside

FIGURE 43
Oliver Strewe, *On the Boards, Kentucky Station, NSW*, 1985, photograph, project for the Australian Workers Union

FIGURE 44
Deej Fabyc, *Wipe Out War Not Women*, c. 1983, screenprinted poster, 76 x 51 cm

FIGURE 45
Graffiti, inner Melbourne

index

Page numbers in **bold** refer to images.